SCHIZOPHRENIA AT HOME

A Guide to Helping the Family

SCHIZOPHRENIA AT HOME

A Guide to Helping the Family

Jacqueline M. Atkinson, PhD
Department of Community Medicine,
University of Glasgow

CROOM HELM
London & Sydney

Croom Helm Ltd, Provident House, Burrell Row,
Beckenham, Kent BR3 1AT
Croom Helm Australia Pty Ltd, Suite 4, 6th Floor,
64-76 Kippax Street, Surry Hills, NSW 2010, Australia

British Library Cataloguing in Publication Data

Atkinson, Jacqueline
    Schizophrenia at home: a guide to helping the
    family.
    1. Schizophrenia
    I. Title
    616.89′82   RC514
    ISBN 0-7099-0565-3
    ISBN 0-7099-0566-1 Pbk

Typeset in 10pt Times Roman by Leaper & Gard, Bristol, England
Printed and bound in Great Britain
by Billing & Sons Limited, Worcester.

CONTENTS

INTRODUCTION

The need to involve the families of schizophrenic patients in therapy and rehabiliation is gradually being accepted at many levels. The relatives themselves, parents in particular, are acutely aware of the nonsense of ignoring such patients; the onset of 'community care' meant that increasing numbers of patients were returned to their families not only to live, but to receive care, supervision, and, ultimately, help.

Such families may have muttered among themselves that they were being ignored, that they were given no information, advice or support. Many may have accepted this as being the normal course of events; some may even have found reasons for the neglect, in terms of the doctor's lack of time and the health service's lack of staff. Others, however, resented the situation and started making demands — after all, were they not relieving the hospitals of the burden of day-to-day care?

As the situation grew ever more pressing, relatives found ways to contact one another and work together. The early 1970s in Britain saw the formation of the National Schizophrenia Fellowship, a self-help group offering support, information and advice to relatives and patients, and acting as a pressure group for relatives' rights.

Therapists, too, became conscious of the need to deal with the relatives of schizophrenic patients and their problems and, since the mid-1970s, a variety of programmes involving relatives has emerged in both Britain and America. There is also some indication that professionals are asking families about their problems and what can be done to help them.

This book sets out to examine how relatives can best be involved in therapy and rehabilitation programmes. Part One looks at the background to the patient living in the community and the effect this has on the patient. The role of the environment and family in aetiology and relapse is examined, and the ways in which the family are involved in rehabilitation and therapy are considered. Part Two looks at the effect of having a schizophrenic patient living within the family and the problems this brings, from both the relative's and the patient's perspective. Part Three considers ways in which the family can be involved and offers practical suggestions and advice. The last chapter considers again the relatives' problems as they describe in their own words their experiences and the help that they want.

PART ONE

BACKGROUND

1 THE SCHIZOPHRENIC PATIENT

Before any help can be given either to patients or their families, some understanding is needed of who the patient is, and where he is to be found. This takes into account the various types of schizophrenia, theories of aetiology and its progress and prognosis. To label a person as a 'chronic mental patient' or even 'chronic schizophrenic patient' is to miss his individuality and to ignore the diversity of the group, thus obscuring his potential for, and ability to, change.

The approach taken to schizophrenia in this book will be that of the fairly standard, medical model as used in most hospitals and caring agencies. However, there is considerable debate about what schizophrenia actually is. For example, it has been described by theorists such as Laing (1960) and Szasz (1970) in more existential and social terms, although this is not the commonly used approach. Schizophrenia *can* mean different things to different groups of people, but there is widespread general agreement over many issues.

The World Health Organization Project (Sartorius, Shapiro and Kimura, 1975; WHO, 1975, 1979) suggests there is a mutual coming together and agreement over diagnostic criteria, although in the initial diagnosis of schizophrenia 11 per cent of patients labelled schizophrenic were unlikely to be so diagnosed outside that particular diagnosing centre. The two centres particularly disposed to such idiosyncratic diagnosis were Washington and Moscow. The American psychiatrists tended to see schizophrenia as a much wider concept than the British and also to rate all symptoms at a higher level of abnormality. In effect, they were describing more behaviour as being pathological than were the British (Cooper, 1975). The American's revision of diagnostic criteria in the *Diagnostic and Statistical Manual of Mental Disease III* (American Psychiatric Association, 1980) has resulted in a tightening up of the American definition of schizophrenia, making it similar to that of the British. Practically, the difference means that care must be taken when reading American research as the groups of schizophrenic patients being considered do not always correspond to British groups.

3

One attempt to explain schizophrenia has suggested that it might most usefully be seen as a spectrum of disorders (e.g. Reich, 1971; 1976). A cluster or spectrum of psychological states is proposed, some of which are a psychosis and some not, but all of which share a genetic aetiology with schizophrenia. The diagnosis of 'schizophrenia', therefore, may be applied ultimately to a wider population.

However schizophrenia is viewed, there are a number of symptoms that are always indicative of the condition, generally referred to as 'core symptoms'. Possibly the best known grouping of core systems are Schneider's first-rank symptoms (Schneider, 1957; Taylor, 1972); they are of major importance in British diagnosis. Research (Mellor, 1970) suggests that such symptoms may only delineate a nuclear group, but Schneider has always been aware of this: 'The presence of first-rank symptoms always signifies schizophrenia, but first-rank symptoms need not always be present in schizophrenia.' The 'second-rank' symptoms he describes can and do occur in other disorders, of both a psychotic and neurotic nature.

Schneider identified eleven pathogenic symptoms for schizophrenia, namely: audible thoughts, voices arguing, voices commenting, thought insertion, thought withdrawal, thought broadcast, made feelings, made impulses, made volitions, delusional perception and somatic passivity. These were chosen for pragmatic rather than theoretical considerations; the ease with which they could be diagnosed and their discriminative ability between diagnostic groups. Carpenter and Strauss (1974), in the International Pilot Study of Schizophrenia carried out in nine countries, showed that first-rank symptoms 'do occur with sufficient frequency to have potential diagnostic usefulness and that each of the nine first-rank symptoms analysed is highly discriminating for schizophrenia. However, since first-rank symptoms were also reported in patients receiving other psychiatric diagnoses they cannot be considered absolutely discriminating for schizophrenia'.

The Career of the Schizophrenic Patient

From epidemiological studies (presented in Chapter 2) it is possible to build up a picture of the 'average schizophrenic patient'. Such information may be useful in planning services, but is rarely helpful on an individual basis.

The incidence (occurrence of new cases in the population) of schizophrenia might suggest that it is an illness of the young adult, but its prevalence (the number of cases in the population) indicates that patients experience problems or relapses throughout adulthood. Although the initial breakdown in schizophrenia is more likely to occur in younger age groups than older, it can occur at any time. Schizophrenia is either a progressive or a recurring illness for most patients. Deterioration and recurrent relapses mean that the patient will be in need of treatment or care at various stages of his life; thus a wide range of problems are involved. The early age of onset can compound problems. Florid symptoms, for example, are not only a source of difficulty in themselves, but can lead to secondary problems such as disturbed (or even unfinished) education and socialisation. Incomplete education can be an especial problem for patients of above average intelligence who are unable to cope with the stresses of further or higher education and are consequently disappointed and frustrated by lost opportunities.   ·

The numbers of men and women becoming schizophrenic are fairly similar, but are slightly higher in men. The main difference lies in age of onset: the rates for men up to the age of 34 are higher than for women, but the pattern reverses after this (Wing and Fryers, 1976). Cooper (1978) indicates that age- and sex-specific rates show a peak within the ages of 20 to 39 years, and a smaller, secondary peak for the over-65s, men being more likely to have an earlier onset. At onset, men are less likely to be married than women: this is likely to be due to differences in both age of onset and in social roles. Women are able to perform their traditional role more easily after onset than men.

The 'New Chronic' Patient

The new approach to care and rehabilitation of mental patients during the 1960s meant that many patients were discharged from mental hospitals, when previously they probably would have been considered to be there for life. The popular belief was that patients would spend less time in hospital and that there would be little or no need for facilities for long-stay patients.

For a time it appeared that this might happen and the number of long-stay patients decreased (Early and Magnus, 1966; Early and Nicholas, 1971; Allodi, 1973). The effects of institutional living were examined and found to be contributing to the problems of long-stay patients. This added to the impetus to move patients from long-stay wards (Wing and Brown, 1970). Despite the discharge of large numbers of patients, there were still some who could not be discharged. Furthermore, there were still patients being admitted to hospital who were becoming resident, a group which became known as the 'new long stay' (Todd, 1974; Todd, Bennie and Carlisle, 1976).

In addition, another new group of chronic patients was emerging: those who were still 'ill' in some way, but who were now living outside the hospital, either with their families, in sheltered accommodation or in lodging houses of some kind. Simply leaving hospital did not solve all their problems, and the facilities and services in the community were not there in sufficient numbers to deal with them. This undoubtedly has contributed to many of the difficulties encountered in community care in general and the problems of families in particular, and will be developed in later chapters. One of the results of the shortened length of hospital stay has been multiple admissions for many patients as they have repeated relapses or crisis points: the 'revolving door' phenomenon.

Prognosis

The cause and outcome of schizophrenia are thus highly variable in the schizophrenic population. A major difficulty in comparing studies or making use of outcome data concerns the type of criteria used to measure outcome. Many studies refer to 'global outcome' without specifying what is meant, others rely heavily on the concept of social outcome, again with little detail. More detailed criteria may be provided, for example, in terms of improvement in symptoms, adjustment to work or ability to handle relationships. Improvement in one area does not necessarily correlate with improvement in others (Brown, 1959; 1960) and thus may be of little help prognostically for the individual patient. The use of length of hospital stay as an outcome measure may have more to do with hospital or social policy, the attitudes of particular psychiatrists, or the presence of support in the community and other factors not directly related to the patient and his symptomatology, than to 'illness'.

Variables taken into account when considering prognosis include: individual factors in the patients' symptomatology, and development of illness, social and life history variables, treatment variables and cultural variables. Demographic diagnostic factors may interact with premorbid adjustment to such an extent that it is difficult to separate them in terms of their effect on the individual. For example, marriage may be important in prognosis as either an indicator or premorbid social and sexual adjustment or because the marital relationship itself is protective, providing care and support, or both. Generally, though, acute onset and good premorbid adjustment are seen as the two most important factors prognostically in terms of the individual. The sex of the patient may be important, males generally receiving a worse prognosis than females (Lane, 1968; Gittelman-Klein, 1969; Allon, 1971), but this in turn may be related to other variables such as social competence (Salokangas, 1983).

In terms of social factors, the frequency of life crises and life events seems linked to relapse in a fairly immediate way (Brown and Birley, 1968; Birley and Brown, 1970). The type of setting to which the patient returns is important (Brown, 1959), as is the level and type of emotional interaction (Brown, Birley and Wing, 1972; Vaughn and Leff, 1976a, 1976b; Vaughn, Snyder, Freeman, Jones, Falloon and Liberman, 1982). The setting might refer to family or hostel, as in the Brown study, or to a wider concept of environment. Rural areas and societies where techno-logical development has had a low impact would seem to point to a more favourable prognosis for the schizophrenic. A WHO study (Sartorious, Shapiro and Kimura, 1975) found that, although approximately the same number of patients followed a chronic, insidious, deteriorating course within schizophrenia in all cultures, among the non-chronic patients a higher proportion had a more favourable outcome in the developing countries, even among those not treated.

The WHO (1979) study reports on a number of variables which appear consistently as among the best predictors. Of the three best socio-demographic predictors, two are associated with poor outcome, namely social isolation and widowed, divorced or separated marital status; and one with good prognosis, namely being married. The three best background predictors, all relating to poor prognosis, were a history of past psychiatric treatment, poor psychosexual adjustment and an unfavourable environment.

Also associated with some poor outcome measures was a history of behavioural disorder. Of symptom variables, the two best predictors were long duration of the episode prior to initial evaluation, and insidious onset, both of which are associated with poor outcome. Despite having some indications of prognostic features, it is not always certain what the outcome will be for each individual patient. The WHO study sums up the results of previous studies as showing 'no matter how schizophrenia is defined, some patients go on to complete recovery and some go on to chronic, severe psychosis'.

Relapse

The course of schizophrenia indicates that relapses are to be expected in schizophrenia. Despite this, little attention has been paid to defining relapse in any objective, quantifiable way. Falloon (1984) points out that 'everyday usage in clinical settings would suggest a clear consensus on the criteria employed in its definition. However, a close perusal of published reports reveals considerable variation in researchers' notions of what constitutes a relapse'. Definitions include anything from exacerbation of psychiatric symptoms, changes in management or treatment, to social or behavioural problems or disturbance.

It would seem that clearer definitions are needed, including operational definitions specifying the quantitative or qualitative temporal nature of symptom change and a standardised rating scale; such measures thus avoid social variables that might confuse the clinical picture.

A number of factors have been related to relapse rates in schizophrenic patients. One of the most important, the level and type of family interaction, will be discussed in Chapters 3 and 9. Stress is another important factor implicated in the development of schizophrenia, as well as relapse.

Stress

Although stress is usually thought of in terms of something added to the situation, under-stimulation and over-stimulation both have adverse effects on the individual and these can be reflected in relapse.

Under-stimulation

Research on under-stimulation and social deprivation can be divided into two broad areas: those studies which are conducted within hospitals or other institutes, and those where the patient is living in the community. The broad findings are the same.

In an early study on the effects of social stimulation, Wing and Freudenberg (1961) point to the way chronic schizophrenic patients responded to extra social stimulation in an industrial setting, and to the sharp drop in output when this stimulation was discontinued. They conclude that these results are 'difficult to explain in terms of learning theory' and suggest that a psychological process is involved. While this may be true, it seems to be a rather hasty dismissal of the effects of social reinforcement, which could account for at least part of the change in learning theory terms. Wing and Brown (1970) conducted an intensive study on the influence of the environment on schizophrenic patients in three hospitals over the years 1960 to 1968. There were significant differences between the hospitals in terms of the freedom allowed by ward routine, the attitude of staff members towards the patients and their prognosis, the opportunities allowed or created for activities of a constructive nature and the extent to which patients were allowed to have personal belongings. The hospital which showed the greatest degree of 'environmental poverty' also showed the greatest clinical retardation among patients, as measured by social withdrawal, flatness of affect and poverty of speech. During the period of the study, changes in the environment were accompanied by changes in the clinical condition of the patients. Wing and Brown conclude that it is the environment itself which produces much of the morbidity found in long-stay patients in mental hospitals.

Similar findings to these for hospital patients were reported by Brown, Bone, Dallison and Wing (1966) for patients living in the community. The unemployed were spending at least one-third of their time doing 'nothing' whereas the employed and housewives were spending only 13-14 per cent of their time doing 'nothing'.

Hostel accommodation in the community may be no more than the exchange of one large institution for one much smaller, with no real benefit regarding changes in attitude. Apte (1968) found that half the residents of local authority aftercare hostels (of which nearly half the residents are chronic schizophrenics) were either unemployed or were working less than half-time. As the level of national unemployment has increased and continues to increase, this proportion has surely risen substantially. Out of a total of 24 hostels, only seven provided social, educational or recreational programmes as often as once a month. Lamb and Goertzel (1971) show that some sheltered-care houses resemble long-term hospital wards in terms of their isolation from the community.

These studies point to the error of assuming that patients living in the community are no longer subject to the ill effects of under-stimulation found in some hospitals, and that they are leading a fairly normal, stimulating social life (however one chooses to define this).

Later studies do little to change this impression. Korer, Freeman and Cheadle (1978) found that in a sample of 190 schizophrenic patients living in the community, 142 were not working and only 49 of these were actively looking for a job. Social isolation (to be discussed in the next chapter) was the major problem for 48 people; 59 said they did not go out as much as they wanted to; six people said they spent 'all the time just sitting doing nothing'; and 58 spent most of their time with nothing to do. There is, however, wide variation between patients.

Once the move away from hospital to community is made it is more difficult to measure stimulation in the same terms as these early studies. Studies of social integration take their place. In their study of the mentally ill living in sheltered housing, Segal and Aviram (1978) found four dimensions of integration into community life: access to resources in the community; presence in the community; participation in community activities; use of resources and, to a lesser degree, consumption. Only 1 per cent of residents came into the top category, finding access to the community and interaction easy, but 12 per cent rarely or never participated in community activities. The largest group, 40 per cent, are only one step up, finding integration difficult and rarely participating in activities.

Under-stimulation does not lead to relapse in the sense of precipitating an acute attack, but it does seem to exacerbate the problems of withdrawal and retreat into the chronic defect state.

Over-stimulation

Stress is more commonly seen in terms of over-stimulation and is implicated in acute relapse. Venables and Wing (1962) demonstrated the significant relationship between levels of arousal, in this case increased cortical arousal, and the withdrawal behaviour of schizophrenics. There is some evidence that increased arousal affects perceptual activity in chronic schizophrenics so that normal selectivity is impaired. Withdrawal from the social and material environment may be seen as a protective mechanism, but as Wing, Leff, Hirsch and Gaind (1972) point out: 'Without appropriate social stimulation this protective withdrawal may go too far.' If, however, the patient is forced to interact, and is thus prevented from adopting the defence of withdrawal, the result may be the occurrence of florid psychotic symptoms, disturbed behaviour and possibly a crisis which may result in hospitalisation.

Psychophysiological responses have been recorded in patients in interviews with their highly emotional families and show significant increases in heart rate and sweat gland activity, indicating increased arousal (Tarrier, Vaughn, Leff and Lader, 1979). Dawson and Nuechterlein (1984) review the literature on electrodermal anomalies in schizophrenia and conclude that 'heightened sensitivity to aversive stimulation appears to be associated with a genetic vulnerability to schizophrenia'. Tonic hyperarousal, they suggest, may 'reflect a later developmental consequence of the underlying vulnerability'.

It is clear that care is needed to maintain the fragile equilibrium between the two extremes of stimulation. Wing, Bennett and Denham (1964) emphasise the need for an introduction to rehabilitation programmes that is both careful and gradual, rather than suddenly placing the patient in a new and demanding situation. It is possible that therapy itself is stressful and may lead to breakdown. Goldberg, Schooler, Hogarty and Roper (1977) found that for symptomatic schizophrenic patients major role therapy, 'a combination of social casework and vocational rehabilitation', had toxic effects and hastened relapse.

Wallis (1972) investigated the types of stress experienced by men in the Royal Navy in the two months preceding a schizophrenic breakdown. No patient had more than three 'units' of stress, but the more units an individual had, the more they related to physical stress rather than personal stress. Family and marital stress was found to carry a slightly better prognosis than others. Personal stress, which was defined as 'those facets of personality which make living less easy' was also an indicator of good prognosis: a result which Wallis points out as being 'rather unexpected'.

But perhaps this finding is not so unexpected since a fuller description of personal stress includes the statement that it is 'more frequently applied to personnel who, irrespective of service and other stresses, disliked service life and felt unhappy and poorly integrated in it'.

Serban (1975) was able to demonstrate that in four general areas — social performance, family interaction, social-personal interaction and social maladaptive activities — non-schizophrenics experience significantly less stress in dealing with life events than do schizophrenics. Within the schizophrenic group, the chronic patients showed more stress than acute patients. These findings led Serban to suggest that the present community after-care treatment is contra-indicated for chronic patients who will be unable to function under the high levels of stress they will experience, and thus will be unable to live in the community for any reasonable period of time. Some of the work in the area of stress and schizophrenia emphasises not so much the stress as a causal factor, but stress as a contextual antecedent of symptom behaviour. Levy (1976) thus describes both intimacy avoidance and emotional intolerance in an interview as producing schizophrenic symptomatology.

These last studies begin to use the concept of stress in a different way from the Venables and Wing, and Tarrier *et al.* studies, where stress is seen as the interaction of stimulation and arousal, and leads to the consideration of stress in a wider context, particularly as it relates to life events.

Life Events

There are numerous methodological problems in research into life events and schizophrenia, not least that of diagnosis itself, the insidious onset of schizophrenia in many instances, retrospective data, the combining of first and subsequent admission data, a clear definition of independent events, critical time periods and interaction with personality and lifestyle. Brown (1974), however, suggests that the root of the problem lies in the nature and meaning of life events to produce illness.

There is general agreement that there is evidence to link life events with acute episodes and relapse in schizophrenia, but whether this is of major importance or only a trivial consideration is open to debate. Brown and Birley (1968) first demonstrated that important life events or crises play a considerable role in precipitating both onset and subsequent severe acute episodes. Newly admitted schizophrenic patients and a control group of non-schizophrenics were compared over a three-month period on a variety of life events. The three months preceded onset of acute symptoms in the patients. Events recorded included positive events such as promotion or marriage; negative events such as losing a job, involvement in crime, and death in the family; others could be either positive or negative events, depending on individual circumstances. Events were also divided in those that were outside the patient's control, 'independent' or not. Findings showed that the onset of the schizophrenic episode was preceded by a fairly sharp increase in life events that were not attributable to abnormal behaviour by the patient.

Later studies broadly confirm this finding (Birley and Brown, 1970; Brown, Harris and Peto, 1973; Leff, Hirsch, Gaind, Rhodes and Stevens, 1973; Jacobs, Pinsoff and Paykel, 1974; Jacobs and Myers, 1976), but the interpretation which is put upon it varies. Leff concludes that 'outpatients on a maintenance therapy are ... unlikely to relapse unless exposed to some additional stress in the form of one or other life event'. Life events can be categorised into two causal roles: 'formative' and 'triggering'. The formative role means that life events are more important than other predisposing factors such as genetic factors, personality traits, early experience and current social problems, including support. Brown *et al.* (1973) conclude that these predisposing factors are more important in the development of schizophrenia than life events, which are more likely to 'trigger an onset which might well have occurred in any case'.

Schwartz and Myers (1977a) find that the areas in which schizophrenics experienced a greater number of life events than a control group were interpersonal, health, work, legal and community crises, and that these events were more likely to be exits from the social field and socially undesirable. They also suggest (1976b) that the non-psychotic symptoms such as anxiety, depression and somatic preoccupations are more affected than psychotic behaviour. In conclusion, Schwartz and Myers (1977b) suggest that, while their results do not directly support the model that the schizophrenic illness is triggered by the number of life events, they 'may increase vulnerability to the more severe symptoms characteristic of schizophrenia'. They suggest that the schizophrenic individual has some measure of coping when life events are within the individual's psychological control.

Other studies have considered the quality of life events and their relationship to stress and thus to illness. Streiner, Norman, McFarlane and Roy (1981) showed that negative events, that is those which were undesirable, uncontrolled and unanticipated, correlated with measures of strain; positive events, however, namely anticipated, controlled and desirable, did not.

The role of life events in schizophrenia remains unclear. In a review of the research literature, Rabkin (1980) indicates that schizophrenics do not report more events than other psychiatric patient groups, although more events are reported by relapsed than unrelapsed patients. She concludes that life events 'are not in themselves sufficient, either quantitatively or qualitatively, to account of illness onset'. Spring (1981) indicates that although it appears 'that stress *may* play some causal role ... its impact is smaller than we might have wished and certainly less specific than the role of loss in depression'.

Dohrenwend and Egri (1981), however, re-analyse some of the previous case-control studies and include literature on schizophrenia and combat conditions. They conclude that 'the consensus that stressful life events play only a trivial role in causing schizophrenic episodes is premature'.

Interactional Models of Stress in Schizophrenia

The causal stress model for schizophrenia is an appealing one, but is fraught with problems, both of a theoretical and practical nature. One major difficulty seems to arise over the definition of 'stress' itself: whether what is meant is the psychobiological response of the individual, as in the Selye (1956) model; whether it is used synonomously with the term stressor; or whether it is an interaction between stimulus and individual factors, which is a broadly social science approach. As Spring (1981) comments, this approach makes 'excellent common sense and splendid clinical sense' but needs to be used with other types of definitions to make it a useful way of looking at stress and schizophrenia. If not, then the cognitive peculiarities of schizophrenia itself will interfere with the measurement and experience of stress as the patient's perception of reality may be distorted.

This in part ties in with the definition of onset of schizophrenia; whether this is at the point when psychotic symptoms are in evidence and diagnosable, or at some point before this. Thus, high geographic and job mobility may be part of the pre-schizophrenic process but will also contribute to a high life events score.

The studies which demonstrate a triggering effect for life events in the three to four weeks before an acute episode would seem to fit a single vulnerability/stress model. Other studies, however, would indicate that the interaction is unlikely to be this straightforward.

Marsella and Snyder (1981) present a conceptual model in which schizophrenia or schizophrenic-type disorders are modified by the simultaneous interaction of stressors, social supports and stress states. The model is complex and proposes a number of categories for each of the three components in the model. Stressors have three parameters: stressor category, stressor content and stressor descriptors. Social supports have four parameters: structure, interactional properties, qualitative properties and functional indices. Stress states have three: dimensions of overload-underload, positive-negative affect, high arousal-low arousal. These three components are 'assumed to be relevant to understanding, describing, and predicting the aetiology, expression, course and prognosis of various dysfunctional profiles associated with schizophreniform disorders'.

A vulnerability model has been proposed by several researchers, but with varying emphasis and parameters. Zubin and Spring (1977), for example, propose a second-order vulnerability model as being the common denominator between the models. They suggest that 'each of us is endowed with a degree of vulnerability that under suitable circumstances will express itself in an episode of schizophrenic illness'. These 'suitable circumstances' presumably include the genetic inheritance of the individual vulnerability, which is described as 'a relatively permanent, enduring trait', as distinguished from schizophrenic episodes, which are 'waxing and waning states'. Highly vulnerable individuals, therefore, will have repeated episodes, whereas the 'relatively invulnerable' will have 'one brief episode or none at all'.

Nuechterlein and Dawson (1984) outline a 'tentative interactive vulnerability/stress model' of the development and course of schizophrenia, with four major categories of primary components, namely, enduring vulnerability characteristics, external environmental stimuli, transient intermediate states and outcome behaviours. The model highlights the individual vulnerability factors, and Nuechterlein and Dawson raise the question of whether these might be related to the subtypes of schizophrenia.

Social vulnerability factors such as coping and competence may be separate from, and follow on from, psychotic periods rather than being identified as part of them.

Lukoff, Snyder, Ventura and Neuchterlein (1984) emphasise that schizophrenic individuals seem 'less adept than most persons at coping skilfully to resolve the environmental threat through behavioural coping techniques, to reduce their resulting stress level through cognitive coping techniques, or to recruit social support during times of crisis'. This might be of importance since, as they point out, none of the parameters in life events and stressful family interaction are exclusive to schizophrenia and occur in other disorders.

2 THE PATIENT IN SOCIETY

The role of the social environment in schizophrenia can be approached from two viewpoints: the effect that society has on the patient and the effect that the patient has on society. Both are complicated and there is likely to be interaction between the two; for example, the way in which patients behave may affect the way society sees and treats them, which in turn further affects them. Of primary concern to clinicians will be the effect of the social environment on the patient, in terms of factors implicated in aetiology, relapse and rehabilitation. This chapter will deal with the demographic variables involved and on the view society has of the schizophrenic patient. The problems the patient has in dealing with life in the community will be dealt with in more detail in Chapter 7.

Epidemiological studies reveal something about the demographic features of the schizophrenic patient. However, these studies collect their information in such a variety of ways that comparisons may be difficult, particularly with regard to studies of incidence and prevalence, first and subsequent hospital admissions, and patients in the community, patients receiving treatment and those not. Methodological variables of these types can lead to confusion both in interpreting the basic data and in the hypotheses and theories associated with them. Since many of the classic studies are now between 20 and 40 years old, changes in hospital admissions policy, employment trends and housing should be borne in mind.

Factors in the physical and social environment which relate to schizophrenia are many and varied. Although certain variables may be found in time to have an instrumental role in the aetiology of schizophrenia, we can be more certain at present about the role played by particular variables in the course of the illness, particularly relapse rates. Such research is also relevant when considering policy, administration and the planning of services, both within the hospital system and as part of community care.

The variables considered in such studies are frequently difficult to measure independently. There is necessarily much overlap and interaction between variables. Thus the implications of these studies, and the hypotheses and theories about schizophrenia which have developed from them, will be discussed together later in the chapter.

The Urban Environment

Most studies considered here are those relating to Western culture, and much depends on whether incidence or prevalence rates are considered.

The first epidemiological study of schizophrenia was included in a study of psychiatric admissions, and the parts of the city from which they came, in Chicago between 1922 and 1934 (Faris and Dunham, 1939). It was found that people with a schizophrenic diagnosis were not randomly distributed throughout the population, but were concentrated in the inner city areas. For example, there were 111 cases per 100,000 of the adult population in the high-rental flat area, while the poorer central business district had a rate of 1,195, the median rate for the city as a whole being 322.

Most later studies support this early finding. In the United States Schroeder (1942) at St Louis, Milwaukee and Kansas City; Gerard and Houston (1953) in Worcester, Massachusetts; Dunham (1965) in Detroit; Gardner and Babigan (1966) at Rochester, New York; Klee, Spiro, Balin and Gorwitz (1967) in Baltimore, and Rowitz and Levy (1968) in Chicago, all found higher rates of schizophrenia in central city zones. European studies are also in substantial agreement; Hare (1956a) in Bristol, England; Sundby and Nyhus (1963) in Oslo, Norway; Walsh (1969) in Dublin, Ireland; and Häfner and Reiman (1970) in Mannheim, Germany.

Although the general finding is towards higher concentrations of schizophrenic individuals in city centres, there are variations. Clausen and Kohn (1959) were not able to show a relationship between rates of schizophrenia and either occupation or residential area. In a later paper, Kohn (1968) re-examines data from other studies and suggests that the larger the city, the stronger the relationship between indices of social class and rates of schizophrenia. He suggests that there is a body of research evidence to support the claim that socioeconomic differentials disappear where there is a smaller population. Rural or agricultural areas, and societies where technological development has had a low impact, would seem to point to a more favourable prognosis for the schizophrenic, as has been mentioned in Chapter one.

It should be borne in mind that many of these studies use correlations between group parameters as though this is the same as correlations between individuals within that group. Individuals who develop schizophrenia may vary from the group described on important characteristics. In the Faris and Dunham (1939) study, for example, although Negro areas of the city had high rates, it was the white members of these areas who showed the particularly high rates for schizophrenia. Kramer, Van Korff and Kessler (1980), however, estimate that there is a lifetime prevalence for schizophrenia at age 55 years of at least 3 per cent for whites and 4 per cent for non-whites in Monroe County, New York, although they consider morbidity measures of secondary importance to incidence and point-prevalence data.

Social Class and Occupation

Although social class and residential area are linked, the formal definition of social class in Britain at least, is dependent on occupation. Since the early years of the century, a large number of studies in both Europe and America have supported the findings of an over-representation of schizophrenia in the lower classes (for example, Nolan, 1917; Clark, 1949; Hollingshead and Redlich, 1953, 1954; Frumkin, 1955; Hare, 1955, 1956a, 1956b; Ødegaard, 1956; Clausen and Kohn, 1959; Jaco 1960; Cooper 1961a, 1961b; Goldberg and Morrison, 1963; Thomas and Lock, 1963; Turner and Wagenfeld, 1967).

A study by Hollingshead and Redlich (1958) found that not only were most schizophrenics to be found in social class V, but that the incidence was larger between IV and V than between other adjacent classes. They also demonstrated that the neuroses were not linked to social class in any noticeable way. Not only was incidence inversely related to social class, but so too was re-entry into treatment and continuity of treatment.

Mishler and Scotch (1963), in a review of nine studies in which all show the highest number of schizophrenics in the lowest social group studied, rework some of the data. They suggest that not only are rates for schizophrenia in this group considerably higher than in the social class immediately above, but when male and female rates are assessed separately, then the female rates within the lowest occupational category are considerably higher than the males.

A number of factors influencing female social class status should be borne in mind in considering studies on social class. Of women who work, a significantly higher proportion are found in unskilled or semi-skilled jobs than in managerial or professional occupations; this proportion is higher than for men (Mackie and Pattullo, 1977). Thus, if women are classed by their occupation, there will always be more in the lower classes than men. In referring to a woman's social class it should be made clear whether this is based on her husband's (or head of household's) occupation, as is usual, or whether she is separately classified by her own occupation for the purposes of the study.

Linking schizophrenia to particular occupations beyond a general category 'unskilled' is a difficult task. In a study on occupational prestige Clarke (1949) reports that 'there is a real association between high income and high prestige, on the one hand, and low psychoses rates, on the other hand'. Ødegaard (1956) investigated the incidence of psychoses in various occupations in Norway, but the data is difficult to interpret beyond the general conclusion linking schizophrenia with unskilled workers, particularly seamen and agricultural and other labourers.

In these occupations, schizophrenia was six times as frequent as manic-depression compared with trade and professional occupations where it is only twice as high. This is partly due to certain occupations having a higher proportion of single men and the higher incidence of schizophrenia among the single, and also to such jobs being more accommodating of the casual worker. In the other diagnostic categories the distribution is fairly equal between single and married men.

Social Mobility

Social mobility is an important factor when considering some of the theories linking class and schizophrenia, but there is much disagreement between studies. It can be measured either between generations, comparing fathers and sons, or within the individual, monitoring changes in occupation. Few studies compare social mobility in schizophrenics with non-schizophrenic controls.

Certain features of an individual make upward social mobility more likely, particularly being white, female, middle class and of good education. Lystad (1957) found that among this group schizophrenic patients 'show less upward status mobility than matched, non-mentally ill persons'. This difference is not upheld, however, among those who are negroes, male, lower class and with poor education.

In their study, Clausen and Kohn (1959) found that although 42 per cent of schizophrenic patients had a history of high occupational instability, as shown by intermittent employment and a high number of jobs for a short period, compared with 8 per cent of matched controls, this was not linked to changes in occupational status. They report that '*none* of the schizophrenics moved consistently downward in occupational status from the time of first steady employment until hospitalisation'. Fluctuations in occupational level are shown by 8 per cent, likewise 8 per cent show consistent upward mobility. Although Clausen and Kohn state that 'this record is approximately equal to that of the normal controls', the trend is in the expected direction of more fluctuation and less upward mobility. Lapouse, Monk and Terris (1956) similarly could find no evidence for downward social mobility.

Harris, Linker, Norris and Shepherd (1956) in England suggested downward mobility only for those whose fathers are in social classes I and II. A comparison of occupational status before hospital admission and after discharge shows 78 per cent remaining at the same level. Also in Britain, Morrison (1959) suggests there is a random social class distribution among fathers of male schizophrenics, even though most of these came from the lower classes. He proposed that downward mobility may not be individual but generational, combining both genetic and environmental factors. Goldberg and Morrison (1963) found in England and Wales a high proportion of male schizophrenic patients in social class V, although their fathers were randomly distributed throughout the population.

A total dropout from the labour market was seen most commonly in the highest and lowest social class, particularly if this followed failure in either academic work or training. A work record was more likely to be maintained in those patients who were in social class III or IV and whose work involved some degree of skill. Goldberg and Morrison suggest that schizophrenia's insidious onset during adolescence meant that occupational skills were not attained, leading to downward mobility; for those patients who suffered acute onset, they indicate a drop in social class shortly before admission. Cooper (1961a) found occupational deterioration to be most severe for those patients who were originally in low status occupations.

Turner and Wagenfeld (1967) indicate that not only is there a 'substantially disproportionate number of schizophrenics in the lowest occupational category', but that the fathers of the patients were also over-represented, 'although to a lesser degree'. The finding contradicts the previously cited studies that suggest a normal distribution of fathers, and is further interesting because most patients with fathers at the lowest level (a seven-point occupational prestige scale is used) are themselves from a higher level. Wender, Rosenthal, Kety, Schulsinger and Welner (1974) showed that the socioeconomic status of adopted schizophrenic patients was lower than both their biological and adoptive fathers.

Social Isolation

Social isolation is not an easy concept either to define or measure, as demonstrated by the idiosyncratic ways in which researchers use the term. One approach views social isolation as an aetiological variable, either predisposing or precipitating, and studies of the pre-schizophrenic individual are common and usually retrospective. In such studies isolation is defined either in physical and social terms (such as number of social contacts, friends and so on), or the more psychological isolation described by the psychoanalysts. Both the individual and the community as a whole can be described on a number of social indices and areas, with high and low rates of schizophrenia compared. A second approach sees the isolation of the schizophrenic individual as deriving from the illness itself, and thus describes isolation in the present, particularly as it relates to prognosis and relapse. The early studies tended to concentrate on the aetiological nature of isolation; later studies having a wider perspective. Another factor was introduced in the early 1960s: the change in both attitude and policy towards community care. This means that the population of patients living in the community since then is both larger and qualitatively different from the previous group. This may account for some differences in data.

An Isolated Population?

When community care was first embraced as the principle of care for chronic mental patients, it was easy to assume that once patients lived in the community rather than the hospital then they would automatically become part of that community. Sadly, this did not happen and stories soon appeared of isolation on a scale worse than in the hospital chronic wards. Lack of facilities undoubtedly plays a part, but this is only one factor in a tripartate problem of facilities, the nature of schizophrenia itself, and family attitudes and ability to cope. The definition of social isolation differs from study to study and is, in some part, dependent on the circumstances of the group in question.

Isolation can be seen in terms of actual contact with others, such as family, friends or other groups, but it can also describe confinement to the home or lack of active involvement in the community. Clearly, different 'degrees' of isolation will be found depending on the type of criteria used. Measurement should involve actual behaviour as well as reported circumstances; just because a patient lives with his family rather than alone does not mean that he is necessarily accepted by or integrated into that family. This will be discussed further in Chapters 3 and 5. An additional problem is presented when comparison figures are not given for non-psychotic patients in the same community. This is particularly important where 'active' involvement in community affairs is under consideration. Care should also be taken where class differences exist in patterns of social behaviour.

Often it is not possible to separate social isolation from other social indices. For example, those living in the inner city areas tend to be in the lower social classes and are also those most commonly living alone. Both Gerard and Houston (1953) and Hare (1956b) observed that patients who were admitted from a family setting had a random distribution throughout the city. It was only those living alone who were from the poorer inner city areas and appeared to be forming a separate group of their own which distorted the general distribution pattern. Reasons why there should be ghettos of single schizophrenic patients in inner city areas will be discussed later in this chapter.

That the schizophrenic population is generally isolated can be inferred from the number of single people in its population. Of a total number of discharges in one year amounting to 327, Parker,

Kenning and Welder (1971) reported 222 to be unattached. Although approximately 40 per cent of the women were married, only 20 per cent of the men were. Other studies have also shown a preponderance of single rather than married people, particularly single men (Ødegaard, 1956; Farina, Garmezy and Barry, 1963; Brown, Bone, Dalison and Wing, 1966).

The author reports (Atkinson, 1981) in a study of schizophrenic patients known at a London hospital, and coming from families in social classes III, IV and V, that 51 per cent of the female patients were presently married compared to only 24 per cent of the men. Being unmarried and being isolated are not identical and although there may be some overlap, care should be taken in extrapolating from marital status. In the Atkinson study, although 61 per cent of the total patient group were not presently married, 71 per cent of these were living with at least one relative or friend or in a family group, 9 per cent were living in hostels, and only 20 per cent were living alone.

Living in the community, or even with a family, however, does not guarantee that the schizophrenic patient will not be isolated. Hamilton and Hoenig (1966) estimated the amount of social isolation in an unselected group of new psychiatric patients presenting during 1958 to 1960. Of this group, nearly 25 per cent were schizophrenic. They defined social isolation as the 'degree of confinement to the home'; this being described as a 'sociological state, objectively defined, which is itself distinct both from "social isolation", the state of bereavement or loss of intimates and from the subjective sense of "loneliness" which may or may not be associated with the two previous states according to the habits and outlook of the individual concerned'.

Initially, 60 per cent of the patients were confined to their home completely while another 25 per cent left only to go to work or to do necessary shopping. Only 15 per cent were not confined at all. These patients were reassessed after four years, during which time they had been involved in an extramural type of service. This time only 25 per cent were completely confined, and those not confined at all had risen to 47 per cent. The proportion confined had remained fairly stable at 27 per cent.

Of social factors, neither social class nor living accommodation seemed to be related to confinement which was associated more with the type of household, a point previously noted by Freeman and Simmons (1958a). This important factor will be taken up and discussed in greater detail in Chapter 5. Of the non-social factors, chronicity, organic illness and increasing age all inter-related and affected the degree of confinement. Being schizophrenic appeared to have no effect on the individual becoming confined, which, as the investigators report 'was rather unexpected'. This finding was unusual since elsewhere social isolation has been linked with schizophrenia in a number of ways: it may, in part, be accounted for by the investigators' definition of social isolation.

Cooper (1961a, 1961b) also related social isolation to type of living group and suggests that 'while this was rather an over-simplification of a vague concept, the patients having been in or out of his family setting gave a practical criterion of isolation'. Later he suggests that social isolation is related to socioeconomic stress, although not the same. Social isolation was related to prognosis: those patients who before admission had been living in a family group and who returned to that group had a better prognosis than those who did not. He sums up the possible importance of community integration by saying 'once the schizophrenic patient, of whatever social status, can return to a community which has not forgotten him and offers him a socially useful role, his prognosis will be greatly improved'.

Isolation as a Causal Factor

That social isolation is such an important factor in the development of schizophrenia was first suggested by Faris (1934). He suggests that 'any form of isolation that cuts the person off from intimate social relations for an extended period of time may possibly lead to this form of mental disorder'. His work with Dunham a few years later (Faris and Dunham, 1939) pointed to high rates of first admission for schizophrenia in city areas with high mobility and low socioeconomic status, among immigrant populations in the slums, and among individuals living outside their ethnic group. In all these groups one might expect a large number of isolated individuals. Faris suggests that rejection by one's peer group leads to isolation and from there to psychosis. Thus isolation is seen as a 'causative' factor in a chain of events starting with parental behaviour producing unacceptable social behaviour in the child ('spoiled child' type of personality), leading to isolation from all but family members. This is followed by more active rejection from peers producing unhappiness. There then follows a period, possibly for years, where the child tries to establish relationships, but fails and ultimately there is 'a withdrawal from a hopeless goal'. Sociability declines and the seclusive personality of the schizophrenic develops. Finally, the symptoms of schizophrenia are seen as being due to inexperience in social situations and thus an unconventional or inappropriate response.

Such a theory of the aetiological nature of isolation would suggest that social isolation should be evident in all persons diagnosed schizophrenic. Unfortunately, such evidence does not exist. The evidence, such as it is, is patchy and inconclusive, although this may in part be due to the difficulty in defining both social isolation and schizophrenia. Dunham (1944) provided supportive evidence in a study of catatonic schizophrenics growing up in areas of high delinquency rates.

Kohn and Clausen (1955) studied a group of manic-depressive schizophrenic patients and controls matched with the patient approximately 16 years before hospitalisation. Thus about half the patients had a control who had been in the same class at school. Questions concentrated on two types of social behaviour: who had the respondent played with when he was 13 to 16 years old, and in what type of activities was he engaged? These aspects of sociability were combined to form an 'Index of Social Participation'. Although a significantly larger proportion of patients are found to have been isolated or partially isolated than controls, nevertheless this is only the case for about one-third of the patients. There is no difference between controls and patients for playing with siblings only (although all but one in this group were females). Thus two-thirds of the patients do not differ from controls on retrospective reports of social behaviour in early adolescence.

Kohn and Clausen then went on to compare the adolescent social experiences of the isolated and non-isolated patients. Isolated patients did not differ from non-isolated on external factors such as living in inaccessible farms, childhood illnesses, residential mobility or parental restrictions on either choice of activity or friends. Although a larger proportion of patients than controls report their mother as having been more easily angered, more dominating and more restrictive than their fathers, isolated patients do not report this more often than non-isolated patients. In all other areas of family functioning there is no reported difference between isolated and non-isolated patients.

Hospital case records indicate that, for patients classified as isolated, the relatives were noting signs of personality disturbance by the time the child was 13 or 14, while patients classified as partially isolated appeared normal to their relatives even though, by this age, they report some withdrawal. Finally, Kohn and Clausen could find no differences in hospital career of present functioning between the groups of isolated and non-isolated patients.

Thus it seems that social isolation is neither a necessary nor a sufficient cause for developing schizophrenia. The question is more complex and more individual; why do some people develop interpersonal difficulty, experience alienation and retreat into interpersonal failure? Studies point to the prognostic importance of a good premorbid personality and good social integration, but there are rarely comparisons with non-psychiatric controls as to what can be considered 'normal social behaviour'.

Another approach to Faris' hypothesis of social isolation was taken about the same time by Jaco (1954). Distinguishing between 'precipitating' factors (those which accelerate onset) and 'predisposing' factors (those which present a susceptibility toward acquiring the disorder), he compared an area of high schizophrenic breakdown with one of low rates of schizophrenia on a measure of social isolation, this being defined as 'the cutting off or minimising of contact and communication with others'. The expectation was 'that those communites having high rates of schizophrenia will have a concomitantly high degree of social isolation'. Thirteen out of 19 measures show a difference between the two areas. Communities having a high rate of schizophrenia also showed more social isolation as evidenced by '(1) knowing the names of fewer neighbours, (2) fewer personal friends, (3) fewer acquaintances, (4) more renting than owning homes, (5) less membership in lodges or fraternal organisations, (6) greater unemployment, (7) more job turnover, (8) fewer visits to the central business districts, (9) fewer visits with friends, (10) fewer visits to other areas of the city, (11) fewer trips out of town, (12) less inter-city immigration, (13) fewer friends in remote areas'.

Jaco suggests that from this a more reliable measure of social disorganisation might be constructed and its 'crucial relation to schizophrenia' investigated. His evidence leads him to conclude that 'a high degree of social isolation in these communities known to have high incidence rates ... warrants serious consideration as a precipitating influence in the social aetiology of schizophrenia.

The psychoanalytic approach views psychological isolation as a causative factor in the development of schizophrenia. Fromm-Reichman (1948) for example, describes the patient as destructful and resentful of other people as well as having sensitivity and a 'never-satisfied lonely need for benevolent contacts'. Will (1959) talks about 'relatedness': 'the interaction of humans in social fields ... and to those ties between all humans which cannot be disregarded'. The schizophrenic reaction he believes can be seen as 'the expressions of complicated patterns of behaviour adopted by the organism in an effort to deal with the gross inadequacy in relating to other humans'. This inadequacy he later describes as 'intolerables of anxiety and aloneness'.

Isolation as a Response

The importance of the current social support system is frequently reaffirmed. These social networks can be viewed both from the outside, in descriptive terms, and from the inside 'from the point of view of the phenomenology of the patient's experience of his group' (Beels, 1979). Since we create our own social networks dependent on our motivations, experience and view of the world, this experience might be different for schizophrenics and non-schizophrenics.

Beels suggests that on becoming schizophrenic the individual leaves one network, where he was regarded as ordinary and enters a new system which sees him mainly in terms of this new status. New friends will mainly be 'fellow patients, their relatives and friends'. The social consequences of this, and possible rejection by old friends or relatives may be adverse and sometimes dramatic: 'For some this means a drop in social class, a distressing change of taste and interest, a crisis in social confidence and competence.' Disability becomes the dominant characteristic of the group. This has therapeutic significance, as Beels is quick to note. He suggests that successful halfway houses or rehabilitation groups 'take pride *as a group* in their competence in dealing with this affliction' and this could be made better use of in promoting support groups for both sufferers and relatives.

Such supportive groups are not common for most chronic or ex-patients. Segal and his colleagues have studied community integration of chronic patients in sheltered care facilities in the United States (Trute and Segal, 1976; Segal and Aviram, 1978). Among their conclusions are three of particular importance:

1. The typical sheltered care resident has never been fully

integrated into mainstream society.

2. When residents attend a social event, even if they are few in number and their attendance has been mediated by that group or facility, they are still seen as outsiders. Together these suggest that reintegration into the community will be achieved only in a marginal way, and by a small number of individuals.

3. Community factors are the most important predictors of integration.

Not all residents of sheltered housing are schizophrenic, although the majority usually are. Cohen and Sokolovsky (1978) and Sokolovsky, Cohen, Berger and Geiger (1978) looked at a hostel where only 22 per cent of the residents had no psychotic history, 43 per cent had had schizophrenia but showed no residual symptoms, and 35 per cent were schizophrenic with residual symptoms. There was a progressive decrease in the size of the individual's social network on this categorisation, with the non-psychotic patients maintaining a network with the hostel of twice the size of those with severe symtomatology. No group was totally isolated, however, and Cohen and Sokolovsky, stress that 'there was no evidence to suggest that a "back-ward" in the community existed'.

Contacts outside the hostel for psychotic patients were less than for the non-psychotic group, but nevertheless did exist, making up one-third of their total network; 'only two of thirty-three schizophrenics in the sample had no outside interactions'. There were, however, qualitative differences between the networks formed by residual schizophrenics and non-residual schizophrenics.

Hammer, Makiesky-Brown and Gutwirth (1978) suggest that the structure of the network is at least as important as size. They interpret the data to suggest that as well as being smaller in size than networks of non-schizophrenics, they are structurally and qualitatively different. A theory is put forward which implicates social network processes in onset and relapse in schizophrenia. The network is described as the primary source of social feedback which is essential to both develop and maintain culturally appropriate behaviour. The feedback might be inadequate because of the particular characteristics of the schizophrenic's network.

The pattern of sheltered housing is not the same in Britain as America (see later in this chapter). In a study of schizophrenics living in the community (Korer *et al.* 1978) 30 per cent of the sample described an 'inability to make friends and form meaningful relationships' as their most acute problem. It is important to note that this loneliness was not confined to people who lived alone. Indeed, the investigators report that 'many of the people who lived alone seemed self-contained and said they were satisfied with the circumstances of their living arrangements'. How labelling might work to influence the individual's behaviour will be described in Chapter 7.

The Influence of Demographic Variables in Schizophrenia

From this brief review of some of the literature two major factors emerge, namely that there are more schizophrenics in the lower social classes than the upper, and that social isolation, where it is a factor, relates to poor prognosis. The nature of the interaction between these factors and the aetiology and cause of schizophrenia is open to various interpretations.

Drift Theory

The contention of the drift theory is that patients drift down the social scale because of their inability to be successful socially and particularly economically. As Faris and Dunham point out in their 1939 study 'it is a question whether this drift process, which undoubtedly contributes something to the apparent concentration of rates, is anything more than an insignificant factor in causing the concentration'. They suggest not, showing that younger patients, who have little time to drift, are found concentrated in inner city areas in much the same way as older patients. Goldberg and Morrison (1963), however, suggest that from their data there is clear evidence for the drift hypothesis. Cooper (1961b) suggests that although there is a degree of downward mobility, the higher the patient's original social class then the more likely he was to maintain it.

The drift hypothesis would suggest that mobility would be high, both among schizophrenic and pre-schizophrenic groups. Although data on this would appear to be contradictory, this can be accounted for, at least in part, by looking at the nature of mobility. In areas where mobility is seen as having a downward connotation, studies do substantiate the hypothesis. Thus in the United States high rates of schizophrenia were found among immigrants to New York (Malzberg and Lee, 1956) and to California

(Lazarus, Locke and Thomas, 1963), in both cases this being a move to inner city areas. Immigration can be external, entering the city, or internal, within the city. Even internal migration can show up in rates of schizophrenia; Dunham (1965) found that differing rates in two parts of Detroit could be largely due to migration within the city. Similar findings were reported in England by Hare (1956a). This inequality in immigration remained even after adjustment to incidence rates for differences in socioeconomic status (Lee, 1963).

Other countries have not always reported this finding. In Norway it would seem that the move from rural areas to towns represented an upward mobility, and the incidence of schizophrenia was lower among migrants than those who did not move. Those who migrated to Oslo, however, followed the pattern of other studies (Astrup and Ødegaard, 1960).

Social Stress Theory

Stress is implicated in a number of ways with the development of schizophrenia and relapse. Explaining the demographic patterns they found, Faris and Dunham (1939) suggest that schizophrenia is a product of social processes underlying city and urban growth. The social disorganisation, isolation and general conditions of these poor, declining areas is assumed to have an effect, detrimental in nature, on the more vulnerable of those living there.

Variations of Faris and Dunham's causal explanation are still being proposed. Holzman (1977) suggests that the developing countries do not have the 'special stresses' of the developed; that work rates are more flexible and expectations for achievement fewer. The rigid work and social roles of the industrialised nations lead to more obvious and harsher censure when these roles of expectations are flouted, for whatever reason.

What the 'special stresses' of industrialised living means varies from researcher to researcher. Clearly, different occupations have different types of stress and these may be linked to mental illness by a number of mechanisms and interactions. Clark (1948) for example, suggests that it may be that 'the low prestige aspect of an occupation increases the pre-schizophrenic's negative attitudes towards himself'. This is a very different concept of occupational stress from the more usually acknowledged physical stresses such as noise, pollution and so forth, or the psychological stresses associated with concentration and decision making.

Cooper (1961b) is convinced by the stress hypothesis, suggesting that 'an increased socioeconomic stress is exerted on those in the lower social classes' and he firmly states that prognosis 'is directly related to social status'. He does, however, suggest that social isolation, which he sees as 'related to both stress and social class, but not identical with them' also has an important prognostic effect.

Kohn (1968) in a review of the epidemiological literature also comes to the conclusion that 'present evidence would make it seem probable that some substantial part of the phenomenon results from lower class conditions of life being conducive to schizophrenia'. From here the speculations become wider and wider. He suggests that perhaps 'lower and working class patterns of family relationships are broadly conducive to schizophrenia, although the latter is more a surmise than a conclusion'. This hypothesis was later extended when Kohn suggests that the family transmits a particular view of social reality which encourages the illness (Kohn, 1973); 'The heart of my formulation is the hypothesis that the constricted conditions of life experienced by people of lower social class position foster conceptions of social reality so limited and so rigid as to impair people's ability to deal resourcefully with the problematic and the stressful.' There is, however, little in the way of evidence to support his contention and it still does not explain why only some members of the lower social classes become schizophrenic.

The effect of the family on the schizophrenic individual will be considered in more detail in the next chapter.

Differential Treatment

Another explanation for why more schizophrenic individuals are found in the lower social classes has more to do with the way schizophrenic individuals are treated than it does with the illness itself.

Patients from the different social classes present at different times in their history, complain of different problems and receive different types of treatment. Families tolerate bizarre behaviour differently (this will be discussed further in the next chapter) and it also seems reasonable that different communities will tolerate people with problems and strange behaviour in a variable manner.

In the United States, Hollingshead and Redlich (1954) found, for example, that the prevalence of treated schizophrenics was 11 times higher in the lowest class compared with the highest. The greatest difference was found in chronic hospitalised patients where the incidence of class V was 31 times as high as the combined classes I and II. The main treatment difference found include the upper and middle class patients presenting for treatment earlier, coming through medical channels, being treated in private hospitals, being more likely to receive psychotherapy and to be discharged to the family. On the other hand, lower class individuals present later, frequently through legal channels, are treated in state hospitals, either organically or, for a large proportion, custodial care only, and are likely to stay continuously in hospital for long periods.

Again in the United States Meyers and Roberts (1959) compared social classes III and V, demonstrating that not only did the two classes view psychiatric illness differently, but also psychiatrists. Although in neither class did the patient usually seek treatment voluntarily or independently, families in social class III tended to seek treatment after about one month of symptoms, whereas most lower class patients had been showing psychotic symptoms for three years before being brought for treatment. Psychiatric illness itself was generally viewed much more negatively by social class V than by III.

Moore, Benedcke and Wallace (1963) compared schizophrenic women in social classes I, II and III with women in IV and V, although in reporting the results they suggest that a comparison of all other classes with class V would show 'the most dramatic differences'. Class V patients show much poorer treatment results, where treatment always includes at least supportive psychotherapy, ward management, occupational and recreational therapies. These patients were also more likely to be transferred to a state hospital. An interesting finding was that women from both social classes were equally unlikely to be forced into hospitalisation. Generally, lower class patients were less likely to think of their illness in 'psychic terms' and 'neither like or understand us (*the psychiatrist*) very well'.

Although these studies were carried out for the main part in the 1950s and 1960s, and treatment methods have changed since then (particularly regarding long hospitalisation and the use of more effective drugs), nevertheless they do represent the picture at the time of most of the epidemiological studies cited. Clear differences will be seen with treatment methods in Britain where very few patients are treated privately and where psychotherapy for schizophrenics is uncommon. Even within Britain, though, the data is not uniform; the major disagreements being over treatment and length of stay in hospital.

Carstairs, Tange, O'Connor and Barber (1955) found that the only group where long-stay patients out-numbered short-stay patients was social class III, which contradicts American findings. Wing, Denham and Munro (1959) found that patients whose previous occupation has been unskilled (social class V) did not have a worse prognosis (i.e. for length of stay in hospital) than any other group. Brooke (1959) reported a clear social class gradient for duration of hospital stay, both for single and married men. This was supported by Cooper (1961a) who concluded that: a significantly higher proportion of patients who became long-stay cases came from the lower class; mean duration of hospital stay was related to social class, being longer for the lower class; response to treatment, as measured both by rate of discharge and clinical state at discharge, was less favourable for the lower classes. These findings could not be explained in terms of age or marital status at admission. There was no relationship between class and either formal hospital treatment or with follow-up supervision, unlike American studies. Like American studies, though, mode of referral to the hospital and inpatient status differed, indicating that patients from social classes IV and V were less likely to present for voluntary treatment. Lower class patients also demonstrated less co-operation with treatment.

In a further study, Cooper (1961b) confirmed his finding that length of hospital stay was related to social class, but suggested this could not be regarded as prognostically important since only a small number of patients became long-stay.

3 THE FAMILY IN AETIOLOGY AND RELAPSE

Although a definitive model regarding the aetiology of schizo-phrenia has yet to be proposed, there is a general agreement that both biochemical and environmental factors are likely to play a part. The assumption is that to develop schizophrenia an individ-ual needs to have a genetic predisposition to develop the disorder, which is triggered by an environmental stress of some kind. This stress might come from upbringing, lifestyle, maturation and, indeed, anything in the individual's milieu.

The question, then, is not only what are the relative contribu-tions of environmental and heredity aspects but, as Erlenmeyer-Kimling (1968) points out, 'what kinds of environ-mental input triggers manifestations of the disorder in genotypically vulnerable persons, and why are these important in a psychological sense?' Summing up the proceedings of the Second Research Conference on the Foundations for Research in Psychia-try on the Transmission of Schizophrenia, Rosenthal (1968) concluded that 'everyone agreed that it is the *interaction* which must be our major future concern, but differences of opinion exist regarding the implications of this view'. This would still seem to be the case.

Possibly because of the apparently multifactorial nature of the causes of schizophrenia, and that different factors are relevant for different patients, clinicians seem to develop their own aetiological model for schizophrenia, in that they combine several accepted models (Soskis, 1972). The models considered were genetic, psychodynamic, family-learning, biochemical-neurological, social and existential. The highest correlations were between existential and social, existential and family-learning, and biochemical-neurological and genetic pairs. Although the biochemical-neurological and genetic models were related to each other they were not related to any of the non-physical models. This seems unusual in that most research seems to suggest both physical and environmental factors are of importance and there is a strong interaction effect. Soskis (1972) found that clinicians generally favoured treatments which were logically derived from the aetiological model they used. These were not, however, exclusive preferences, although their choice stayed within the physical versus psychosocial group.

In this chapter the theories of schizophrenia which involve the family will be considered, not because the family is considered necessarily to be of prime aetiological importance, but because the family *is* involved in the care of the patient, and may have something to do with prognosis and the general career of the patient. There is little, if any, direct evidence to link family lifestyle with the development of schizophrenia.

Psychodynamic Theories

The first theories which emphasised the role of the family in the aetiology of schizophrenia are founded in dynamic theory and couched in psychoanalytic terms. They concentrate, however, on interpersonal functioning while other psychodynamic and analytic theories are more properly concerned with individual functioning, and take many and varying forms. That the psychoses are the severest form of psychopathology and, therefore, the regression is deepest, is agreed by all.

The metapsychological disputes surrounding schizophrenia focus traditionally on whether schizophrenia is a deficit or a defence. The latter is derived from Freud's early views on the subject, the former from his later formulations. Psychoanalysis suggests that whereas crucial regression in the neuroses is never earlier than the anal stage, in the psychoses it goes back to the oral period. In schizophrenia the regression to primary narcissism is seen most clearly, as the regression is complete to the early oral stage and because the super-ego is only minimally involved. The break with reality has two immediate causes, an increase in demands and an increase in anxiety accompanying them. Thus reality is rejected because of the temptations which it holds (Freud, 1914).

It was Jung (1906), however, who was instrumental in developing the dynamic theory of schizophrenia. He suggested that the deterioration of the patients in the later stages of the illness was a psychosomatic expression of a pathological libidinal process.

Adlerian individual psychology is concerned with the development of schizophrenia as a style of life by the child. It hypothesises that because regression is so complete we never become aware that each child lays out a life plan for himself and then structures it to a lifestyle by learning and experience. In schizophrenia something forces the child to give up his orientation to social reality. While saying he 'cannot believe that any single form of family structure can produce this', Burton (1974) continues that it does seem that 'the child receives a covert mandate from the family to rescue it from its paradoxes ... It becomes his task to make the family philosophically and morally plausible'.

Searles (1959), from a psychoanalytic orientation, takes the opposite point of view, stating that a person will develop schizophrenia 'partly by reason of a long-continued effort, a largely or wholly unconscious effort, on the part of some person or persons highly important in his upbringing, to drive him crazy'. The motivation for this can arise from either the parent or the child, and Searles identified eight motives. These may arise from: (1) jealousy, where it is the psychological equivalent to murder; (2) a desire to externalise a sense of 'craziness' which threatens the self; (3) a need to find an end to a situation which is filled with intolerable suspense and conflict; (4) transference between parent and child; (5) a desperate need to find a 'soul-mate to assuage unbearable loneliness'; (6) a need to encourage closeness; (7) the child's need to develop as an individual may become expressed as a need to drive the other crazy; (8) the need to attain, maintain or renew 'the gratification inherent in the symbolic mode of relatedness'.

Searles suggests a number of methods used to bring 'craziness' about, including unconscious, or even conscious, emotional conflict, the use of stimulation-frustration, sudden changes in emotion, emotional content or topic of conversation, double-bind and dealing with the other person on several unrelated levels of interaction at the same time. This is not only a highly developed model relating the interaction between two people in the aetiology of schizophrenia, but one of the most extreme.

These psychodynamic theories are only concerned, if at all, with the family at the fringes of the individual. Some, however, regard the family more centrally. All the approaches consider the family's response to and acceptance of that which is seen as irrational or unrealistic. It is not always clear what criteria for describing behaviour as irrational is being used, either by investigators or families, nor whether there is any agreement on this at all. It is assumed that 'rational' is synonymous with 'healthy' or 'normal', although it is rare for data on 'normal' or even non-psychotic families to be presented as a comparison in these studies. Furthermore, it would seem that many children learn to live with a double standard of within-family/outside-family behaviour. Anthony (1972) talks of the 'contagious subculture of psychosis' that some individuals, namely the 'more suggestible, the more submissive and the more undifferentiated', may respond to irrationality within the family more rapidly and more completely than others.

Although most of the psychodynamic theories concentrate on the family of origin of the patient, some research has looked at the psychodynamics of the marital relationship where the patient became ill only after marriage. Alanen and Kinnunen (1974) suggest that three types of marriage are involved, depending on their pathological significance, and are broadly the same regardless of whether the patient is the husband or wife. The most pathogenetic was type I, characterised by a patient who was passive-dependent and a spouse who was dominating but unempathic. The importance of the marriage meant that the patient was in a binding emotional conflict. In type II marriages, the most prominent feature was the unsatisfied infantile dependency needs of both spouses. The marriages caused difficulties for the patient because the spouse failed to provide the necessary support. Type III marriages showed a superficially dominant patient and a passive, but supportive spouse, although such support did not prevent the patient falling ill.

There are several prominent family-based psychodynamic theories that can be considered separately.

Fromm-Reichmann and the Schizophrenogenic Mother

Fromm-Reichmann (1948) coined the term 'schizophrenogenic mother' reconstructing the figure from the experiences related in psychotherapy with the individual patient. This mother was cold and withdrawn from the child, expressing little maternal love, and making little mention of the father's part in the child's upbringing or the marital relationship. This view of the parents was an elaboration of the picture of the schizophrenic parents suggested by Hajdu-Gimes (1940) and derived from the analysis of four schizophrenic women. The pattern he found was of a mother who was cold, rigorous and 'sadistically aggressive', and a father who was soft, indifferent and passive.

Bateson and the Double-Bind

The earliest of the theories to involve the whole family was put forward by Bateson, Jackson, Haley and Weakland (1956) and centres on paradoxical communication in the child-parent relationship. They coined the now famous 'double-bind' to describe a situation when the child, no matter what action he takes, will be construed by the parent as being in the wrong. The focus is essentially a one-to-one communication and for a double-bind to exist a number of conditions are considered essential. These include: (1) the need for two or more people to be involved; (2) the person(s) giving the directive need to be important to the child; (3) the experience of double-bind must be repeated; (4) punishment must be implied or explicit for the 'wrong' choice; (5) the child is unable to escape from the situation, or to point out the contradiction which is denied. The actual communication involves a primary negative injunction, followed by a second which contradicts or conflicts with the first, usually at a more abstract level. Other directives forbid the child from leaving the situation and both injunctions carry with them the threat of punishment. The conflicting injunctions may come in verbal form, e.g. 'do not be so obedient' or may include a mismatch of verbal and nonverbal messages (Bateson, Jackson, Haley and Weakland, 1956; Haley, 1959a, 1959b, 1960).

Approaching schizophrenia from this perspective tends to involve redefining it as something other than an illness; it is better described as a pattern or method of communication (Watzlawick, Beavin and Jackson, 1968). Empirical studies have been conducted into the use of the double-bind, but it is not easy to identify. One study (Ringuette and Kennedy, 1966) compared the letters written by parents to their schizophrenic child and to their non-schizophrenic child in a state hospital, and from volunteers as though their child was in hospital. Not only could no distinction be made between parents of schizophrenics and non-schizophrenics on the basis of the letters, but there was very little agreement on what constituted a double-bind, even among the group of expert judges who were the pioneers of the double-bind theory.

Haley (1968) considered the double-bind situation of parental pairs giving instructions over a microphone to their schizophrenic (adult) child. This was compared with normal and neurotic children and their parents. These two latter groups did equally well and significantly better than the schizophrenic child and his parents. The task was conducted again, allowing the children to question their parents. All improved, the schizophrenic group the most, but probably because they had the greatest room for improvement. Clearly, the confusion in the schizophrenic inter- action could arise from confused communication from the parents, or faulty interpretation by the patient. Both sets of parents then instructed normal children unknown to them with equally success- ful results. This would tend to indicate that the problem lies in the understanding of the schizophrenic individual, or entirely within the interaction of the parent and that particular child. The com- parison which might have shed light on this, between schizophrenic patient and normal parents, was not investigated.

Sojit (1971) suggests that parents of schizophrenics do use the double-bind form of communication more than other parents. Carter (1975) considers therapeutic interventions which are concerned with recognising and coping with the double-bind con- necting the anxiety it engenders with that situation. Gentry (1981) considers brief therapy from the perspective of its 'philosophic origins' and the 'behavioural effects of paradox in human commu- nication' as described by Bateson and his colleagues (1956). The therapy is linked to a behavioural model in that it suggests that psychopathology is repeatedly reinforced in communication between the person labelled 'ill' and significant others.

These and other studies are fraught with methodological prob- lems, and frequently the experimental design does not allow for the emotional involvement which is present and necessary for the double-bind to be effective. This is of particular importance in studies involving normal people, supposedly double-bind messages, levels of anxiety and subsequent performance, since this would seem to be a very different set of circumstances and responses (Smith, 1976; Dush and Brodsky, 1981). Williams (1970) suggested that although schizophrenic patients responded in the same way to congruent film messages, whereas normal peo- ple responded to the two types of messages differently, this need not show any specific effect of the double-bind type of message.

Although the double-bind theory of schizophrenia could provide a hypothesis not only about its origin, but also about the nature of thought disorder and current family functioning, as Olson (1972) points out, a conceptual or operational scheme that accurately reflects the double-bind hypothesis has yet to be developed. This is still the case. Also, still to be demonstrated is the real existence of double-bind communication in families with a schizophrenic member.

Lidz and Disordered Marital Relationship

Lidz (Lidz and Lidz, 1949; Lidz, Cornelison, Fleck and Terry, 1957; Lidz, Cornelison, Terry and Fleck, 1958; Lidz, 1972, 1975) focuses on the triadic relationship of both parents and child. Although the entire family is seen as pathological, it is primarily because of the disturbed parental relationship. The child is forced into the role of 'scapegoat'. Lidz distinguishes between a 'skewed' family when one parent is either very inadequate or excessively dominant, and a 'schism' when one parent is hostile, cold and possibly even destructive toward the other. Essentially, the 'transmission of irrationality' from which the schizophrenia develops is related to difficulties in communication between the parents. These are centred in the parents' ill-defined ego boundaries and a delicate emotional balance both within them as individuals and between them as a couple.

As well as the parents not giving each other support and co-operation, other family roles are altered and the usual distinctions between generations within the family are blurred. The evidence for this hypothesis came originally from a long-term study of 17 schizophrenic patients and their families. Of these, 14 families came from social classes I and II, and the patient had been having inpatient psychoanalysis over a number of years. Thus these families could hardly be described as typical, nor was any control group studied.

The skewed families were found predominantly where the patient was male, the mother being the dominant figure. The father was weak and passive, providing a poor model for his son and little emotional support or satisfaction for his wife, who turned for this to her son. The patients were predominantly female in families where there is a schism. The conflict between the spouses leads them to pursue their own goals, ignoring each other's, and those of the family as a whole, and thus the child's loyalties are divided as they are battled over by the parents for support, affection and to be allies against the other parent. In both cases it is assumed that there is an increase in anxiety, particularly regarding incestuous feelings and behaviour.

This approach to schizophrenia, like that of the double-bind, suggests that it is not an illness as such, but a learnt response to a situation in which the behaviour of the parents is seen as inappropriate, in terms of their sex and age, both to each other and to their child.

There is no objective evidence to support Lidz's theory for schizophrenia. While family patterns have been described of the type identified by Lidz, they also appear in families with other types of psychiatric patient, or with no psychiatric illness at all. In a series of studies, Ferreira and Winter (Ferreira, 1963; Ferreira and Winter, 1965; Ferreira, Winter and Poindexter, 1966; Winter and Ferreria, 1967) compared interactions between parents and child in families where the child was schizophrenic, had some other psychiatric condition, or had no psychiatric illness. Although there was less agreement in families with a psychiatric patient than in normal families, and agreement was worst in schizophrenic families, there did not appear to be any significant mother-child collusion. Agreement between mother and child was the same as between father and child: overall, the father's answer took precedence in the family, and the mother's precedence over the child's.

Despite not producing evidence to support his claim, Lidz continues to assert that he has seen the 'results of research conducted in many parts of the world, and one thing is clear: there has never been a schizophrenic who came from a stable family — at least we cannot find any' (Orrill and Boyers, 1972).

Wynne

If 17 families was a small number for Lidz to base his original hypothesis on, Wynne used an even smaller number, four (Wynne, Ryckoff, Day and Hirsch, 1958; Wynne, 1970, 1972). The suggestion was that the entire family relationship was disturbed, in that they were strongly trying to maintain the concept of mutuality in the family. In other words, there is a reciprocal fulfilment of expectations by family members, even though the observers of the family thought mutuality was absent. Wynne coined the term 'pseudomutuality' for this phenomena. It is characterised by surface stability under which the patterns of communication in the family are disjointed, fragmented and frequently irrational in their progression, and where shifts in terms of the focus of attention prevent any real continuity in the interaction.

This faulty communication by parents characterise the family as a whole and fall along a bipolar continuum with the two basic styles of amorphous and fragmented at either end. These styles of communication are held in conjunction with feelings of meaninglessness and emptiness. The roles held by family members are also out of line, and are either held in a rigid and stereotyped manner or they are loose and ambiguous in their structure.

All these factors influence the development of schizophrenia in a child. The communication patterns affect the child's cognitive development and will be reflected in the variety of schizophrenic thought disorder. The feelings of emptiness and pointlessness are conveyed to the child, leaving him doubtful and uncertain; the rigid adherence to the roles in the family mean that the child cannot experience or develop any sense of self-identity outside the role laid down for him by the family. Thus the child's independent and conflicting needs, demands and expectations are denied or disturbed by the family. This may reach a crisis point at adolescence when the child is making efforts to establish himself in the world outside the family, but only has the patterns of thought and communication that he has learnt in the family.

Wynne (Singer and Wynne, 1966a) adapted the Rorschach test to generate speech from families of schizophrenics and from this described a number of deviant categories of communication. Although there is some overlap and some categories are only loosely defined, these were used to distinguish between parents of adult schizophrenics, adult neurotics and 'normal' adults (Singer and Wynne, 1966b). Over 75 per cent of parental pairs were correctly classified by their child's diagnosis. Mothers and fathers, when compared separately, scored differently. The mothers of schizophrenic children did not score significantly differently from mothers of neurotics, while fathers had a significantly higher score than the fathers of neurotic or normal children. It is interesting to speculate why a test to distinguish between communication patterns in schizophrenic and normal families should put families with a neurotic member firmly between them.

Hirsch and Leff (1971, 1975) attempted to replicate these findings in England. Although they found the deviance scores were much higher for schizophrenic families than neurotic families, and that this was attributable to the father's score, there was a much greater overlap in the scores between the two groups than in the American study. Although there were differences in diagnosis between the two countries, this would not seem to be a likely explanation, the diagnosis in England being much tighter than in the United States. A more likely explanation lies in the subject families used. The Hirsch and Leff sample were a consecutive series of admissions fulfilling study criteria, whereas Wynne and Singer's families were referred to them, from a wide area, specifically because their interest in communication deviancy was known: thus it would seem that, in this case, families had already been described as having communication abnormalities before selection for referral.

Despite this difference in sampling, Hirsch and Leff offer another explanation for the differences found, which again reflect methodology. They found a high correlation between deviance score and the amount the individual spoke. Mothers from both groups spoke equally, but fathers from the schizophrenic families spoke more than fathers with a neurotic child. When this difference in amount of speech was allowed for, there was no difference between the two groups. Although it may be that deviance in these terms may be closely linked to the number of words spoken, why fathers of schizophrenic children should speak more remains an open question.

Roles in the Family

The dynamic family theories discussed above emphasise roles in the family to a greater or lesser extent. Other studies, while not tied specifically to any of these theories, also consider the relevance of disturbed patterns of interaction within the family. Cheek (1965, 1967), for example, found that the mothers of schizophrenic patients were generally 'inactive and withdrawn, permissive but not supportive'. The fathers, while apparently playing a peripheral role, were more supportive than the mother. Cheek also found that there was sex-role reversal in the patients themselves, a finding previously unnoticed or unreported. Thus the male patients were passive and withdrawn, while the daughters were both overactive and dominating.

Her findings suggest that rather than causing the role reversal in the child, the parents' roles are forced on them by the aberrant behaviour of the schizophrenic. For example, 'where schizophrenics were poorly adjusted at the time of the interaction interview, the mothers were low on positive sanctions in their interaction, though low positive sanctions by the mother were not associated with poor adjustment on follow-up'. This, she suggests, indicates that the mother's low sanctioning behaviour appears when the schizophrenics are behaving badly, presumably as a result of such behaviour, rather than before such behaviour occurs.

Likewise, fathers became peripheral and supportive because 'when they have behaved more like normal fathers, that is to say where they have participated actively in their disciplinarian role and not shown a high degree of support, the schizophrenic became worse'. Over time, when the illness is of long duration, this means that both parents are low on negative sanctions and the father is high on support in the interview. This might also indicate that where there is an apparently lengthy onset, it may simply be that the patient has been kept out of hospital by 'accommodative permissive behaviour' on the part of the parents.

Existential Based Family Theory

In his early writing Laing appears to be of the opinion that the contemporary nuclear family is a 'pathogenic' institution in its own right and says that 'without exception the experience and behaviour that gets labelled schizophrenic is a special strategy that a person invents in order to live in an unliveable situation' (Laing, 1960). He does not, however, tell us about specific family psychopathy and its relation to the specific strategy of schizophrenia. Despite the emphasis on family pathology, he is still writing essentially as a psychiatrist concerned with a clinical entity, although he makes no clear distinction between those suffering from schizophrenia and those with a schizoid personality. There seems to be the assumption that, given a sufficient degree of stress, anyone with a schizoid personality can become schizophrenic, and that understanding such individuals gives insight into the speech and behaviour of the schizophrenic.

Later, Laing uses the term schizophrenia in a new way (1961). It no longer refers to a disease entity of any kind; at most it is seen as a form of interpersonal functioning, and the intelligibility of schizophrenia is now seen as being interpersonal rather than intrapersonal. Schizophrenia is still viewed, however, in a negative light.

Finally, he breaks with conventional psychiatry altogether and describes schizophrenia in political terms: 'There is no such condition as "schizophrenia", but the label is a social fact and the social fact a *political event* (1967). Traditional concepts of sanity and madness are questioned and rejected. 'Our sanity is not "true" sanity. Their madness is not "true" madness. The madness of our patients is an artefact of the destruction wreaked on them by us, and by them on themselves.'

This view of schizophrenia has moved a long way from his original, family-orientated hypothesis. Now 'true sanity' involves the 'dissolution of the normal ego' which is described as a 'false self competently adjusted to our alienated social reality.' In its place comes a new kind of ego-functioning, in which the ego is 'the servant of the divine, no longer its betrayer'. Thus schizophrenia is being described as a transcendental experience; the schizophrenic individual is, or is capable of becoming, a mystic, a seer of inner words and universal truths. Madness is no longer a breakdown, but a breakthrough. From this point it becomes senseless to think of therapy or rehabilitation. There is no need.

Despite the mixture and confusion of sociological, psycho-analytic and existential models with clinical insights and assumptions, it would be possible to test certain hypotheses from Laing's suppositions, but this has yet to be done.

Learning Theories and the Family

Although the part of the family may play in the causation of schizophrenia is sometimes described as providing an environment in which the developing schizophrenic learns to be ill, the way in which this is achieved is rarely described in learning terms. The learning models themselves, be they based on classical or operant conditioning, are essentially descriptive theories founded in behavioural data rather than being truly aetiological theories.

Some of the learning theories see the problem of schizophrenia as being one of a basic learning deficit, whereas others see schizophrenia as learnt, adaptive behaviour. It is these latter models which might have relevance for a family approach.

A specialised area of learning, social skills, may have a part to play both in the development and maintenance of schizophrenia. Social incompetency and social isolation have been described as important factors in chronic schizophrenia (e.g. Jaco, 1954; Wagner and Hartsaugh, 1974). Zusman (1967) refers to the 'Social

Breakdown Syndrome' to describe both the behaviour and symptoms of psychotic patients. It is still unclear as to whether these social learning difficulties pre-date the schizophrenia, contribute to it or are a result of it, as is any interaction between such deficits and vulnerability to life changes and environmental stresses.

Social skill deficits may be of importance in determining the career of the patient, especially whether he is hospitalised or not. They might also relate to the work on social isolation previously described.

Genetic Studies

It would not be appropriate here to discuss the genetic models put forward to account for how schizophrenia may be inherited. However, it would be misleading to consider some of the family and environmental data without looking at some of the genetic studies. Data on the influence of genetic factors in schizophrenia come from a variety of types of studies, each of which consider the family in a different way. To be considered here is a brief overview of family, adoption and twin studies. Gottesman, Shields and Hanson (1982) suggest that the data from West European studies are particularly important because of the similar, conservative diagnosis, relatively immobile populations and relative homogeneity for race, religion and social class.

Family Studies

Compared to a lifetime morbid risk of 1 per cent, Gottesman *et al.* suggest that the morbid risk ranges from approximately 46 per cent for offspring of two schizophrenics, to nearly 13 per cent for children of one schizophrenic, 10 per cent for siblings as a whole, to approximately just over 3 per cent for second degree relatives, and just over 2 per cent for third degree relatives. However, these studies do not record whether there is a closer relative who is also schizophrenic. Thus someone who is recorded as the grandchild or nephew of a schizophrenic may also be the son of a schizophrenic. The risk for finding the parents of a schizophrenic to be schizophrenic is low at less than 6 per cent. This would seem to be due to assortive mating which leads to the 'selection' of mentally healthy mates. Bleuler (1978) indicates that those parents of schizophrenics who were themselves schizophrenic had a later onset and a mild end state, and thus form a subgroup of schizophrenics; unlike the majority of the schizophrenics who do become parents twice as many are female than male. This might account for the emphasis placed on the mother in some of the psychodynamic theories as being the agent of transmission in schizophrenia.

Although some of the relatives of a schizophrenic individual are, or become, schizophrenic, it is clear that the overwhelming majority are not, nor are likely to become so. This should be borne in mind against the frequent assumptions that relatives of schizophrenics are in some way 'odd', even if not schizophrenic. Kallmann (1938) suggested that at least two-thirds of the children of schizophrenics were 'eugenically doubtful' while Hoover and Franz (1972) suggest that over half the siblings of a schizophrenic were in a category defined as 'struggling'. Many were seen to have neurosis or character disorders of various kinds, and a further 5 per cent were borderline schizophrenic and 5 per cent delinquent in some way. Bleuler (1978), however, suggests that these types of figures were essentially artefacts born out of investigations 'aimed specifically at deviant personality characteristics' which came about because of the stressful situation in which they found themselves.

As Gottesman *et al.* (1982) point out '89 per cent of schizophrenics *do not* have a schizophrenic mother *or* father, and 81 per cent of schizophrenics do not have a schizophrenic parent *or* a schizophrenic sibling'. This does not, however, equate with a low level of genetic influence of types of schizophrenia, but it should be seen as hopeful for those individuals contemplating having children.

Twin Studies

Since the late 1920s, studies have been reported comparing the rates of schizophrenia in monozygotic (MZ) twins with dizygotic (DZ) twins, the assumption being that if family environment were to cause schizophrenia then MZ pairs should be the same as same-sex DZ pairs in their rates for schizophrenia. If genetics play a crucial role then MZ pairs will be more concordant for schizophrenia than DZ pairs.

It has been shown repeatedly that MZ twins have a considerably higher concordance rate than do DZ twins; this figure is usually about three times higher (e.g. Kallman, 1946; Kringlen, 1967;

Gottesman and Shields, 1972; Tienari, 1975). The methodology of such studies is subject to intensive criticism and rates have to be corrected for age which in turn leads to further controversy and dispute over the 'final' rates. Gender does not appear to play a part, opposite sex DZ pairs being as concordant as same sex pairs, and neither does the sex of the schizophrenic patient seem to affect the risk. MZ twins transmit schizophrenia to their offspring at the same rate, even if they are discordant for schizophrenia.

Early studies especially were used in support of a particular socio-political stance. Gottesman, Shields and Hanson (1982) point out that 'social Darwinism and unwarranted eugenic fervor were a political-social policy by-product of the Mendelian revolution in genetics'. Marshall (1984) casts doubt on the scientific integrity of Kallman's work and reminds us that he was 'emotionally committed to eugenics and regards any opposition as based on prejudice in contrast to his own purely scientific approach', this despite the fact that he was a Jewish refugee from Hitler's Germany.

Studies which are particularly interesting and important in terms of teasing out strands of the genetic — environment tangle are those in which MZ twins, one of whom is schizophrenic, have been reared apart in unlike environments. Sadly, for researchers at least, such occurrences are extremely rare. Gottesman, Shields and Hanson (1982) suggest that there are known 'only some dozen authenticated pairs'. They compute that the chances of being both schizophrenic and a MZ twin are 53 in one million; the chances of separate — home adoptions reduces this figure drastically. Although it is frequently accepted that 'MZ twins do not have to be brought up together in an extremely similar environment for them to be alike, (Shields, 1978), it would seem that the circumstances under which this is likely to happen make them a curiosity, in all senses, rather than crucial to the central thesis.

Despite methodological uncertainties the twin studies have been taken very much to heart. Reade and Wertheimer (1976) found that providing the information of a schizophrenic twin doubled the likelihood that a patient would be diagnosed as schizophrenic when the other information given was only moderately consistent with schizophrenia.

Adoptive Studies

Like the twin study, adoption studies are fraught with methodological difficulties and idiosyncratic interpretation. Nevertheless, as a whole, they support the notice of a genetic base for schizophrenia. The children of schizophrenics who are adopted away from the family while young still have an increased risk for schizophrenia (e.g. Heston, 1966; Kety, Rosenthal, Wender and Schulsinger, 1968; Kety, Rosenthal, Wender, Schulsinger and Jacobsen, 1978; Wender, Rosenthal, Kety, Schulsinger and Welner, 1974). Also, biological relatives of the schizophrenic have the expected raised rate for schizophrenia, but adopted relatives do not. In the few cases where a child from a non-schizophrenic family has been fostered or adopted into a home where a parent has schizophrenia, the child does not have a raised rate for schizophrenia.

Among methodological problems with such studies is the likelihood that the parents of those placed for adoption, whether the parent or adoptee is schizophrenic, are unlikely to be typical of their group. In particular, there may be a high rate of assortive mating for psychiatric and social problems. Gottesman and Shields (1976) enumerate the problems that the researchers had not only in diagnosis, but also in determining or not, as the case may be, illness or abnormal behaviour in the non-schizophrenics in the study. Some of these categories seem to be extremely vague and ambiguous, and Lidz (1976) draws attention to them: 'I believe it is fair to consider that it must be somewhat difficult to know just who should be categorised as a *definite* latent schizophrenic, and that how to judge with any certainty who may or may not be an *uncertain* latent schizophrenic is a rather extraordinary feat.'

High-risk Studies

A currently popular research methodology is the 'high-risk study' or prospective longitudinal study of children with one or two schizophrenic parents (e.g. Neale and Oltmanns, 1980; Watts, Anthony, Wynne and Rolf, 1982).

A rationale for this type of study was that while, retrospectively, some premorbid schizophrenics appear to be normal, others have always been clearly disturbed, while still others have been described as 'different' or 'odd'. It has been suggested that about half of all adult schizophrenics show signs of abnormality before the overt signs of schizophrenia develop (Bleuler, 1978). But while pathology in childhood is often associated with mental illness in adults, it is generally a poor predictor of adult mental health or adult diagnosis (Rutter and Hersov, 1977). It is also clear that being raised by a sick parent can lead to behavioural disturbances in children for reasons which are entirely environmental (Rutter, 1966).

Although such studies may provide us with information in three important areas, to date all evidence and leads are tentative. Mednick and Baert (1981) suggest that such studies should: (1) define the range of specificity of the characteristics that precede adult schizophrenia; (2) determine the usefulness of predictors in relation to outcome; (3) determine whether valid childhood predictors of adult schizophrenia can specify the aetiology of schizophrenia.

As in the other types of genetic studies there are many intervening variables which confuse and confound the issue. Childhood predictors might be the earliest signs, or even effects, of the illness itself. Alternatively, the seeming predictor might be related to the child's general genetic or environmental background in such a way that it is neither a consequence of being at-risk for schizophrenia, nor does not, on its own, represent incipient schizophrenic breakdown.

Other methodological problems arise over the diagnostic criteria used to identify the schizophrenic parent sample, and the fact that less than 10 per cent of schizophrenics have schizophrenic parents.

An Overview of the Genetic Studies

The evidence considered here for genetic factors having a causal role in schizophrenia comes from clinical-population genetics data and not from molecular genetics. This assumption is, however, that this data implies a biochemical or other physical malfunction of the brain which then leads to the development of schizophrenia. Great strides are being made in this direction, but are outwith the scope of this book. As yet, no individual gene has been identified which is related to schizophrenia, let alone described biochemically or biophysically, and nor has a satisfactory model of transmission been proposed. Neither can the premorbid schizophrenic be identified in any way reliably, nor which of a schizophrenic's other relatives might also be sufferers. Nevertheless, the fact of some genetic link is clear.

Gottesman *et al.* (1982) look to the future with hope: 'The schizophrenia puzzle is in the process of being solved, and we are

optimistic that it will be solved before the twentieth century ends.'
Others, however, are more pragmatically rooted in the present. As
Kessler (1976) points out, there is an ever-widening gulf between
the researcher-academician and the clinician. The former have not
made clear the importance or relevance of the genetic studies,
either in terms of treatment of the individual or the family, or of
understanding the schizophrenic process itself. 'To most clinicians
the psychological environment in which the patient has functioned
and is currently functioning appears to have a more direct connection to the development and maintenance of schizophrenic
symptoms than the fact that he or she may have some intangible
vulnerability on account of genetic factors.'

The Family and Relapse

While it might be true to say that the evidence implicating the
family environment in the aetiology of schizophrenia is sketchy,
the data suggesting that it plays a role in relapse and the career of
the patient is more substantial. Such evidence comes from a
number of different sources and types of study.

   Brown, Carstairs and Topping (1958) and Brown, Monck,
Carstairs and Wing (1962) found that schizophrenic patients who
returned to live with their parents or spouses or in hostels relapsed
significantly more often than those returning to other relatives or
lodgings. These findings held true even where there was control for
clinical state at discharge. Behaviour deterioration was more
severe among those returning to parental or marital homes. A
similar pattern was found by Freeman and Simmons (1958a,
1958b, 1963); male patients who were sons and returned to their
parental family had lower work and social performance scores than
did patients who were husbands returning to the marital home.
Despite this, patients were more likely to be returned to hospital
by their spouses than by their parents, probably due to the parents
showing 'greater tolerance of deviant behaviour and lower role
expectations'. This was true even though the 'objective burden' on
the family due to the patient's presence in the home was greater
for parents than for other relatives. (Burden will be discussed in
detail in Chapter 5.) Goldberg (1967) judged the majority of
schizophrenics living with their parents as 'unsettled' when compared with patients living in lodgings. She suggests that the

non-familial environment is more conducive to success in the community than living with the family.

Only very few researchers have not supported these broad findings. Pasamanick, Scarpitti and Dimitz (1967) found no significant difference in the relapse rates of patients regardless of the family group to which they returned. Niskanen and Pitikanen (1972) found unfavourable attitudes toward the patient in almost the same degree in both families of patients treated in hospitals and those treated in the community. The general outcome of their study, they suggest, does not support the hypothesis that it is the unfavourable attitudes of family members that lead to the admission or readmission of patients to hospital, or to his becoming institutionalised in the long-term.

Studying yet another family variable, Klein, Person and Itil (1972) found that family agreement with current treatment and payment by them of hospital inpatient fees were strong predictors of a favourable outcome.

The size of the group or groups returned to will vary, and with this the patient's ability to cope with life and stresses. Civrezu (1975) suggests that to give the returning patient the best choice of coping with the problems involved, the optimum size of the social field should be three to five people. He also suggests that the interpersonal relationships should be neutral.

This latter point is a finding which has received more attention over the last decade and deserves consideration in its own right.

Emotionality in the Family

Much of the evidence from family studies suggests that the pressures put upon patients returning to their families are greater than those experienced by patients who return to a non-familial environment. The emotional atmosphere of the family seems to be a crucial parameter. Brown's early study (Brown *et al.* 1958) and its follow-up (Brown, Bone, Dalison and Wing, 1966) showed a significant difference in hospital readmission between those living with their family, of whom over half were readmitted in the last three years of the follow-up, and those living alone, of whom only 30 per cent were readmitted during the same period. This finding seemed to indicate that a link existed between relapse and the atmosphere surrounding the patient.

Believing it to be the emotional atmosphere that was crucial, Brown tried to evaluate this objectively (Brown, Monck, Carstairs and Wing, 1962), measuring dominant behaviour, hostility and a global measure of emotion. This was then refined and elaborated to include a measure of hostility, warmth, critical comments and emotional over-involvement (Brown and Rutter, 1966; Rutter and Brown, 1966). These rating scales involved non-verbal, as well as verbal, communication; for example, for a statement to be rated as 'critical comment' both content and tone of voice were included, and hostility had to include rejection or generalisation of criticism.

Using these measures, a later Brown study (Brown, Birley and Wing, 1972) found relapse to be significantly correlated with the three measures of critical comments, hostility and over-involvement. Together these were described as a measure of 'expressed emotion' within the family. From these scores families were rated as being either high in expressed emotion (HEE) or low (LEE). The relapse rates of patients from the two types of families differed markedly, being much greater from HEE families. By controlling for EE, the association between impairment and disturbance of the patient and relapse almost disappeared; controlling for impairment and disturbance did not affect the association between EE and relapse. This would support the hypothesis linking expressed emotion to relapse rather than to the idea that the emotion was generated by the patient's deteriorating state. Most importantly, this work also considered the medication which the patients were taking. It seemed that drugs made little difference to relapse for patients living in LEE homes, whereas there was a trend suggesting that the drugs were beneficial in preventing or postponing relapse in HEE homes. A third important variable was the social contact between relatives and patients. Again this appeared to have no bearing on patients in LEE families but was significant in HEE homes; the cut-off point was made at 35 hours face-to-face contact per week.

This study was replicated by Vaughn and Leff (1976a) using a modified version of the family interview (1976b). Hostility was dropped from the scoring since it was not found in the absence of critical comments. Critical comments did not differ significantly between parents or spouses. They showed that relative's expressed emotion was the most important factor, of those considered, in a patient's relapse, including lack of preventive or maintenance drug treatment.

The data from both studies were pooled, from which the inter-action of the three variables, EE, maintenance drug therapy and face-to-face contact, should be assessed. In low EE families drugs made little difference to relapse, but had a significant effect on HEE homes, whether there was high contact or not. Where contact is above the 35 hour limit, the number relapsing in HEE homes is higher than where it is less. These two protective factors work together to make some dramatic differences in relapse rates. In HEE families where both protective factors are at work (less than 35 hours contact and maintenance drug therapy), only 15 per cent of patients relapsed compared to 92 per cent who relapse when neither factor was operating. Where only one factor was operating, 42 per cent relapsed when not on drugs (but with low contact) and 53 with over 35 hours contact (but on medication).

This work has important theoretic and practical implications and these, plus further research on expressed emotion in families, will be considered in Chapter 9.

The Family in Aetiology — Some Comments

In summing up the theory and research a number of general, or more or less general, comments can be made. The family theories of aetiology seem to have had a fairly popular appeal. Why this might be so is an interesting point. It may have something to do with the language of the theories being intelligible to the public in a way that the genetic theories are not, or it may have to do with the concepts themselves being readily accessible. If, however, people can look at the concept of, for example, double-bind and see it in their own lives or families, and thus understand it, it weakens its power as a likely aetiological factor in schizophrenia, because this negates its specificity.

These theories also take away the stigma of madness by present-ing the 'illness' as a reaction to family pressures, which again may be a more easily understood concept than madness. The voluntary self-help groups organised by relatives, however, are more likely to favour the biochemical theories, for fairly obvious reasons, in terms of their own self-protection. Many of the theories that are suggested as a total explanation of the aetiology of schizophrenia are so complex that they are difficult to test at an empirical level. Despite their level of complexity they cannot usually explain why it is one child who becomes ill and not a sibling. The nature of schizophrenia appears to be determined by the theory of family pathology and thus may be true of some patients but not of others. Concepts such as 'role', 'dominance', 'hostility' and 'submissive behaviour' are defined separately by each researcher. Therefore it is difficult to compare studies although there may be overlap.

One important problem that the high-risk studies are trying to overcome is the reconstruction of the past in the light of the current illness, leading to possible unintended exaggeration or mis-representation.

A major problem still exists in teasing out the strands of cause and effect. Any characteristic that parents of schizophrenics share, and that is not held by parents of non-schizophrenic people (and more work needs to be included on this group), could be a result of the problem having occurred in their family, either in an acute or pre-morbid form. Or it could be the expression of some shared genetic characteristic.

Regardless of whether the family's role is a cause or an effect of schizophrenia, the family *is* involved. By the time an individual has had a breakdown, been in hospital and then returned to his family, relapsed and returned to hospital, come home again, and so on and so forth, the whole problem has certainly become a matter of and cause for family concern and, if for no other reason, they should be considered in the rehabilitation of the patient.

4 THE FAMILY IN THERAPY

Why Involve the Family?

The preceding chapters have outlined the position of the schizophrenic patient in society, the part the environment may play in the development of the illness and career of the patient, and the role of the family in aetiology and relapse. All of this leads to the conclusion that for patients who live with their family, to attempt therapy or rehabilitation without involving the family will be, at best, less than optimal. The burden on the family and the problems they have, as described in the next two chapters, adds weight to the argument that the family should be involved in therapy. Their difficulties affect the patient directly and indirectly and, although often ignored, should not be.

That the families of psychiatric patients have been ignored by professional groups and their role in caring for the patient underestimated, is increasingly recognised. The relatives themselves, not surprisingly, have been pointing this out for some time. In a document presented to the Rt Hon. Barbara Castle, MP then Secretary of State in the Department of Health and Social Security, the National Schizophrenia Fellowship (1974) made ten major recommendations. The first of these was that 'relatives of the chronic schizophrenics living in the community who accept a caring responsibility for them are "primary care" agents and should be recognised as such in policy-making and administration'.

A number of professionals have added their voice to the families. Watt (1975) strikes a cautious note when he suggests that 'enthusiasm for extra-mural care of schizophrenic patients must be tempered by the substantial evidence of financial hardship, emotional strain and restricted life imposed on the relatives who support them'. Hatfield (1982) acknowledges that families 'have become the primary resource for patients' and that 'good collaborative relationships' are necessary between relatives and professionals if community care is to be maintained and be successful.

Appleton (1974) talks of the 'mistreatment of patients' families' indicating that psychiatrists often blame and mistreat relatives either through 'open hostility', 'vague innuendo' or more subtly by 'ignoring the relatives'. This usually results from their belief that the family has played a part in the illness. He suggests that such an approach leads to the family becoming even less willing to co-operate in the patient's treatment, to change their behaviour towards the patient, to tolerate his problems and to give information. To overcome this means changing the professional's attitude to the family, to use the same techniques used to help patients and 'to go out of one's way to win the family's confidence and co-operation'.

In a study of relatives' and staff's attitudes toward the involvement of the family in the treatment of hospitalised, chronic psychiatric patients due for discharge to the community and their families' care, Smets (1982) found that of the highly selected group of relatives involved, more than two-thirds felt that the family plays an important role in the aetiology, course and prognosis of the illness. Furthermore, these relatives wanted to be involved in treatment, but their responses were ambiguous when asked how much they felt involved presently. There were significant differences between relatives and staff, and within the staff group in relation to treatment variables which 'make it difficult to implement consistent family involvement'. Smets suggests the need to screen staff groups for internal disagreements and to 'sell staff on the necessity of involving families' by a system of in-service training and exposure to existing family-oriented groups.

The third part of this book considers how best to work with the family, how to involve them in therapy programmes, and what areas are most appropriate for inclusion. This chapter deals with research on the current involvement of the family in therapy.

What Type of Family Therapy?

Family participation in therapy occurs in a number of guises. The theories of family involvement in aetiology have not given rise to any strong, formal family therapy, but to a number of different approaches. Psychodynamically oriented family therapy emerged during the 1950s and gained acceptance during the 1960s; its use in schizophrenia always being considered of importance. During the 1960s and 1970 behaviour therapy began to be used with schizophrenic patients and some of these programmes included the patient's relatives. Since then the types of therapy or involvement offered have expanded considerably, ranging from full family therapy, to support groups, relatives as therapists and educational groups for relatives. The family or relative might be involved with just their ill relative, or in groups with either other relatives alone or relatives and patients. The patients may be either acute or chronic. As a supplement to the services offered by professionals there are also the voluntary organisations.

A further difference, possibly underestimated, is the difference between male and female patients and the impact of their illness on the family. Seeman (1983) points out that the earlier onset of schizophrenia in men than women makes a number of crucial differences in this area. Families of male patients tend to have higher expectations, and for longer, than do families of female patients, and are concerned about the unpredictability of the son's violence and unacceptable sexual behaviour. Families of female patients are more likely to be concerned about the sexual exploitation of their daughter. Counselling must take account of these differences and need individually tailored family programmes.

Beels and McFarlane (1982) review the family treatment of schizophrenia from an historical perspective, and indicate that 'the initiative in designing family therapy for schizophrenia has passed from an early group of innovators with strong family-theory ideological commitments to a more pragmatic group, trained in the research methodology of several disciplines, including the medical model'. Therapy might thus be seen as aetiology-oriented or outcome-oriented.

The way in which relatives are involved with the clinical team varies both with the philosophy of the therapy and the objectives behind family participation. In some instances the latter will dictate the former. The major division in goal orientation can be based on whether the patient or the family is the primary client. As Haley (1970) suggests, family therapy is not a method but an orientation. Thus some family involvement may be directed at changing relative's behaviour or attitudes because of the effect this has on the patient, or it might involve relatives in helping the patient to change or control his behaviour. Fewer relatives find themselves involved for their own sakes, where the aim of the programme is to deal with the problems of the relatives, the benefits to the patient being indirect.

Methodological Problems

Massie and Beels (1972) reviewing the literature conclude that 'outcome studies of the family therapy of schizophrenia are relatively limited and inadequate in scope'. Things have improved since then, but there are still a number of studies being reported with small numbers and using subjective or anecdotal evidence. There are a number of problems in reporting on the methodology of some of the studies, since they admit that reported procedures are sometimes changed to suit family circumstances, and 'family' can vary from one relative to all family members, the number who are involved being variable, even within a research group.

It is difficult to separate studies on the basis of therapeutic or theoretical intervention, since there is a tendency for many to use a number of techniques, even if they emphasise one. The most obvious division lies between approaches which see the family alone, and those which see them as part of a larger group, multiple family therapy

Most of the family interventions assume that the patient will be maintained on the most appropriate regime of chemotherapy, that the family therapy is additional to this, and that the medication will reduce patient sensitivity and vulnerability to environmental stimulation and stress.

Outcome is also difficult to measure, since it depends on goals, and these vary with type of therapy, and at whom it is primarily directed. Many studies content themselves with broad generalities of 'improvement' in global terms. How easy it is to involve the family, their compliance, and the effect on other treatments will be discussed in Chapter 8.

Individual Family Programmes

An early study by Esterson, Cooper and Laing (1965) reports family and milieu therapy with hospitalised schizophrenic patients. The principles and aims of therapy were 'a systematic clarification and undoing of patterns of communication that we take to be "schizogenic" within the family' and also between patients and between patients and staff. In addition, there was to be a continuity of personnel working with the family during inpatient to outpatient phases, and the patients were on 'comparatively small doses' of tranquilizers. They report that 17 per cent of their patients were readmitted compared to 43 per cent in an MRC study. Of those not readmitted, approximately 70 per cent were 'capable of a sufficiently reasonable social adjustment to be able to earn their living for the whole of the year after discharge'.

Alanen, Hagglund, Harkonen and Kunnunen (1968), following upon their work on the dynamics of marriages in which one partner is schizophrenic, report on conjoint psychotherapy of schizophrenic men and their wives. They consider that such therapy is of 'considerable preventive importance' because of the high number of couples who had children.

Mosher (1969) describes a case study of family therapy which attempts to bridge the gap between 'the psychotherapeutic context of family therapy and the "communication theory" of schizophrenia'. The aim is to 'establish and maintain clear, consistent, constantly focused communication within the family group so that invalidation is minimised'.

A highly structured family therapy is described by Mueller and Orfanidis (1976) in which male and female co-therapists work with the entire family weekly for six to nine months, and subsequently, less frequently with subsystems of the family for a number of years. Two issues, they suggest, must be dealt with from the beginning, namely, the tendency to blame others in the family, and the differentiation between feelings and behaviour. The aim of the therapy is to ameliorate 'the difficulties and autonomous development' within the families. This involves two main areas of attention; first, the differentiation of family members, particularly in respect of generational and sexual boundaries, and second, the resolution of separation and loss, especially that regarding 'the unresolved mourning in the families of origin and the concomitant stress of giving up the fusion relationship with the identified patient in the nuclear family'. Thus the model of family functioning involved uses a 'three-generational hypothesis that defines schizophrenia as a lifelong, restricting mode of relating'. Comments are made about various families, but no data are presented on outcome or follow-up.

Despite generalised early enthusiasm for dynamic psychotherapy with families of schizophrenics, some warning notes are sounded. Rubinstein (1974) reports that the schizophrenic's family is extremely complex and that it 'frequently functions at levels which escape our comprehension'. He cites as common and obvious dynamics, undifferentiation of ego boundaries, distortion of self-image and interpersonal relatedness, cognitive dysfunctions, deficiency in decision-making processes, resistance to change and deficits in the family's developmental tasks. Most of these are common themes throughout family therapy with this group of patients; the differences occur in how they are dealt with and the rationale behind the therapy.

Beels (1975) reports an involvement in the family and social management of schizophrenia since 1962. Part of the rationale behind the programme is that 'the schizophrenic and his family usually lack a network of connections with society'. One of the aims is to establish such a network, and to do this it is necessary to experiment with new relations between the family and others, these being the extended family of the patient himself, families of other patients and 'the professional "family" of the treatment team'. Emphasis is laid on the family and social system surrounding the patient and report that the patient often gets better 'while nobody is looking at him so intently'. Furthermore, it is stated that this 'is the theory behind the treatment approach'. Although there is talk of 'the success of our operation', there are only four descriptive case histories to substantiate it. Beels develops the work on the social networks of schizophrenics (1979) and suggests the need to introduce the patient and his family to a variety of groups and increase their ability to develop networks. It is suggested that 'these network building experiences ... are less demanding of professional attention in the long run than the alternative'.

A systems approach to family pathology is described by Fleck (1979) that forms the basis of including the family in treatment, which he regards as 'essential', and following dyadic psychotherapeutic treatment and medication for the patient. Fleck suggests a 'relatively neutral but participant stance' particularly if the patient is to be included, with 'special technnical manoeuvres' being included where necessary. As an aim of therapy, he states that the 'major and general tasks are usually to improve communication and help family members to establish more workable boundaries, promoting their respective individuation to the greatest possible extent'. The affectivity of the family system and proneness of a particular relative to be over-involved with the patient are considered to be important if the patient is to return to live with the family. Fleck presents his case histories but no data on the therapy.

Kanter and Lin (1980) found that it was possible to involve

families as 'allies in the long and difficult process of psychodynamically oriented psychotherapy and resocialisation' of the
schizophrenic patient. Although the families were seen initially
alone, the parents were encouraged to attend the relatives group. It
is suggested that parents can be encouraged to improve their own
relationship if necessary and 'provide several of the major functions of a vital therapeutic milieu including containment, support
and structure'.

Goldstein and colleagues (Goldstein, Rodnick, Evans, May and
Steinberg, 1978; Goldstein and Kopeikin, 1981) describe a
programme of drug and family therapy in the six-week period after
hospitalisation for an acute schizophrenic breakdown. The crisis-
oriented family therapy is described as 'brief, concrete and
problem focused'. It has four treatment objectives: the main one
being the identification of stressful events, from which two or three
more follow which cause the most problems for the patient. The
therapy then moves on to developing strategies for avoiding and
coping with stress. The third part of the programme involves the
implementation, refining and evaluation of these strategies and,
lastly, the anticipation of a plan for future stressful experiences.
The treatment programme was studied comparing four treatment
conditions, moderate- and low-dose maintenance phenothiazine
with or without family therapy; 96 patients took part.

Short-term effects indicate that at the end of the six-week
controlled trial there is already a significant difference between the
two groups on relapse rates, despite this number being small. The
low-phenothiazine — no family group had a 24 per cent relapse rate
compared to the high-phenothiazine—family therapy group which
had no relapses. The other two groups were intermediate and did
not differ significantly from each other or from the two extremes.
At the six-month follow-up, this had increased to 48 per cent
relapse, while the high-phenothiazine—family therapy group still
had no relapses. Considering symptomatology, at six weeks those
patients in family therapy showed significantly less overall
psychopathology. The greatest differences were noted with withdrawal, but at six months this effect is only related to the
high-phenothiazine—family therapy group. Long-term effects are
reported but are complicated by the number of lost cases and the
fact that the follow-up period represented between three and six
years after the programme. Continued use of the mental health
services was only related to one variable, premorbid adjustment,

and not to drug or therapy status.

An unusual approach to the family of the schizophrenic patient is taken by Waring (1981) who, observing that the parents of schizophrenics display a lack of intimacy, offers the parents alone cognitive family therapy, the patient receiving individual help from another therapist. The aim of the therapy is to understand why the parents are not close and to increase their intimacy through a series of ten one-hour sessions. This follows an initial introductory session, which all family members attend, and which focuses on each family member's explanation of why the problem has occurred. In both the initial session and the marital sessions only 'why' questions are asked; feelings and behaviour are not identified, confronted or interpreted. Waring discusses briefly ten families and presents one case study.

A few studies which use only behavioural techniques with individual families can be separated from the more general approaches.

Behavioural Programmes with Individual Families

One of the criticisms directed at behavioural programmes centred on the problem of the generalisation, or lack of generalisation, of behaviour learned and rewarded in the hospital setting to other environments, particularly the home and family. In an early review of behaviour modification techniques with adults in institutional settings, Davison (1969) concluded that there were problems with such programmes, 'primarily because of the failure of at least the operant approaches, thus far, to make an appreciable contribution to the goal of equipping adult mental hospital patients with the means to cope successfully in the outside world'.

A change of emphasis to behaviour necessary in the community and to social reinforcement rather than tokens or other material reward was suggested by Kanfer and Phillips (1970). Coupled with this was the understanding that some behavioural problems would only show themselves in one setting. For example, Byrne, O'Connor and Fahy (1974) indicate that the behaviour of some patients may differ significantly between the home and the day centre. This seems particularly true of aggressive patients and the difference in behaviour could be in either direction. Thus relatives, most often parents, found themselves included in the behavioural programmes (e.g. Cheek, Laucius, Matincke and Beck, 1971). In such studies, the family, acting as the 'therapeutic agent', is given varying amounts of information as to basic principles, and emphasis is put on the relative's behaviour as much as the patient's. Not all the relatives involved were adults. Miller and Cantwell (1976) used siblings as therapists when treating children's problems, where the child's maladaptive behaviour was being maintained by other children in the family.

A pilot study with adult schizophrenic patients and their relatives involved an operant approach in the home setting with some success (Hudson, 1975). Atkinson (1981, 1982) used a variety of behavioural interventions with adult chronic schizophrenic patients, comparing effectiveness when a relative was included in the programme with the patient being seen alone. On a behavioural checklist the two groups of patients improved by about the same amount of change-score, although there was a wide range of individual change in both groups. There was, however, an important difference in where the improvement occurred: the patients seen with a relative improved more in areas which involved the family or social behaviours; the patients seen alone changed more in personal areas, such as their ability to deal with depression and neurotic symptoms.

As well as influencing the target behaviours for change, the other important effect the relatives had on the therapy programme seemed to be their ability to get the patient to accept the programme in the first place, and then to maintain the involvement in rehabilitation. Other studies have not always found the relatives to be co-operative (Hudson, 1975).

A different approach to the family was taken by O'Brien and Azrin (1973) when they tried to reinstate patient-family relationships using response priming. This views the complex behaviour as a chain of events, the probability of completion of the chain being higher the closer one gets to the end of the chain. Three chronic patients are reported, having been hospitalised for over 18 months with virtually no contact with their relatives for at least the last year. These patients were to be discharged and thus the need to reinstate relationships was strong. Patients were taken on visits home and a reinforcer sampling procedure used showing the families that being together was enjoyable. Thus using response priming and reinforcer sampling it was hoped that the relationships would be maintained. The visits home were evaluated by a staff member in terms of the behavioural needs of the patient. Ward programmes were then set up to develop such skills in the patient.

Multiple Family Therapy

A number of studies have included schizophrenic patients and their families in various forms of group therapy or, as it is sometimes called, multiple family therapy. Little attempt has been made to compare the use of individual family therapy with multiple family therapy. One study that attempts this suggests there are no differences on a global outcome measurement (Gould and Glick, 1977) but there are a number of methodological comments to be made.

Four groups were compared, two involving family therapy and two not, the patients having inpatient status. Individual family therapy was given to one group, A, in weekly sessions for at least one month. Group B had the same individual sessions plus weekly multi-family sessions for at least a month. Group C not only received no family therapy, but also had no family living near them. In Group D, although the family was physically available, they either refused to co-operate or were not seen as being clinically relevant. Thus, although Gould and Glick compare family therapy with no family therapy, the type of families with which the patient was involved presumably differed significantly between the two groups, although details are not given.

It is thus interesting to note that the researchers find no significant differences between groups A, B and D. They conclude that 'family therapy in addition to the presence of a family does not seem to be associated with better outcome'. It might be argued that four sessions does not constitute a fair trial for the therapy and, indeed, most other research reported has a longer period of intervention.

Laqueur, La Burt and Morang (1964) report data on 80 patients and their families. About 15 per cent of families dropped out within the first week or two, but few after that. Patients were involved as inpatients and they continued in the groups on discharge, for anything up to two years. Approximately 40 per cent of the patients showed clinical improvement and 67 per cent of families reported subjective benefit. Atkinson (1969) reports working with families whose ill relative was the member of a therapeutic community in a hospital. The group sessions were seen as mainly supportive, becoming more formal and with less leadership from the professionals as contact between the families grew.

Lurie and Ron (1971) developed a counselling group for young, recently discharged schizophrenics and their parents. The groups, of five to six families, meet weekly for one and a half hours for about a year. Four major themes developed: the stigma of psychiatric hospitalisation; conflict between the adult child's independence and parental control; conflicting child-parent expectations; and communication problems within the family.

Atwood (Atwood and Williams, 1978; Atwood, 1983) presents a model of group support for families of the mentally ill which is said to be similar to many self-help groups, despite having professional leadership. The group lasted for eight sessions and families were expected to attend regularly. The avowed aim of the group was 'to bring about interpersonal communication among a group of people showing a common problem', namely, the understanding of the mental illness, its effects on the family and how to cope with this. The subjects covered at the meetings were determined by the group itself. All the patients were involved in a local rehabilitation programme and, although the programme was discussed at the meetings, individual patients were not. Atwood and Williams report that the therapeutic elements of the group include 'catharsis, identification with others, the creation of an interpersonal community, the stimulation of pride in existing strengths and assets, and the recognition of the legitimacy of personal needs and of keeping resources outside of the family'. The authors report that the family gain in support and guidance and that this benefits the ill relative, but they present no objective or subjective data.

Family groups can be usefully employed even when the conviction of the rehabilitation agency is that the psychiatric patient usually functions better when not living with his family (Dincin, Selleck and Streicker, 1978). A parents' group was started after some years of considering 'the parents of members (*of the rehabilitation agency*) to be an impediment to the rehabilitation efforts ... we decided that the process of members' independence might accelerate if parents were converted from enemy to ally'. One of the prime objectives of the parent group was to 'promote independent living', but the relatives were able to discuss matters of importance to them which they may not have had an opportunity to talk about before. The group was open-ended, but parents were expected to stay in the group only for about 12 weeks. Although Dincin *et al.* report a significant improvement in the parents' attitude and behaviour towards the patient in 60 per cent of their families, based on 'the clinical judgement of the staff who led the group', it would seem at least possible that the change in attitude of the staff to the patient's relatives contributed to the change in attitude of the relative to the patient and the rehabilitation programme.

Anecdotal evidence presented by Mass and Odaniell (1958) on group casework with relatives of adult schizophrenic patients again supports the value of such an approach. They suggest that the 'most impressive results ... were the great reduction of irritating occurrences between the patients and family members, and the more comfortable and relaxed atmosphere in the homes'. The most striking feature of the group is reported as the 'key which unlocked the door to a real change in behaviour turned when the members spoke about *themselves* — often with great emotion and relief'. Mass and Odaniell report that they gained a greater insight into and understanding of the relatives and their problems, which in view of their reported prejudice, a result of witnessing 'their earlier unknowingly destructive actions', was not easy. As a consequence of the group sessions the relatives 'seemed much more human and understandable'. This change in attitudes, and presumably behaviour, on the part of the social workers towards the parents may in itself be responsible for some of the lowering of tension in the home.

The group does not always have to have a primary therapeutic task. Scharfstein and Libbey (1982) describe the use of a multiple family group to help patients and their families adjust to the fact of psychiatric inpatient status. Groups were made up of five families over a two-month period with a range of psychiatric diagnosis. The groups met once only, for an hour and a half, and were divided into a social stage for introductions, and an educational stage for discussion of problems and the involvement of the family. Like many other studies, no hard data is presented, but the authors report 'we have the distinct impression that parents and families were helped by the orientation meetings' and that the families who attended the group meetings 'quickly became open and available to both staff and patients'.

Multiple Behavioural Family Therapy

Although the Atkinson study (1981, 1982) involved a family member (in some instances the only other family member) in a behavioural programme which involved possible change in the relative's own behaviour, nevertheless the major area of concern was influencing the patient's behaviour and did not consider the family as a whole. This contrasts with behavioural family therapy where the family system as a whole is subjected to behavioural analysis. Since there is an underlying assumption that family members are performing optimally in the specific situation, this means that coping mechanisms labelled undesirable, whether by the family, observer or therapist, must be assumed to be the best that the person can do at that time (Falloon, Boyd, McGill, Strang and Moss, 1981; Falloon and Liberman, 1983).

Behavioural analysis both precedes and continues throughout therapy and concentrates on three main areas. First, the behaviour of individuals must be recorded, especially in terms of specific assets and deficits, or what might be described as adaptive or maladaptive behaviour. Second, repeating this for the functioning of the family as a group and, third, clarifying the role that the 'problem' behaviour has in the family as a whole. From this baseline attempts to change the behaviour of one person or family interaction can be assessed in terms of their possible positive and negative consequences for the functioning of the family group.

Liberman and his colleagues have been responsible for much pioneering work in the area of behavioural family therapy with schizophrenics. Liberman's first report (1970) was based on case studies with marital and parental families, and from this have developed further studies. Falloon and Liberman (1983) report that use of an 'education workshop' in 1971 to teach relatives the basics of social learning principles and the reformulation of mental illness as 'problems in living'. This approach was extended in Britain during the latter 1970s to include a specific skills training component, but only three families are reported. The intervention centred on the communication of feelings within the family (Falloon, Liberman, Lillie and Vaughn, 1981; Snyder and Liberman, 1981). They report this 'structured educational behavioural treatment method' as useful in 'reducing emotional intensity in families with adult schizophrenic members' and that 'all three patients showed substantial improvement in their nonverbal and verbal communication', but no details are given. Again, therapy was presented in a group setting and involved educational seminars, training in problem-solving and communication with the families being given homework assignments.

Following this pilot study a comparison was made between an at-home family therapy and a clinic-based individual supportive psychotherapy (Falloon, Boyd and McGill, 1982; Falloon, Boyd, McGill, Razani, Moss and Gilderman, 1982). At nine-month assessment only one patient (6 per cent) had a clinical relapse in the family-treated group compared with eight (44 per cent) who were treated individually.

McGill, Falloon, Boyd and Wood-Siverio (1983) repeat the family education aspect of this programme. Relatives' knowledge in the home-education group improved compared to those whose child had been in individual psychotherapy, despite the authors commenting that 'there was often considerable contact with family members'. Information given to them, although of the same type as the home-based group, was presented less formally. Although patients in the educational sessions improved their overall knowledge, it was not significantly greater than that shown by patients in the supportive psychotherapy groups.

Behavioural family therapy as described above, in a multi-family group format, was offered to young, male, schizophrenic patients and their families, and in addition the patients were involved in an inpatient-based, intensive social skills training programme. The social skills training is described elsewhere (Liberman, Neuchterlein and Wallace, 1982; Wallace, 1982). This was contrasted with similar patients taking part in insight-oriented family therapy plus holistic health therapy (Liberman, Wallace, Falloon and Vaughn, 1981; Liberman, Falloon and Aitchison, 1984). A variety of outcome measures were used including in the latter study an assessment of the relative's expressed emotion (EE). Of the relatives involved in the behavioural family therapy, 73 per cent of the relatives moved from high EE to low EE rating. Patient relapse figures were 21 per cent for patients in the 'behavioural family therapy plus social skills training' group, compared with 50 per cent from the 'insight-oriented family therapy plus holistic health therapy' group. While these differences may appear large, because of the small numbers of patients involved, they do not reach statistical significance.

Both relatives and patients in the behavioural family therapy group improved their knowledge of schizophrenia on a questionnaire test. The content of behavioural family therapy as described by Liberman and his colleagues varies over the studies, but the emphasis is on education, communication and problem-solving skills. Other behavioural paradigms are also employed. The description by Falloon and colleagues of the behavioural approach in various articles includes positive reinforcement, shaping, extinction, modeling, rehearsal, homework, and an 'essential feature of the family therapy is the around-the-clock availability of each therapist during crises. At these times, the therapist may make home visits or conduct sessions by telephone to resolve the crises promptly and effectively'.

Crisis intervention and the availability of a therapist on 24 hour call subtantially alter the nature of the therapy provided and are important therapeutic procedures in their own right. Their inclusion makes an assessment of the family therapy itself difficult. In terms of structured problem-solving, Moss, Falloon, Boyd and McGill (1982) describe the strategies as identifying a specific problem, listing alternative solutions, discussing pros and cons, choosing the best solution, planning to implement the solution and reviewing efforts. This is a preliminary description of the clinical study reported in later papers.

Two elements, education and communication training, to reduce expressed emotion have been discussed as approaches in their own right by other authors and will be considered separately now.

Educational Programmes

Anderson (1977) stresses the importance of recognising and meeting the needs of the family of the schizophrenic patient by providing 'information, structure and control in a time of chaos and crisis'. She advocates the importance of having a professional assigned to represent the families' needs and interests, and discusses a variety of treatment formats including multi-family groups, task-oriented groups and home visits.

From this, Anderson, Hogarty and Reiss (1980, 1981) describe the rationale behind a 'psychoeducational family treatment' of schizophrenia as including the perceptual and cognitive deficits of the patients which seem to make them sensitive to environmental stresses and the family communication styles which might exacerbate this condition. Thus, again, the modification of the expressed emotion of the family is one of the goals of therapy; or, an 'increased predictability and stability of the family environment, to be achieved by a decrease in the anxiety of family members about the patient, an increase in their knowledge about the illness, and an increase in their confidence regarding their ability to manage it'.

Four overlapping phases are described as the process of intervention, covering 18 to 30 months: connecting; survival skills workshop; re-entry and application of survival skills themes to individual families; continued treatment or disengagement. Phase I, connecting, is held with family members only, to give them an opportunity to discuss their feelings without the acutely ill patient being present. Various issues are discussed, including the family's experience of the illness, establishing a treatment contact. Phase II, a multiple-family workshop lasting a day provides information about schizophrenia and its treatment, and describes the issues and themes of the whole programme. Its goal is to 'decrease the family's anxiety, sense of helplessness and feelings of stigma and isolation'. It concentrates on four major areas, giving information about the illness, about medication and about management, and concern for the family, both as individuals and a group, to maintain their own survival. As a part of this the family are presented with a series of concrete principles and techniques to help them manage the patient. The need for creating psychological space is emphasised, provided by decreasing family expectations of the patient and, by setting reasonable limits for patient behaviour, as is the need to develop support networks for all family members.

It is only at the third phase that the patient is introduced to the family programme. It begins when the acute phase is under some control and lasts between six to twelve months. Two main areas of intervention are involved, family boundaries and patient responsibility, and sessions are highly task-oriented. The last phase offers the family a choice of two options, and is presented when the goals for effective functioning have been attained to the maximum degree possible, 'considering the patient's abilities and the current family structure'. The choices are: a more traditional intensive family therapy on a weekly basis with the aim of improving effective family interaction; or a gradual disengagement, with maintenance sessions decreasing in frequency.

The programme is still being researched, but a preliminary report presents relapse data from 33 patients indicating that family therapy with social skills training decreases the likelihood of relapse (Anderson *et al.* 1981; Anderson, 1983). Already, changes have occurred in the programme (Anderson, 1983), notably that phase III is longer than originally envisaged but less intense.

The education of families of schizophrenic patients was undertaken by McLean, Greer, Scot and Beck (1982) in a 'multiple family 12 weeks support and education' group. The group was organised with speakers scheduled every other week to provide information on the illness, hospital care, community care and disability income. Written information was distributed to group members, including advice and suggestions for setting up a group for families, and articles by patients and families. The parents received support and advice about communicating with their ill child and managing psychotic behaviour. The parents made a number of suggestions regarding hospital procedures which were implemented and, as a result of the first group, a local voluntary group was organised with monthly meetings.

Reducing Expressed Emotion

The work on expressed emotion described in Chapter 3 has clear implications for treatment. One approach has already been discussed under behavioural family therapy, as described by Liberman and colleagues. A further rationale and approach is by Leff and colleagues (Leff, 1976, 1979; Berkowitz, Kuipers, Eberlein-Fries and Leff, 1981; Berkowitz, Kuipers and Leff, 1981). One effective way of dealing with the problems of high expressed emotion would be to reduce face-to-face contact by removing the patient from his home to some other form of community accommodation, but this is judged to be unacceptable for many families (Leff, 1976, 1983). Within a package of strategies subsumed under the heading of social intervention is a form of family therapy for relatives only. Both high and low EE relatives are included in a group of up to eight people, with the aim of exploring coping behaviour. Low EE relatives are involved because it was hoped that any helpful coping strategies used by such relatives would emerge and be discussed in the group 'both to enlighten the professional members and to instruct the high EE members in better management of the patients'.

Joint family sessions and a mental health education programme were also part of the intervention. This was presented as a series of four lectures, read to each relative at home, with unlimited time for questions. The lectures deal with aetiology, symptoms, course, treatment and management of schizophrenia. This is described in detail by Berkowitz, Eberlein-Fries, Kuipers and Leff (1984). The aim of the education package was described as twofold: to provide the relatives with information about schizophrenia and, through this, the hope that their attitudes would change. The relatives were tested on a 'knowledge interview' before and immediately after the education sessions and then at a nine-month follow-up. Although there are some changes in knowledge and attitudes at follow-up, the conclusion must be that 'there is little doubt that relatives remembered only a fraction of what they had been told'. Immediately after education they know the diagnosis and something about management, but they have no knowledge of aetiology, 'the tendency to retain their own version of causes of the illness is consistent across all groups'. Only one change in attitudes was found among high EE relatives who had received education, and that was that they became less pessimistic. In practice, the programme of intervention has been modified as some relatives either would not, or could not, attend group meetings. Home visits were introduced for these relatives. The results from this study are reported (Leff, Kuipers, Berkowitz, Eberlein-Fries and Sturgeon, 1982; Leff, Kuipers and Berkowitz, 1983). Twelve families were assigned to the social interventions package and 12 to routine outpatient care. All patients were on medication and judged to be at high risk of relapse. During the nine-month follow-up six of the control group and one of the experimental group relapsed, a statistically significant difference. The aims of the social intervention programme were to lower expressed emotion and/or face-to-face contact. This was achieved in eight families.

The problems of involving the family in a therapy programme, of working with relatives and their effect not only on outcome measures but compliance and drop-out rates will be discussed in Chapter 8.

PART TWO

SCHIZOPHRENIA AT HOME

5 THE FAMILY SITUATION

Perhaps only those who have faced it (*schizophrenia*) in their own households can fully grasp what it can mean, the problems of managing the unmanageable, of coping with the inexplicable alterations between a known and loved person and an apparent stranger, the headaches over money and the sufferer's mainten-ance, the nagging anxieties over the long term outcome. Nor are they problems which can be faced, dealt with, finished with. They may drag on for years. Finally, since the disease commonly strikes people in their teens and twenties, parents can be well on in life, with correspondingly reduced resilience and capacity to cope.

National Schizophrenia Fellowship, 1975

With hindsight it would seem obvious that discharging mental patients from the hospital to the community, either to live there alone or with their family, would create numerous problems and place a heavy burden on the community, particularly on the family. The policy of community care may be laudable in its inten-tions, but the reality is often very different. Living at home with their families provides additional stresses for both patient and rela-tives, and these will be discussed in some detail in the next two chapters. This chapter concentrates on the global problems of the family and the situation as a whole.

Type of Family Household

Not all patients return from hospital to living with their families. Some will live alone in accommodation owned or rented by them, or go to digs or lodging with various degrees of services provided (e.g. meals), or to hostels. Of those who return to families, some will return to parental homes and others to marital homes. In an analysis of chronic schizophrenic patients known to a London hospital, Atkinson (1981) found that out of a total of 195 chronic schizophrenic patients, 71 per cent were living with relatives or friends, 9 per cent were in a hostel, 17 per cent were living alone, and a further 3 per cent were living alone but with some sort of supervision. The population as a whole was composed of 55 per cent women and 45 per cent men. Comparing living accommodation by sex of patient, 76 per cent of women lived with a relative or friend compared with 67 per cent of the men. Only 4 per cent of women lived in hostel accommodation compared with 14 per cent of men; 19 per cent of the women and 15 per cent of the men lived alone, and 2 per cent of women and 5 per cent of men lived in supervised accommodation. The difference in numbers living in hostel accommodation is probably accounted for by the differing number of available places in the area rather than more individual factors.

Of the 140 patients who lived with a relative or friend, 48 per cent were living in a marital home, 34 per cent in the parental home, 11 per cent with a sibling, 4 per cent with their adult children, 2 per cent with friends and less than 1 per cent with another relative or young children (i.e. as a single parent). There are some clear differences between the male and female patients: of the women, 59 per cent are presently living in a marital home, compared with 32 per cent of men. Marital home includes living with a spouse or cohabiting, and may include children living in the home, who may be young children or adult. Fifty-nine per cent of men, but only 16 per cent of women, live in their parental home. More women live with siblings than do men, 16 per cent compared to 3 per cent. The numbers living with other relatives are too small from which to generalise, but it should be noted that it is only women who were living with their children. One of these was as a single parent with young children, the other 6 per cent were living with adult children. This probably reflects the greater likelihood of women in this group having children (Sturt, Wykes and Creer, 1982).

The study reported by Sturt *et al.* (1982) describes 67 people using day-care services, of whom 3 per cent lived in a marital home (including cohabiters), 28 per cent were living with parents or other relatives, 31 per cent lived alone, and 9 per cent in a hostel. No separate data are given for men and women except to say that all the hostel residents were men, and that those under 40 years in both sexes were more likely to be living in a marital home. Other information has to be inferred from the data that more women (25 per cent) than men (17 per cent) were currently married. This picture of the chronic population as a whole is important to bear in mind when considering the family situation. It is easy to fall into the habit of considering the family of the schizophrenic patient to be parents and forget the special problems of other types of families. This in part probably stems from family theories of aetiology concerning themselves with the patient's family of origin. One important group for consideration are patients living with elderly relatives (of pensionable age) and who are dependent on these elderly family members. The special problems of this group have been described by Stevens (1972).

Family Burden

The concept of burden on the family has been well documented over the last 25 years. What is meant by 'burden' varies across studies, but a broad division between 'subjective burden' and 'objective burden' is useful (Grad and Sainsbury, 1966). Hoenig and Hamilton (1967, 1969) use this approach to assess the burden which falls on the family as a result of an extramural service provided by the hospital rather than an inpatient service. They report that from 'the point of view of the psychiatric administrator, the picture that has emerged so far is an encouraging one'. By this they mean that a 'completely unselected group of psychiatric patients' had been managed in the community for four years, and that this 'relief of the inpatient services was not achieved at the expense of other branches, such as the outpatient, day-patient, or domiciliary services, nor at the expense of the general hospital service, not yet of the general practitioner.' Yet since the patients themselves were 'by no means all recovered' the care of them had to come from somewhere. This 'somewhere' was the family.

The objective burden concerns 'adverse effects on the household due to the patient's illness' under four headings: financial, health, effects on children, and effects on family routine. The disruption of the lives of individual family members was the highest area of burden, with 42 per cent of families with a schizophrenic patient being affected, although only 8 per cent were severely affected. Financial effects were the next most important group of burdens, followed by health problems and strain in family members. In both these categories, twice as many families with a schizophrenic member reported problems as they did in the sample of families with mental patients as a whole. In 12 per cent of households there was separation of children from their parents, and in 2 per cent of cases the child 'seemed disturbed or frankly neurotic'.

The other aspect of object burden studied was the presence of abnormal behaviour in the patient. This type of burden occurred very much more often with schizophrenic patients than it did in the sample as a whole. 'Other unusual behaviour' occurred in 49 per cent of families; 'used odd speech or expressed unusual ideas' in 48 per cent; and 'apparently wilfully unco-operative' in 32 per cent. In all these cases, the majority fell into the 'constant or periodic' category, very few having only the occasional problem.

The two types of objective burden were combined into a single measure indicating that in 69 per cent of households there was objective burden of some type and degree; only 31 per cent had no objective burden. This was a higher percentage than in the psychiatric sample as a whole, suggesting that schizophrenia is more likely to cause difficulties for the family than some other types of psychiatric problems.

Age and sex were positively related to experience of objective burden, younger male patients being over represented in families reporting burden. This was probably more due to the unemployment of the patient and resulting financial loss than it was to their disturbing behaviour. Type of household also seemed to effect the experience of burden. Parental homes were the group reporting objective burden the most often, then marital homes, followed by other relatives. The differences were not, however, significant.

'Subjective burden' was essentially an inquiry into the attitudes of the family whether they thought that 'as a result of the patient's illness the household had suffered a sense of burden'. Sixty per cent of the families reported some degree of subjective burden, which was slightly higher than the whole population group, but only 9 per cent of the schizophrenia sample reported severe subjective burden which was less than for the total psychiatric sample as a whole. Sex of the patient and duration of illness made some difference to the experience of burden but did not reach statistical significance. Again male patients were over-represented in the burden group.

Comparing data on objective and subjective burden, of the 81 per cent of families who were assessed as having periodic or constant burden, 29 per cent of these did not complain of subjective burden, 60 per cent experienced some, and only 11 per cent severe subjective burden. Of the 19 per cent of households with no, or only occasional objective burden, 13 per cent reported some subjective burden, but there were no reports of severe subjective burden. Compared with the sample as a whole, Hoenig and Hamilton report that 'what we have called "tolerance" of the household towards schizophrenic patients seemed if anything to be greater than that extended to psychiatric patients in general'.

Grad and Sainsbury (1963) concentrated on the 'objective' aspects of the problem when assessing the effects of the patient's illness on the family. This included disruption of the household routine, social and leisure activities and employment of other family members. At least one-fifth of the families were found to have a severe management problem. They conclude that 'schemes for treating patients outside the mental hospital will have to take account of the health and economic peculiarities of families: and in deciding whether treatment inside or outside the hospital is preferable, family attitudes will have to be considered'.

It may be that, in part, the experience of burden is related to the amount and type of care provided in the community and extended to the family, and the family's satisfaction with the services provided. This issue will be considered later. A study by Fenton, Tessier and Struening (1979) found no difference in burden between a hospital-based and a home-based group of patients. The home care provided included pharmacological and other physical treatments, psychotherapy and a 24-hour on-call service.

Wing and colleagues (e.g. Wing 1982) report on the experience of long-term community care, and suggest that for many patients the care and support provided by families and friends is more important than the services provided locally by the various agencies. In attempting to assess the complex interaction between objective and subjective burden, Creer, Sturt and Wykes (1982) rate relatives as 'content', 'resigned' or 'dissatisfied' in four areas of patient behaviour: self care; housework; management of money; and socially difficult behaviour. Although only four out of 52 relatives (8 per cent) rated no objective burden, 60 per cent rated themselves content with the situation and their responsibilities. When a 'satisfaction score is compared with the amount of support the relatives give, there is a significant association between providing a lot of support for the patient and dissatisfaction or resignation on the part of the relatives providing this support'.

This study considered the chronic psychiatric population as a whole. Of these, 62 per cent of patients needed some help and 19 per cent much help in terms of self-care from their relatives. As Creer *et al.* (1982) point out it 'should be emphasised that *no* help would normally be thought necessary'. In terms of socially difficult behaviour, which included embarrassing behaviour in public, violence and talk or threats of suicide, 40 per cent of patients required some and 33 per cent much 'caring attention' from relatives in at least one category.

A survey completed by the National Schizophrenia Fellowship gives verbatim reports of 'living with schizophrenia — by the relatives' (1974a). Complaints feature strongly, as would be expected in a report from a group one of whose aims is getting more help for relatives. The major complaints centred around the lack of facilities, for example day centres, hostels, sheltered employment and occupational therapy, and lack of fast readmission to hospital at the relatives' request. They also complain of lack of help from the various professional groups, such as social workers, mental welfare officers, social security officers and doctors. This includes the doctors not discussing or giving reports on the patient's condition and progress without the patient's permission.

No amount of research data on families, expressed as percentages of the group bearing a burden, can convey what it means in real terms to the family. Nothing takes the place of talking to individual family members about their lifestyle, and how it has changed to accommodate their ill relative. Very often major changes or sacrifices are made by relatives without the professionals knowing this. Often the adjustments made by the family seem excessive to the professional, and might fall into the category of 'overprotective'. Even if this is pointed out to them they may feel that there are special circumstances which justify their position. This might be further complicated by what the professional knows, or thinks, the patient can do, and what the patient actually does. For example, there is a difference between the patient being able to wash and shave himself, and him doing this willingly, naturally and daily, and only doing this when nagged, pressurised or otherwise persuaded by relatives on a daily basis. Even a checklist which rates this as 'with prompting' does not begin to describe the emotional impact on the family, or indeed, on the patient.

The changes families may make to their lifestyle, or to their plans may frequently strike the professional as extravagant, if they even know about it, but they are not unusual. These may be 'one-off' changes or a more permanent adaptation.

Mrs K

Mrs K, the widowed mother of a schizophrenic son, had been trying for a number of years to find some kind of day facilities for him to attend. In the meantime they had developed a very close, interdependent relationship, with the son becoming increasingly withdrawn, unwilling to leave the house and having day–night reversal. After much effort, a place at a day centre was found for the son to start in a matter of two weeks. No help was given or offered in helping the patient to adjust to the changes he would have to make in his lifestyle to attend the day centre, 'at 9 a.m. prompt' as he was told.

Both became increasingly agitated, he at the prospect of attending the day centre, and his mother by the stress he was under. He was due to start while she was on holiday with a friend, her one break in the year. She felt that if she was not at home he would never get to the centre, so she cancelled her holiday, with the attendant loss of money and ill feeling between the two friends, as the other woman was unhappy about now having to make a trip abroad on her own. None of this was conveyed to the therapeutic team, who had not made any enquiries about coping with this new development. When the son attended the day centre for only three days before refusing to go back, the staff at the centre were annoyed at his 'inconsistent and inconsiderate behaviour' but could not understand the mother's bitterness at what she saw as their lack of concern and caring and generally unhelpful manner. Her bitterness was fed by disappointed expectations, albeit unrealistic in the first place, but also by the financial and personal loss she had suffered to no good end, sacrifice that the professional team still do not know about. It is too easy to label her overprotective and dismiss her actions, or only to see them in terms of the stress they place on her son; but without considering their meaning to her, much of their impact is lost.

Family Attitudes

As has been noted, researchers have looked at the family attitude to the care of the patient in terms of subjective burden. The concept of 'tolerance' or the ability of the family to deal with the patient, their problems and the effect on family members themselves is postulated. As in so many other areas, the research evidence is equivocal.

Freeman and Simmons (1958a) believed that 'the tolerance of deviant behaviour on the part of family members is a key factor affecting the course of post-hospital experience' for male psychiatric patients. They report (1958b) differences in patient's performance levels depending on the type of family in which the patient lives: patients showing lower levels of performance in parental homes than in marital homes. This, they suggest, is related to the relative's expectations of performance. Mothers were more likely to have lower expectations than wives, and patients with a low performance were more likely to live with a female relative 'atypical' in personality, by which they meant 'authoritarian, anomic, frustrated, rigid and withdrawn'. A further interesting finding related to other male family members. Where the patient had low-level functioning he tended not to be seen as 'either a breadwinner or potential breadwinner' and that there were other male relatives who could 'supplement or replace the patient'.

Other studies have also considered the interaction between family attitudes and outcome. Kelley (1964) found no difference between the favourable or unfavourable family attitude groups on background and treatment variables which were considered relevant to outcome. Even when married and single patients were evaluated separately, there was no relationship between family attitude and outcome.

Niskanen and Pitikanen (1972) compared the families' attitude toward their schizophrenic member when the patient was receiving either hospital or a home-based treatment. Interestingly, the patient was rated a burden more often in the hospital based group, 47 per cent compared with 26 per cent of families rating the patient a burden. In both groups the families were equally satisfied with the care provided. Both groups showed a similar degree of unfavourable attitude to the family, and thus it was thought unlikely that this affected whether the patient chose hospital- or home-based treatment. There were, however, more women in the home-based group, which 'may be connected with the known, less tolerant attitudes of the families towards male patients'. This might have led male patients to choose a hospital-based service.

A study of relatives visiting inpatients in mental hospitals

(Rawnsley, London and Miles, 1962) indicated that visiting was higher for married than single patients. Married schizophrenics in hospital for less than two years 'attract greater interest' and are more likely to be given a home on discharge than are single schizophrenic patients.

In a further study, Freeman and Simmons (1963) consider the feelings of the relatives to the patient. Tolerance of deviance is defined as 'the continued acceptance of the former patient by his family members, even when he fails to perform in instrumental roles'. They report that 'feelings of stigma on the part of the relatives' are 'significantly correlated with performance levels among males and show a fairly strong trend among females' but do not seem to have a relationship with the patient's ability to remain in the community. Patients who were returned to hospital with a low performance level were more likely to come from marital than parental homes. Thus Freeman and Simmons introduce the notion of differential tolerance of deviance. Based on the family data reported above, their premises about tolerance of deviance are divided into four categories: structural (of family), personality (of family and patient), cultural and attitudinal.

Whether or not the family experiences shame, embarrassment or stigma is again a debatable issue with varying research evidence. Although it is often assumed that the family would feel either shame or embarrassment, Doll (1976) did not find this to be true. In fact he reports that 80 per cent of relatives 'denied avoiding friends out of embarrassment'. As one might expect, from common sense if not other research data, the severity of symptoms causes problems. The picture, however, is not straightforward. Thus Doll reports 'our findings showed that the families of the mentally ill often display a high tolerance of deviant behaviour with little shame', but in the next paragraph continues 'what does trouble them and even seems to turn the return home into a mutually painful and unwanted experience, is the continued presence of psychiatrically severe symptoms'. What the difference is between the 'deviant behaviour' which is tolerated and the 'psychiatrically severe symptoms' which are not, is not made clear.

As might be expected, the least sympathetic reactions come from family members whose patient–relative presented the most symptoms. These families reported significantly more embarrassment than the relatives of the less disturbed group; 67 per cent compared with 35 per cent. Since, out of the total sample only 12 per cent of the patients returned to hospital within a ten-month period, Doll concluded that the relatives would physically tolerate psychiatrically disturbed behaviour in the home. Most of the patients considered to be seriously disturbed, 72 per cent, however, were considered to be a management problem in the home. Regarding the isolation of the patients within the family, Doll reports that less than 20 per cent of relatives 'engaged in leisure-time activities with the former patient, such as going to parties or sports events or belonging to the same clubs'. Since we are not told how many relatives were engaging in such activities on their own, or with another relative this data is difficult to interpret. We are told, however, that 71 per cent of those relatives living with a severely disturbed patient said they wanted to exclude the patient from their social life.

Doll acknowledges this confused state of attitude and behaviour. There is a difference between the standard measures of social distance which show the relatives to be amenable to, and accepting of, the former patient, and beneath these gives a picture of 'people who feel trapped or who carry strong feelings of antagonism and fear'. What comes clearly out of this study is that living in the community as a criterion of adjustment is nonsensical. 'We see here a fairly representative sample of former mental patients who are socially and affectionately rejected while not being hospitalised and while failing in the community ... The reassuring findings that families show little shame and avoidance of the mentally ill obscures much of the reality of coping with the mentally ill. The reality is woven of feelings and patterns of response that are destructive for the family as well as the patient'.

Doll, Thompson and Lefton (1976a, b) stress the important distinction to be made between tolerating deviant behaviour and accepting it. Thus 'psychiatrically disturbed behaviour' may not lead to rehospitalisation and symptoms are 'put up with', but this carries a very strong negative charge and may have a serious emotional impact upon the family. The effect of this impact is not formally explored in this study, but other research, for example on expressed emotion, attest to its harm and effects.

The extent to which a family feels guilt, shame, blame and other identifiable expressions of stigma will, naturally, depend in part on the way their particular reference groups view mental illness. One way of dealing with the shame and guilt, and reasons for this, is described by Juni (1980) for an Orthodox Jewish family. The mother's concern is to prove the schizophrenic son is brain-damaged and, therefore, that the condition is not inherited, and thus will not affect any children her daughters might bear and, therefore, will not hinder their opportunities for marriage. To deal with such a family and to be able to help them would not be possible without an understanding of their religious and cultural beliefs.

The previous studies do not indicate a difference in experience of stigma associated with social class, but in one study, Kennard, Clemmy and Mandlebrote (1977) this is an important variable. The study uses a semantic differential with two scales of 'pleasantness' and 'illness'. In a mixed diagnostic group the level of contact with the hospital was clearly related to how much the patient and his 'closest other person' differed in their perception of how 'ill' the patient was. It is probable that both interested parties are looking to the hospital for confirmation of their outlook, and for the hospital staff to convince the other party of this.

It is interesting to note that this study showed that 'patients who had little or no contact with the hospital were seen as less "ill", but less "pleasant" than those who had more'. The association came from middle-class families (social classes I and II). In this study the patients were in a therapeutic community, and it seemed to be working-class patients rather than middle-class who attended group meetings on discharge. The middle-class group of patients are seen as less pleasant, both by themselves and by their relatives, and 'quickly terminate their contact with the Unit'. Kennard *et al.* conclude that this 'suggests that middle-class households have a less indulgent or accepting attitude to psychiatric patienthood, expecting nicer behaviour from the patient and greater independence from the hospital.

It seems that relatives' attitudes to schizophrenia itself, as an illness, may influence their attitude towards the patient. One might expect that not blaming the patient for his illness would mean the family would tolerate the patient's problems more. Freeman and Simmons (1963), although expecting this, found the opposite to be the case. They found a 'strong association between expressing doubt that patients can recover from mental illness and attributing blame to the patient for his illness'. Furthermore, the view that patients are not to blame for their condition was more prevalent among relatives of successful than unsuccessful patients, as well as among relatives of patients with higher performance levels among both successful and unsuccessful patients. Freeman and Simmons suggest that 'refraining from making demands for instrumental performance on the patient can be rationalised by placing the blame for inadequate performance on the patient himself rather than on his interpersonal situation'. They also suggest that the more educated the person the less likely they are to blame the patient for his condition, 'which may in part reflect a greater concern with interpersonal orientation gained in the process of higher education'.

The general pervasive attitude to schizophrenia as an illness is clearly described in an article in *The Times* (1970), written by the parent of a schizophrenic, which led ultimately to the formation of the National Schizophrenia Fellowship: 'They excite none of the sympathy which surrounds other classes of the disabled. Even close relatives, let alone official bodies or employers, find it not always easy to choke back the feeling that there is something *morally* culpable about people apparently fit and rational who fling up work without an excuse.'

In the report by the National Schizophrenia Fellowship (1974a), relatives describe feeling forced to 'put on a false front', both to the patients and to the community, to cover up feelings of guilt, but particularly shame. This causes the family strain, and may be perceived by the patient and add to his stress. It may thus be conducive to an exacerbation of the patient's present problems.

Another report by the National Schizophrenia Fellowship (1975) describes the problems of stigma to the relative reader. 'As regards stigma, your family has to live in the world as it is — a world in which the popular press and television "image" of a schizophrenic is mostly of a rapist or a child-murderer, in which a hostel cannot be established in a "better class" district without protest from the neighbours that their wives and daughters will not be safe. It is useless for families of schizophrenics to reflect their poor, frightened lad would not hurt a fly ...

'Do not be surprised, therefore, if your family, with the abnormalities of its home-life, shrinks from introducing too many outsiders into the home. To be thereupon typecast by the investigator with the clipboard as "introverted family which finds social contacts difficult".'

The author of this passage clearly expects the experience of feelings of stigma to occur and, furthermore, to be acted upon by relatives and to be perceived and possibly mislabelled by professionals.

The Patient's Attitude to the Family

A much neglected aspect of the family dynamics in schizophrenic families is the patient's attitude towards their family. It is interesting, although not necessarily fruitful, to speculate on why this might be so. One possible reason may stem from the past emphasis placed on the family's role in aetiology, and later in relapse. The emotional atmosphere of the family is presented in terms of the relatives' response to the patient who is described as, if not passive, then a collection of symptomatology and problems, rather than a dynamic part of the family group. It may be that professionals see the patient as fairly passive, someone to whom things are done, rather than as someone who plays an instrumental role in the doing. Family therapy may involve the professionals' attitude changing to the role of the patient, as well as to the role of the relatives.

One research programme that has considered the family relationship from a more equitable position is that of Scott and Montanez (1971) who describes the relationship between the schizophrenic patient and parents as being either tenable or untenable. Tenability depends on 'whether or not the patient confirmed certain parental expectations and values'. If the patient denies or violates parental expectations he threatens 'the core of the parent's identity, thereby creating an untenable situation, which if it persists after the acute disturbance is over, may lead to prolonged hospitalisation'.

Scott and Montanez compare community-centred and hospital-centred patients, although the cut-off point of less than 70 per cent of the two years after first admission in hospital seems high; this suggests that even the community-based patients may spend less than half their time out of the hospital. The relationship between patients based in the community and their parents is described as tenable, whereas the relationship between hospital-based patients and their parents is seen as untenable. There is, however, only one scale on their family relationship test which differentiates the two groups, namely 'how the patient sees his parents'. Both sets of parents see themselves as being 'good or "well" parents, and expect the patient to see them likewise. Community-based patients do support their parents in this view of themselves, whereas the hospital-based patients do not, seeing their parents 'as being "ill" or disturbed'. These are the patients who are likely to be readmitted to hospital fairly quickly, a crisis having developed.

Further analysis reveals more to the situation than this simple position. It is not enough for patients not to see negative aspects in their parents. 'Further to this the parents require confirmation, in specific terms, that they are good or "well" parents. They require to be seen as secure, self-confident, responsible parents who mix well out and have a place in the world. Also that as a further distinction of their roles as "well-parents" the patients shall not see themselves in these terms.'

Scott (1976) later discontinues the use of the word 'tenability' but the meaning remains the same. The 'tenability score' becomes the 'agreement score'; a 'tenable score' being a 'confirming score' and an 'untenable score' being a 'contradicting score'. The patients in the first study (1971) were first admitted in 1963 or 1964 and were followed up for four years. It would seem unlikely that patients are admitted for such a long period now, which means that patients who have an 'untenable' relationship with their parents are either having to live with their parents and face the consequences (possibly repeated admission or requests for admission), or live alone. It may be that this research gives us one explanation for why some families refuse to co-operate in family therapy programmes. Such families may be looking for confirmation that they are 'well' and see the suggestion of therapy as a threat, or colluding with a patient who has defined them as disturbed.

The patient's attitude to the family may also have a bearing on the influence of expressed emotion on relapse. Not every patient in this condition relapses, and the view the patient takes of the criticism or hostility may be a relevant, intervening, protective factor. Whether or not he sees it as justified, whether or not this attitude has only appeared since be became ill, may be important. Criticism from all the family may be a very different thing from criticism from one person if there is support coming from elsewhere. Whether or not the patient thinks he is being singled out may be crucial. Criticism may have a more arousing effect if the patient sees it aimed only at him in the family, rather than if it is seen as that person's habitual mode of communication, when it may be more easily shrugged off or otherwise dealt with.

Perceptions of Problems

When describing the problems in the family, the previously discussed studies either use an assessment made by the researcher based on observation of the family, or a report by the family of their problems. Even where patient's behaviour is included in the area of problems, their assessment of the situation is rarely sought. Clinically, most therapists will be aware that the patient and his relatives have a different perspective on what constitutes a problem, and part of the therapy process may be to explore and deal with that issue.

One study that measured both patients' and relatives' perception was that by Atkinson (1981), although only patient behaviour was assessed rather than the family situation as a whole. A behavioural checklist was used and at pre-test the relatives scored the patient as more handicapped than did the patient, although this did not reach statistical significance. Although after the therapy programme both groups reported a significant improvement in the patient's functioning, the difference in perception of the problem still remained.

Since the same behaviour is being rated it would seem that it is being seen in different ways by the people concerned. These different views of the same objective reality are important in therapy and may be an obstacle which has to be overcome. A discussion on the nature of reality would be out of place here, but it is useful to consider that 'reality' is best used and understood with 'perceived' as an unspoken but understood prefix. It is fruitless to argue which of the two views, relative's or patient's, is the more accurate. They are both telling the truth (one assumes) as they see it. Whether one provides a better base for therapy than the other is a separate issue and will be discussed in Chapter 8.

A number of factors will affect the perception of the 'facts'. One of these will almost certainly be the relative's attitude towards the patient and his illness. Some of the research on this has already been discussed. If the patient is viewed as 'ill' then the relatives may expect less of him in performance terms. It may be that for some areas of behaviour or problem it is appropriate to view the schizophrenic patient as ill, but not in all cases. A bad temper or a tendency to argue may have pre-dated the onset of illness, and may be a 'problem' in anyone, but in the context of someone being labelled ill such behaviour may come to be seen as part of the illness and, therefore, something for which it is legitimate to demand change, and for a doctor or therapist to work to bring this about.

For example, the husband of a 40-year-old schizophrenic patient who was well stabilised on fluphenazine decanoate (Modecate), would suggest that she saw a doctor or get her medication changed at any show of irritability on her part, or whenever she expressed a wish to do something he did not want to. In general he seemed to see any change in her mood as being attributable to her illness, and possibly the beginnings of a relapse, rather than as an acceptable, normal variation. A result of this was that the patient tried to appear as placid as she could, particularly when she was with him. In other circles this would have been (and was) termed 'blunting of affect'.

A second consequence of this perception of someone as ill is revealed in expectations of behaviour. Often families accept the conditioned concept that people who are 'ill' should not do too much, and should be looked after. This is expressed in comments like: 'There is time enough for that when he's better'; 'She is not really well enough to do any housework'; or 'I don't mind doing it for him while he is ill'. It seems that some families express this view frequently to their 'ill' relative and stifle any initiative on his part; often with the best intentions that this might be too stressful for them.

Sometimes this occurs simply through a passive lack of encouragement; in others may take the form of a more active discouragement. For example, 'you will only be ill again if you ...' may or may not have some basis in truth from past experience, but makes current progress for the patient difficult. The result is that the patient can be forced into a role of low performance, a role which leaves him little to do but sit in a chair and 'concentrate on getting better'. Such an approach can make the setting of targets difficult in therapy or rehabilitation. This view of the patient may also colour the reporting of behaviour and problems. Behaviour that would be described as inadequate for a 'normal' family member may be viewed as quite adequate or even appropriate for someone who 'isn't well'.

Not all relatives see the patient as ill, of course, and some are reluctant even to admit that the patient has a problem. This does not necessarily prevent them enumerating the problems he causes and the difficulties they have in dealing with him. Common complaints are likely to be of laziness, idleness, sullenness and stubborness, rather than the psychiatrist's less emotionally laden terms of apathy and withdrawal. Relatives frequently do not appreciate the difficulty the patient has in doing some things, possibly whatever the family deemed normal or necessary. They may focus on one particular issue as being the central problem, from which they see everything else stemming. For example, the belief might be 'he would be all right if he got a job/girlfriend/went out more'.

An important complicating factor in assessment of behaviour is that everyone tends to exaggerate their relative participation in tasks (Hoffman and Lippitt, 1960). Thus we might expect a reporting of greater involvement or higher performance levels from patients about their own behaviour than from relatives reporting on the patient. Patients, clearly, are going to be aware of the difficulty they have in doing certain tasks and of the amount of effort involved, in a way that their relatives are not. Thus they may view themselves as functioning at capacity, while relatives may see only that there is room for improvement. This might lead patients to over-value or over-estimate the amount they are accomplishing and its relative importance to the family.

Rutter and Brown (1966) in a questionnaire on participation in household tasks found good across-interview agreement between husbands and wives when using an 'intensive interview' to obtain data. Nevertheless, they still found that compared with their husband's account, wives who were categorised 'dissatisfied' tended to under-estimate their husband's participation by, on average, 16 per cent, and wives who were satisfied over-estimated his participation by, on average, 11 per cent. 'Put another way, eight out of twelve dissatisfied wives under-estimated their husband's performance, but only five out of sixteen satisfied wives did so'. Similar findings occurred in the husband's reports. It should be noted, however, that under-estimation does not refer to an observed, 'true' figure, but only to the other partner's report.

In view of the small differences, Rutter and Brown felt justified in concluding that 'the emphasis on facts rather than feelings, largely eliminated attitudinal biases'. If, however, it is true that an individual over-estimates his own participation, it may be that dissatisfied partners are reporting closer to the 'objective reality' and that satisfied partners share their spouses rosy picture. A similar effect might be expected in relatives' and patients' reporting behaviour, depending on the relative's satisfaction with the patient and the situation.

Feldman (1960) found that an individual reporting for himself will record more illness than a family member reporting for him. While this is no doubt reasonable, it may be more difficult for an individual to report or admit a problem connected with mental illness than it would be for a relative, where this was manifest in the patient's behaviour. In the Atkinson (1981) study, on the part of the checklist dealing with 'illness problems', the relative's average ratings were more than twice that of the patient's.

An interesting corollary to this is that a group of patients whose families were not involved in assessment and therapy scored themselves twice as highly as the patients in the family group, although on clinical examination (present-state examination, PSE) there was no difference between the two groups. It would seem reasonable to conclude that the presence of a family member influences the way the patient reports illness behaviour and symptoms.

A possible explanation would be that the patients are aware, presumably, of the effect both socially and in the family, of admitting to 'mental' problems and do not want to become involved in a discussion of these with the relative. The patient may have realised that his relative would present him in a 'poor light', possibly more than he felt was justified, and he wanted to redress the balance, particularly if family friction stemmed from some of these areas. The patient, knowing the relative is to be involved in therapy, might have felt that pressure would be brought to bear to change in some of these areas where they either felt it was not possible to change, would be too difficult to change, or where simply they did not want to. The patient without his relative's involvement may have experienced a greater sense of freedom in his ability to negotiate with the therapist.

A question is not a stimulus presented in a vacuum, expecting a response in a similar vacuum. Getzels (1954) suggests three stages in a question-answer process. First, a question arouses a 'previously established personal hypothesis', the question is put into a context and the personal hypothesis checked against this and, lastly, an answer formed that 'will facilitate or at least not threaten the respondent's adjustment in the light of personal needs relative to situational demands'. Getzels suggests that the situational context of the therapeutic interview is 'permissive' and that there is 'no value judgement anticipated'. It would seem likely, however, that where the family is present the situational context of the questions is altered and a value judgement is presumed.

Differential Effects on Family

Not all the family are affected in the same way by having a schizo-phrenic family member. Like the patient's attitude to the family, this is another neglected area of research. Anecdotal clinical evidence shows us that different family members respond to the burdens on them in different ways and, indeed, acknowledge the burden differently. Typically, it is the mother who shows most concern, and on whom most of the burden falls. This is clearly demonstrated in membership of and attendance at meetings of the voluntary bodies, and in some of the therapy groups with family members.

In terms of day-to-day caring where the patient is a child, the main care falls upon the mother. It is she who may have to give up a job or outside activities to care for him, and she who spends most time with him. The rest of the family may not appreciate the stress this places on her, and the alterations it makes to her life. Some of the changes that may be required of the family may involve changes in the role structure of the family, particularly that of the mother as 'carer'. How this might affect therapy is discussed in Chapter 8.

Even if some of the family accept the patient as 'ill', usually not all do. Typical patterns would be the father viewing the patient as 'lazy' or 'difficult' while the mother sees him as ill. This in itself can lead to problems within the marital relationship which might then be exacer-bated by the mother being tired and stressed by the extra burden on her. If this is further complicated by other siblings, possibly divided among themselves and taking one or other side, then disharmony in the family becomes widespread and the very structure of the family becomes threatened.

A neglected group in research terms are relatives other than parents of the schizophrenic. The effects on a spouse of their partner being ill will be very different from a parent. Where the ill spouse is the husband this may have a severe financial impact as well as devas-tating psychological and emotional ones. The wife may find that she has to bear the whole burden of child-rearing alone and that her ill husband may assume, in both their minds, the role of another child within the family. Parents of an ill child, if they are fortunate, will receive and give support to one another, whereas the spouse of a patient may have no one to turn to for support and help apart from their parents. Support may be difficult to obtain where these are elderly or geographically distant. If the ill parent's behaviour is affecting the children of the marriage then the spouse might find themselves torn between impossible choices. As one wife put it 'the best thing for the kids is to go. The best for him — to stay. I promised "for better, for worse". but how can I ignore the kids? . . .' This wife's dilemma was made worse by her own parents encouraging her to leave her husband, and her in-laws blaming her for their son's breakdown.

Although parents often feel to blame for their child's illness, spouses are not exempt from this belief. This is especially true when there has been no sign of illness before the marriage. In-laws, in seeking to absolve themselves, may make this blame apparent. As well as guilt, spouses may experience shame in terms of 'will people think I am odd because I married this person?' Or they may see their own self-worth devalued because of their spouse's illness.

The differential effects on family members may become more pronounced as other changes occur in the family. For example, in one family where the mother and patient son had evolved a reasonable pattern of daily life together over the years, there was great disruption when the father retired, because he could not cope with having his son at home all day. It was almost as though he was having to confront the son's illness for the first time, being presented with this evidence that his son was not 'like other lads his age' and was not doing 'normal things — like a job'. To deal with this the father took himself off for long walks, which became less feasible as the weather worsened into winter. The parents, who had not argued over the son before, now found that their attitude and approach was totally different and had problems themselves confronting this.

The next two chapters consider the particular problems confronting families who have a schizophrenic relative living with them, first from the relatives' position and then from the patient's.

6 THE RELATIVES' PROBLEMS

The previous chapter has shown how caring for a chronic, psychiatrically ill patient affects the family in terms of the burden, both objective and subjective, that is put on them. The consequences of this burden affect different types of families and individual family members in different ways, as has been described. However, this research only begins to outline the problems the relatives experience. It deals primarily with the relative's difficulties in managing the patient and his behaviour rather than on problems the relatives *themselves* have and have to learn to cope with as best they can.

The research gives us details, in global terms, of the amount of burden families might carry, but this does not help us understand how this affects the family in their day-to-day life. This is probably best described in a number of first-person accounts, written by relatives (e.g. NSF, 1974a; Reed, 1976; Duval, 1979; McDonald, 1980; Ogdon and Kerr, 1981; Willis, 1982). The probability that professional staff do not understand the reality of living with a chronic schizophrenic patient, of the disruption to family life in terms of restrictions, tensions and disharmony might be contributory to the finding that relatives value their natural network of family and friends as more supportive than they do professional services (Hatfield, 1981).

The research tells us a burden exists; this chapter sets out to describe the effect, in individual terms, on the family. The problems are both in dealing with the patient and their own experiences. This chapter concentrates on the problems the relatives themselves have in coming to terms with the illness and the disruption to their daily life, rather than the difficulties they might have in dealing with the patient, which will be dealt with in Chapter 10.

There is very little direct research on these sorts of problems with the relatives of schizophrenic patients. What there is concentrates on broad terms and tends to be subsumed under the heading of subjective burden. There is little concern or detail about what this actually means in terms of how the relative's life is affected on a day-to-day basis or what, if anything, is being done, or can be done, to improve the relative's position. The research also suggests a host of interactions between the clinical state of the patient, the type of family to which he returns and the problems experienced.

Problems overlap and there is rarely only one area of difficulty. Feelings of embarrassment may lead to social isolation; lack of information may add to a feeling of helplessness; everything will probably create emotional problems. Nevertheless, some broad areas can be established which have been described as problems for relatives and, if this is supplemented with anecdotal evidence, the pattern and picture of the relative's life becomes clearer.

Lack of Information

Relatives complain of lack of information on many levels, ranging from not being told the patient's diagnosis and not understanding this when they are told, to not being told about the patient's treatment, discharge or what they might expect in the future. This lack of often very fundamental information can interact with or cause other problems. Lack of recognition by professionals is one important area and this is discussed below. Lack of information can also affect relatives' satisfaction or otherwise with treatment, if they have expectations based on wrong information. Holden and Levine (1982) describe lack of information about both the illness itself and its management as one of the preliminary sources of relative's dissatisfaction with help received. The three major complaints about the explanation of the diagnosis were that it was 'too vague' (35 per cent), 'not thorough enough' (31 per cent) or 'completely avoided' (24 per cent). Only 4 per cent were given an explanation which was 'too technical'.

The educational approach to relatives groups described in Chapter 4 is aimed at improving the relative's knowledge of schizophrenia and thus relieving some of the difficulties or dissatisfaction that may come through ignorance. In some instances, however, where dissatisfaction has become a 'habit', it is likely that more than straightforward information will be needed to change attitudes and behaviour. Most clinicians will find examples of this type if they look for them.

Mrs M

Mrs M's son had been diagnosed schizophrenic 15 years previously and although she accepted he was ill and had a number of very handicapping problems, she was less than happy with the diagnosis. A frequent complaint and an ever-present doubt was 'he has never been diagnosed properly'. On asking her what she meant by 'proper diagnosis' and what she felt had not been done, she replied 'he has never been given a blood test'. This indicates a misunderstanding of what schizophrenia is and how psychiatric diagnoses are made at a very basic level. Years of doubt and complaining had never been dealt with by giving her appropriate information: no one had thought to ask her what she wanted or was expecting.

Lack of Recognition

The lack of recognition of relatives by families has been mentioned in Chapter 4 as one of the reasons for including the family in therapy. Its impact should not be underestimated in adding to relatives' burden. The relatives' views reported by the National Schizophrenia Fellowship (1974a) show, in many cases, an ambivalent feeling towards the health care and social services professionals with whom they come into contact. While a particular individual may be well-liked and respected, most relatives can point to at least one area where they are, or feel they are, being ignored, mis- or ill-informed, treated as the cause of their relative's illness, put-upon and generally dealt with in a less than helpful or sympathetic manner.

This comes through clearly in dealing with relatives, either in the form of formal or informal complaints, continual requests for help, a general reiteration about their inability to cope and lack of anyone caring, and the demand for someone to 'do something'. As any clinician who has been faced with such relatives will know, many of the demands are either unrealistic and impossible to meet, beyond the present facilities of the hospital or immediate area, being made to the wrong agency, or not in the best interests of the patient. It is all too easy to forget, or ignore, that without such relatives the patients would require some form of supervised care, including hostels and day care, and in some cases inpatient facilities. In many instances, relatives are taking the place of paid workers of various types. Their desire to be recognised as agents of primary care has been documented previously.

It would be fair to say that over the last decade, although lip service has been paid to including the relatives more in treatment and rehabilitation (as described in Chapter 4), it is still a very common complaint of relatives that they are not being included in decisions regarding the patient's future — a future in which they are expected very often to play a prominent part. The problem remains a major concern of the National Schizophrenia Fellowship, to the extent that they have produced a booklet for professionals (1983) which sets out areas of concern to the relative, and about which they think they should be informed.

One of the difficulties in involving the relatives in some discussions centres around the issue of confidentiality. While it would seem self-evident that, if a patient is to be discharged to the care of a relative, it should be discussed in advance with this person, other issues which might impinge on care might be more difficult. In its 1983 document the NSF asserts: 'Professional roles of practice as to confidentiality should not normally place the caring relative in any less privileged position than other members of the primary care team as regards the doctor's information respecting the treatment and course of the illness. Any confidential information to be disclosed should only include that relevant to the care and management of the patient. The doctor would naturally have regard to the caring relative's capacity to appreciate the nature of such information. Other persons and authorities should have no greater right than the doctor to withhold confidential information affecting treatment and management from caring relatives.'

What the relatives consider they need to know and what professionals think they can tell them may differ widely in some instances. Where this is the case, explanation and discussion with the relatives about confidentiality may help them to appreciate the professional's ethical and legal position more clearly. Thus relatives may realise that they are not being deliberately ignored, even if they still feel dissatisfied with the amount of information they are being given.

Some relatives seem to feel that their wishes regarding the patient's future should take precedence over everyone else's. While this may always be difficult to resolve satisfactorily for all concerned, their position may seem more understandable when one considers all the problems they are faced with, even if it is not always reasonable or capable of resolution.

Helplessness

A problem closely allied to lack of information and of recognition is helplessness. Having to deal with a chronic, deteriorating illness may cause relatives to feel helpless, demoralised or weak. Helplessness may both arise from and contribute to, depression. Support for relatives may need to include a specific element to counteract these feelings and to enable the family members to acknowledge, and then live with, the realisation that they *are* helpless in some respects.

Emotional Problems

Inevitably, relatives of chronic schizophrenic patients are worried about the present and the future, in terms of the patient's treatment and management. The past may also be of concern to them and provide an additional source of worry. Not infrequently there is a 'search after meaning' as relatives try to understand why this should have happened to their family. Many parents will feel that it is something they have or have not done that is at the root of the problem. They may search for anything in the ill child's upbringing that distinguishes him from his siblings, and will recall anything from traumas and illness, to real or imagined rejection by other family members as being of possible significance.

This can lead to a number of problems. A relative can suffer with guilt feelings and this may contribute to depression. Both guilt and blame can feature in or contribute to family disharmony when the situation is assessed differently by the various family members, as has been discussed in Chapter 5.

Grief is generally associated with the physical loss of a person whether through death, divorce or other circumstances. Although in the schizophrenic's family the patient is still physically with them, nevertheless the family may need to grieve over the psychological loss of their ill relative. This grief may need to encompass loss of potential and loss of companionship. The grieving process is made doubly hard by being faced with the physical presence of the person they are mourning the loss of, and by having to accept this psychological stranger into the family. Added to this, the episodic nature of schizophrenia creates a series of false hopes and dashed expectations as the patient seems to improve only to become ill again. It is the apparent 'waste' of a young life that so frequently fills parents with grief.

Other emotional problems the family might expect to experience are anger at the patient's behaviour where it intrudes into their life and prevents them doing what they want, and frustration at their inability to get the patient to change. The anger can, in turn, feed the relative's guilt if he also believes that the patient is 'ill and cannot help it'.

Anecdotally it would seem that more than a few relatives suffer from anxiety, depression or associated emotional states, apparently caused by the stress of living with a severely disturbed patient. They often receive treatment, usually medication, for their condition. Whether some of this emotional distress could be relieved in other ways is open to debate and research.

One area of emotional difficulty which has been researched involves the embarrassment and shame experienced by family members, the so-called experience of stigma.

Stigma and Isolation

Research on the stigma felt by relatives of schizophrenic patients has included different aspects of the experience, such as feelings of shame and embarrassment and also attitudes towards the patient. Some studies are only concerned with what the relatives report their attitudes to be, others go further and relate reported attitude to reported behaviour. It would seem from the contradictory evidence that this is one area where reported beliefs need to be compared to *actual* behaviour. The research is considered in some detail in Chapter 5.

The general picture that emerges from such research is one in which relatives are struggling to deal with their feelings of shame or embarrassment, and succeeding only partially. Few patients are behaviourally integrated into the family, which produces additional problems for both sides. The patient may find himself isolated within the family and the relatives isolated from friends and acquaintances outside the family.

Mr O

Mr O had been ill for a number of years, but was now living at home with his wife and three teenage children. He was maintained on Modecate and suffered from side-effects, including restlessness, which made him pace up and own, and mouth movements, which involved him continually blow his cheeks in and out and make loud sucking noises. Both his wife and children felt embarrassed at being seen with him in public. The children refused to go out with him, but their mother insisted he accompany them on occasions as a way of dealing with her guilt feelings. Nevertheless she felt embarrassed; her main concern was that other people would think she was 'odd' for having married 'someone like that'. Arguments developed between mother and children which led to the children refusing to go out with either parent, and seeking to leave home as soon as they could.

Mrs B

Mrs B was living at home with her husband and two children aged six and eight. Although maintained on fluphenazine decanoate (Modecate) she still experienced hallucinations and talked to her 'voices' as a matter of routine. The children's friends had teased them about their 'crazy mother' and eventually they refused to invite friends to visit them at home. Gradually, they stopped mixing with other children and the boy, aged eight, got into a number of fights with children at school who called his mother names. This, in turn, got him into trouble with the school authorities who labelled him 'difficult', 'aggressive' and 'antisocial'.

Physical Effects

It is possible that some family members will experience physical reactions to caring for their ill relative. Tiredness and fatigue may result from the extra burden of work, but these feelings are likely to accompany depression. In many cases it will be difficult to know which comes first. Being tired adds to the feeling of depression and depression can create feelings of apathy and fatigue. Sleep patterns may be disrupted by a patient who has day-night reversal, and exhaustion may follow.

Someone who is stressed and fatigued is likely to have less resistance to illness and succumb more easily. This may come as a surprise to some people who have been previously fit and healthy, and this will only aggravate the condition. Relatives may need help in establishing and maintaining a healthy lifestyle for themselves as well as for the patient.

Privacy and Time Away From the Problem

This can be a crucial issue for some families, and is not always dependent upon the degree of 'ill' behaviour exhibited by the patient. Hatfield (1978) describes intrusive behaviour as taking the form of, among other things, 'careless or deliberate destruction of objects around the house, incessant argumentativeness, and physical threats and attacks'. Patients' strange eating habits and patterns can lead to a total disruption of family and social life, and may lead to the family avoiding eating with him in public, or inviting people to the house. It may mean that special meals have to be cooked, or that the patient takes over the kitchen in order to prepare his own 'uncontaminated' food (as he sees it), thus disrupting the preparation of other meals.

Having the opportunity to have a break from the problems seems vital, and is one of the recommendations that Creer, Sturt and Wykes (1982) make. They suggest three types of provision seem to be needed: short-term residential accommodation; overnight accommodation that could be regularly used; and a 'sitter' to stay with patients who cannot be left.

Hereditary Aspects

Whether other family members will develop the illness must be something that worries many relatives and patients. Self-help groups tend towards supporting a genetic or biochemical theory, for example the National Schizophrenia Fellowship and the Schizophrenia Association of Great Britain. In a study with a small number of people Schulz, Schulz, Dibble, Targum, van Kammen and Gershon (1982) report that over 80 per cent of parents say that they would not have children if they knew there was any risk of developing schizophrenia.

They were asked if they would have children with the probes 'knowing what you now know about schizophrenia' and 'if you had to do it over again'. Mothers were generally prepared to take a greater risk than fathers, three-quarters of whom would take no risk at all. Over two-thirds of patients, however, and nearly 90 per cent of siblings said they planned to have children. Schulz *et al.* point out that both parents and relatives knew of the biological bias of the research unit before the study and that they would have been unlikely to have sought treatment there if they did not accept this bias.

Attitudes toward genetic counselling again differed, with siblings and patients being more alike. However, the picture is not clear since multiple responses were allowed. For example, although one-third of patients and one-half of siblings think that genetic counselling might be 'potentially harmful', 58 per cent of patients and 63 per cent of siblings also say that it would be 'helpful'. Parents seem to be more consistent, with three-quarters seeing it as being 'helpful' and only 4 per cent believing it to be 'potentially harmful'. Over 50 per cent of the parents think genetic counselling is 'necessary' whereas only a quarter of patients and just over one-third of siblings do.

Despite these equivocal findings Schulz *et al.* conclude that 'the wish for genetic counselling exists' and this would seem to be reasonable. Whether our present knowledge enables us to give as detailed or accurate breakdown of risk as relatives might want is a separate issue. Little is being done in the way of counselling families with a schizophrenic member. Indeed, in one recent book on genetic counselling (Emery and Pullen, 1984) schizophrenia is mentioned only once, and briefly.

Worry about whether or not to have children is not the only issue. Family members may also worry about themselves or other people in the family. This in itself can lead to a person being treated in such a way that difficulties or behavioural problems might occur.

Mrs A

Mrs A is a trained nurse and midwife and has two young children, a boy of four and a girl of 18 months. Mrs A's sister has been in hospital with schizophrenia for the past nine years. Mrs A reports that she thought her son was slow in reaching some of his developmental milestones and she began to worry whether he might develop schizophrenia like her sister. She says that, although she knows that it is the wrong thing to do, she watches every move he makes, evaluating whether it is 'normal' or not, and that she is becoming increasingly protective and 'nags him a lot'. Her son is becoming increasingly difficult to manage and she often tries to curb what, in more rational moments, she knows to be 'only childish curiosity, adventure or naughtiness'. She sees the problem as escalating as the child gets older, but has had no help in dealing with this. She has no problems with her daughter.

The Future

There are many chronic schizophrenic patients living in the community entirely dependant for their care on elderly relatives (Stevens, 1972). Although in many cases there are advantages to both patient and relative in this situation, there are also a number of disadvantages, not least of which is the worry to both of the future of the patient, either on the death of the relative or when the elderly relative is himself in need of care. Stevens also suggests that this dependence should be emphasised 'since it appeared to be an obstacle to successful rehabilitation', the patients recognising and accepting their social withdrawal more than did the relatives.

Even parents now in their forties or fifties may worry about the future of their ill child; siblings who feel that they might be expected to take on the care of their ill brother or sister may worry and become involved in the family disputes about the future, or withdraw from the family. Some of the issues and problems in family disharmony have been discussed in the preceding chapter. Counselling with the family may be useful to help them discuss these issues. Practical advice should be available for the parents about making financial provision for their schizophrenic relative after their own death.

Implications for Treatment

Chapter 4 considered the various types of therapies which include a family member or even the whole family in the therapeutic process, as well as groups, both educational and supportive, for the families themselves. From the published reports of such groups, however, it would seem that the major emphasis is on the patient, his problems and how the family can best deal with this. That this is the case should not be surprising, and to some extent it is only natural and right that this is where the emphasis lies. The aim, even if unspoken, is to improve the patient's circumstances and condition, and this may be facilitated by helping the relatives. If the aim is to help the relatives then some of the emphasis of the groups might need to change, to concentrate more directly on some of their problems. It is quite possible that such improvements in the relative's feelings and ability to cope might indirectly benefit the patient. Part Three of this book, Helping the Family, looks at some of these areas more closely. Management problems, decisions about goal-setting and the impact of the illness on the life of the family will be discussed.

Simply having some understanding of how schizophrenia affects the lives of those who live with it should be of importance in planning treatment and rehabilitation programmes and in terms of setting goals. One of the reasons why a service for relatives may not have developed is because of lack of trained staff and available staff time being spent directly with patients. Atwood (1983) suggests that 'supportive counselling for relatives' may be 'preferable' to other types of intervention 'for staff members to use who are unfamiliar with family treatment, but who wish to expand the range of family-oriented services'. She describes a short-term, closed group whose aims are to: validate the relatives' perceptions of the problems; enable relatives to share problems with others; build morale by focussing on the manageability of the problem; give information and peer support. By concentrating on the relative's problems, Atwood suggests that supportive counselling in such a group 'legitimises the role of relatives as care givers, identifies the purpose of intervention as supporting them in performing this function, and restricts the focus of the meetings to a specific problem area common to all the members'. How best to work with the family will be discussed in Part Three.

7 THE PATIENT'S PROBLEMS

The patient's problems in living with schizophrenia can become submerged when considering his management by family and professionals, the problems only being seen in terms of illness symptoms or as a direct consequence of these. Other problems or aspects of the situation, dealing with the more indirect aspects of being schizophrenic are largely ignored, if not always in clinical practice then very much so in research. The patient has to live in a society which, at best, misunderstands the problems of mental illness, and, at worst, fears, shuns or incarcerates the mentally ill.

Thus the patient's problems can be seen as falling into three broad areas. The first of these involves all areas of dealing with symptoms, residual symptoms, drug side-effects and the secondary symptoms and difficulties resulting from schizophrenia. In practical terms such problems can be divided into five major cateogories:

1. Coping with residual symptoms such as delusions, hallucinations, disturbed thought, and their effects such as poor concentration or uncertainty about reality.
2. The effects on the patient's personal skills and habits, in terms of caring for self on a daily basis, for example, personal hygiene, shopping, cooking or budgeting, and knowing how to spend time.
3. Social skills and the patient's ability to communicate verbally and nonverbally, to hold conversations, and to join in social and communal activities.
4. The effects of the illness on the patient's employment or educational prospects. This may involve training or retraining and may be seen to include housework, child-rearing and employment skills.
5. The more indirect psychological aspects of the illness. How does knowing that they are schizophrenic affect patients? Does it change their perception of themselves and affect self-esteem or evaluation? Each of these might interact with problems in other areas.

The second major area results from the particular living circumstances the patients find themselves in as a result of their illness; for example, living with parents long after they would normally have left home, or living in group homes or hostels. The new role the patient plays in the family as its 'ill member' may cause problems, as can living with people who do not know and do not understand what is happening.

The third major area concerns difficulties arising from living in the community as a mental, or ex-mental patient. Feelings of stigma and isolation may have to be dealt with, resulting from society's inability to deal with that which it cannot immediately understand.

This chapter concentrates on problems that arise from living in the family and in the community, although there is little research on this.

Roles in the Family

Adult Children

One of the major problems centres around the issue of adults versus children, or rather young children versus adult children. Although the work of family therapists is expanding, much of the published behavioural family work, particularly using operant methods, involves parents and young children. Issues which are clear in this relationship are blurred when the relationship is that of parent and adult child. When this relationship is that of husband and wife (or, less commonly, other relationships) similar problems will be raised, although the conventions of marital therapy may apply more. The parent–adult child relationship probably has more inherent difficulties for therapy than the husband–wife relationships, as will be discussed.

The adult son or daughter has typically never left home, and in the parent's eyes remains a child for whom they are responsible. It is easy for the parent to maintain their adult son or daughter as a child as they are so often more responsible for a schizophrenic than they would be for a 'normal', unmarried child living at home. There has often been no movement away from the child role, particularly when the first schizophrenic episode occurred early on. The child has never had to, or never been able to, take responsibility for himself and his own day-to-day living arrangements. In some instances, the child may have left home for a period and then returned, either due to difficulties preceding a breakdown or in its early stages or, more typically, upon discharge from hospital. Sometimes this return home will follow the break-up of a marriage, often of short duration, when the spouse is no longer able or willing to cope.

In such circumstances, the parents frequently take on much of the responsibility for their child, which can include the responsibility he should take for himself. They remind him to attend the hospital, collect his social security payments, take medication, indeed, often to wash and change. The adult is still essentially in the role of a child and an effort from both parties is needed to change this situation. However, the motivation to change may be lacking on both sides. Patients do not always want to accept responsibility for themselves but, since independence is a goal in most rehabilitation programmes, it will usually be encouraged. On a practical basis, patients will not always have their parents to care for them and therefore need to be able to take responsibility for themselves. From the parents' viewpoint, some are loath to lose their 'child' and wish to keep him dependent. They may genuinely believe, or know, that he is incapable of being responsible for himself at present. They see their behaviour as being helpful, loving and caring and do not understand when professionals label it overprotective or a barrier to rehabilitation.

If an aim of rehabilitation is to enable the patient to take up a coping adult role, then parents and adult child must be encouraged to see each other as peers, and to interact as adults rather than as parent to child. Involving parent and patient on equal terms in a therapy programme can teach them new ways of relating to one another. The therapist can provide a role model for the parents, showing them how to treat the patient as an adult.

Indeed, the therapist's attitude and behaviour may be part of the patient's problem, if it encourages the patient to be seen as, and to think of himself as being in, a 'child' role. This can be done in subtle and unconscious ways, without due notice being given to its impact. Possibly the most common and simplest example is referring to an adult woman as 'girl', with the implication that this is someone not yet ready to fulfil an adult role. That male patients are only occasionally referred to as 'boy' (or its equivalent) and that women who are non-patients are called 'girl' reflects society's attitude to women in general, and is not an issue for discussion here.

Some types of therapeutic intervention might encourage the child role more than others. For example, the issuing of instructions and use of rewards seems to be counterproductive to the aim of adult responsibility, and to perpetuate the controlling role of the patient and, indeed, to add another controlling figure, that is, the therapist. This may happen in some behavioural programmes and the practical implications will be discussed in the next chapter.

Marital Relationships

Although the ill person in a marriage is not placed immediately in the child role as when living with parents, this role can come about. When a husband takes over responsibility for an ill wife, it is often the result of norms and expectations about the husband's role, i.e. that this is his 'job' and is 'right and natural'. Thus sick and female roles might be combined. For example, if the wife is not capable of budgeting, then this is seen as part of a more generalised norm of women not coping with family finances, and is not a legitimate cause for concern. In these cases, the wife might otherwise be treated as an adult, and be seen as fulfilling an adult role, but it is a second class role. Another pattern, more common where the husband is the patient, is that he becomes dependent and the wife feels she has another child to look after. This is usually more a problem for the wife than the patient, and she may come to resent her husband's dependence and having to provide support rather than having someone with whom she can share family responsibilities, everyday events, dreams and problems.

Dependency

Patient on Relatives.   The patient may, then, become dependent on relatives, be they parents or spouse. This relationship is most commonly described in terms of the burden it places on the relative; the patient is seen as wanting to maintain dependency. Although this might be true in many cases, it is not true of all. The patient may find himself held in a dependent position by relatives out of a sense of protection. In such cases he might be dissuaded from trying anything new or different or, in extreme cases, anything at all, on the grounds that it 'might make you ill', 'you were ill last time you did ...', and 'you're not well enough to ...' The patient may be encouraged to 'concentrate on getting better', which seems to imply 'do nothing until you are better'. In such cases it is the relative's behaviour that is causing problems for the patient and it is the relative's overprotection which needs to be dealt with in therapy.

The patient's dependence on relatives may not be only psychological but may include many practical aspects, such as having meals and other services provided automatically, having financial support, and being given accommodation since the patient may have nowhere else to go. The patient may also worry about his future if his parents are old; it may be a pressing problem and a continuing source of anxiety.

Relative's Dependence on Patient.   Many patients are dependent on elderly relatives (Stevens, 1972). In some instances, however, the patient may play an important role in caring for his elderly parent. For example, shopping and doing chores which the relative can no longer perform, helping an arthritic parent to dress and get about, or simply providing company. Although the patient may not always be capable of full independence and may rely on the relative for help in some areas such as managing money, in other ways the patient may be trapped by a responsibilty to his elderly parents. This might have come about because the patient, through his illness, never married and left home. Such a problem is not restricted to patients: those involved will find themselves with all the problems that come with caring for an elderly relative, and such a burden may be undertaken more, or less, willingly.

Exploitation by Family

In a few exceptional cases the patient may be in a situation where he is neglected or even exploited by the family. There are some patients, living with relatives, whose lives are as restricted as the worst of the 'back wards', who get little help, comfort or company from their family. In very rare cases the patient might be exploited or even abused by a relative, who may, for example, take charge of a patient's finances and use the money for his own ends. Roy-Byrne, Gross and Marder (1982) cite three examples of this and discuss how it might come about. It is easy to dismiss patient complaints as 'imagination', paranoia or delusional beliefs; care should be taken to investigate such complaints with sympathy and concern for all involved. Some patients may be unwilling to complain for fear of losing the only support they have and professionals should be alert to the possibility, although rare, of neglect or exploitation.

The Effect of the Label 'Schizophrenia'

The social creation of mental illness through a process of labelling, social reaction and deviancy from social norms has been explained by a number of theorists since the 1960s (Szasz, 1962, 1970, 1979; Becker, 1963; Scheff, 1966; Laing, 1967). An important aspect of labelling theory, as proposed initially by Becker, is that not only are the causes of deviance within social forces, but that social groups themselves 'create deviance by making the rules whose infraction constitutes deviance, and by applying those rules to particular people and labelling them as outsiders'.

This is not the place to evaluate theories of how and why the labelling system exists and works, nor to examine how far schizophrenia is, or is not, an 'illness' in the sense of the medical model. However, observations can be made about how the label may affect the patient at a practical level on a day-to-day basis. One important aspect of labelling theory highlighted by Scheff (1966) is that the person labelled accepts this label of himself and integrates it into his self-image. While this is true of some patients, it is not so of all. Whether a patient can ignore or hide his 'label' will depend to a large extent on whether he still exhibits behaviours labelled 'ill' or 'deviant'. In certain instances there may be sanctions or penalties regarding the disguising of the label, e.g. in some job applications. Regardless of whether the patient himself accepts this label, it will be accepted and acted upon by society as a whole. The patient may have to balance any possible benefits of admitting the label with the disadvantages. For example, in a job application, the benefits of admitting to schizophrenia may be honesty and freedom from anxiety about being 'found out'; the disadvantages may be that the schizophrenic is immediately excluded from the job.

Some attempt has been made to look at the effect of the label of mental illness on the behaviour of others. Kirk (1974, 1975) uses the standard method of presenting a case vignette with college students as subjects. A social rejection index was used to measure subject's reactions. Labels and labellers did not affect rejection, which was only influenced by the behaviour of the person described. There are limitations in this type of study: Kirk suggests that in the natural environment 'the behaviour would have appeared more ambiguous' and thus the labels and labellers might have produced a significant effect. Labelling in this study was represented by 'a single interpretive written statement', whereas labelling theory is concerned with series of interactions.

In Kirk's study, then, even if people believed a psychiatrist has labelled the person mentally ill, there was no negative reaction unless the behaviour described indicated this. Other studies have looked at public attitudes in general to the mentally ill, and although some suggest that mental illness is not always recognised, attitudes are generally negative (Cumming and Cumming, 1957; Nunnally, 1961; Lenikan and Crocetti, 1962). The 'unpredictability' of the mentally ill person's behaviour and its supposed 'dangerousness' were two important categories in contributing to the negative attitude.

Another question to be asked is whether those individuals labelled as mentally ill accept this label for themselves. One of the difficulties with this is that, ideally, a person should be assessed before, during and after the labelling process: clearly, this is not possible unless very large numbers are used, since at outset it would not be known who might be labelled mentally ill in the future. Patients already labelled and in hospital will usually believe their stay in hospital has helped them and, since both clinical symptoms and social functioning should improve, this will be seen to be true. Since labelling theory predicts that deteriorations in terms of psychological symptoms, social functioning and ability to adjust to other roles is a factor of time spent in hospital, one would assume that patients already in mental hospitals would believe that hospitals are therapeutic as part of their patient role. Thus to try to evaluate the effect of hospitalisation labelling and self-image in such a group is probably not sensible.

It is possible, however, to consider in certain cases whether an individual adopts a label. To do so it is assumed that the individual must be in a suitably receptive frame of mind and that the label offered must conform with or confirm the individual's prior self-conception, and that the individual accepts the general category from which the label is drawn. Rotenberg (1974, 1975) has explored these issues and suggests that if a person has a negative or confused perception of self then he might be more amenable to accepting the label of mental illness. Since it is likely that people who seek help from psychiatric services may have this self-image, they will be a particularly receptive group to this label. Rotenberg also suggests that the person must believe in the category used, that is, that it is culturally acceptable and culturally defined. Thus in cultures where schizophrenia is believed to be a permanent category with only temporary symptomatic recovery, individuals who accept this label will be likely to become chronically mentally ill. However, in cultures where the schizophrenia is seen as a transitory state, it is likely that those so labelled will experience only a transitory disorder. This might account, in part at least, for findings such as those by Murphy and Raman (1971) who showed that the course and outcome of schizophrenia is better in Mauritius than in Britain. J.M. Murphy (1976) in a study of Yorubas and Eskimos suggests that 'symptoms of mental illness are manifestations of a type of illness shared by virtually all mankind', rather than being 'simply violations of the social norms of particular groups'. Thus labelling might be more important for prognosis and outcome rather than diagnosis.

There is, then, some evidence both to suggest that the label given to the person may affect his or her behaviour and perception of self, and of a model to describe how this may come about. Although research suggests that aberrant behaviour is at least as important as a label in determining the behaviour of others to the mentally ill, the possible practical consequences of the label cannot be ignored. A further consequence of the label is that patients may expect others to react to them in terms of that label and thus attribute not getting a job to the fact that he was known to suffer from schizophrenia, when poor job skills and high unemployment may be equally, if not more, important.

One woman patient reported being made anxious when greeted with remarks like 'How are you?' or even 'How do you do?' as she assumed that the speaker knew of her psychiatric history and was making either a pointed remark or an enquiry as to her mental health. Although on an intellectual level she could accept that they were merely standard phrases used in a greeting, emotionally she could not.

Perception of the Illness

It is only to be expected that relatives and patients view the illness differently. For patients, schizophrenia is an intensely personal experience, whereas relatives can only observe its effect on someone close. As well as having to deal with bizarre happenings which form the symptoms, the patient is also likely to experience grief, despair, sorrow, anger, fear, anxiety and a sense of loss for self. The knowledge that what one believes in or experiences is not believed in or experienced by others must be traumatic and difficult to accept.

To accept that this has happened in the past and that one was mistaken is one's perception of reality; to accept that it might happen again must be a disorienting experience. As one patient put it: 'It's the uncertainty of reality that's the real problem. When is reality real, and when it isn't, how do I know? And since it's the only reality I've got, what do I do?' This man was talking about hallucinations which he experienced regularly and frequently, but it could apply to any of the primary symptoms.

Relatives, however, are more likely to describe schizophrenia in terms of how it appears to them, usually in terms of the patient being antisocial and withdrawn, lacking confidence and friends, and possibly being lazy or deliberately awkward. This difference in perspective may in itself cause problems of communication, as the relatives cannot understand why the patient has any difficulties.

The type of work discussed in Chapter 4, teaching relatives about schizophrenia, would be useful in helping with this problem.

Myth of the 'Before' Person

The phrase 'the inexplicable alterations between a known and loved person and an apparent stranger' from a relative of a schizophrenic patient (see Chapter 5) highlights a further problem, one that is very common to the families of schizophrenics. Relatives make references to the patient as he was 'before', that is, before he became ill, even if the 'before' was 30 or more years ago. Atkinson (1981) found that this was a common problem when asking relatives to assess the patient's personality. A frequent response was 'as he is now, or as he used to be', and expressed disappointment at having to describe the person now. It seems that many families have an extra member, the 'ghost of patient past'. Coupled with the idealised 'ghost of patient future', the patient of the present could be seen as occupying an insignificant family role.

This approach seems to colour the relative's attitude to, and expectations of, therapy. There is often an all-or-none type of response. The family wants the patient to be as he used to be, rather than wanting changes in his present behaviour. This can lead to failure to notice or accept any improvements the patient makes, even over a few years. This may be an exaggerated form of a normal process. It is often difficult to perceive changes in people one is living with until something happens to cause a reassessment of the individual, his personality, or some aspect of it. It has already been suggested that many parents never fully recognise, or accept, their child's adult status and thus never reassess their child's behaviour and their own expectations in the light of this.

Although in the Atkinson study several families did accept or point out that 'he's much better than he used to be', this tended to mean that the patient was more easily managed than he had been. Bizarre and distressing psychotic symptoms, violence, aggression and hostility, and noisy and embarrassing behaviour were likely to be noticed when they ceased; the patient's docility, even apathy and withdrawal, is then seen positively. Whereas most relatives wanted, and indeed often expected, the outcome of therapy or rehabilitation to be that the patient returned to his 'old self', most patients saw this as impossible or almost so. Patients might refer to the changes that had occurred to, and in, them, and to their 'old self', but tended not to experience this as the dichotomy that the relatives saw.

This differing perception must cause problems, not only in the interaction between the patient and his family, but also within the patient. Even the most sane must surely doubt their own sense when told 'you're not the person you were'. This must be doubly difficult for someone who is aware that reality for him is not always the same as it is for others. Patients often report fighting to retain their own identity or control of themselves when faced with outside, inexplicable forces. Yet at the same time, relatives may be suggesting to the patient that he is *not* the same as he was, that he is a different person. Furthermore, they may imply that this new person is someone they don't really like, or don't approve of, and would prefer the 'old one' back. Faced with such messages from people close to them, it is hardly surprising that some patients say they don't know who they are. That so few patients talk of a former existence seems remarkable since this is the picture of their lives constantly laid before them.

As with overprotectiveness, the solution to the patient's problems lies not with changing their own behaviour, but that of their relatives. The family needs to be encouraged to accept this 'new' family member, rather than always looking back, and to accept that their 'old' relative has almost certainly gone for good, much in the same way that a child has gone, to be replaced by an adult. A role must be found in the family for the patient as he is; affection, if it is given, must be given for him as he is now, and not with the qualifications of a former personality to be attained, or merely because of that former personality.

Work and Leisure

Employment and Unemployment

Possibly one of the greatest problems that the chronic, unemployed schizophrenic patient has to face up to is what to do with his time. Many patients who show no interest in looking for a job are only facing up to a grim reality: that they are not able to work, and that they could not maintain the routine, discipline or concentration needed to hold down a job. Others are facing up to the fact that although they might be capable of working, they are unlikely to find jobs easily because of high unemployment levels and their own unstable employment history.

On a slightly more positive note, the high numbers of unemployed have made it easier for the schizophrenic patient to 'hide' the reason for his unemployment should he so wish. Unemployment has become an accepted (however unwanted) fact of life and some patients find it easier to accept their unemployed state when accompanied by three million-plus others.

Employment is often an area of conflict between relatives and patients, since many relatives find it difficult to accept that the patient cannot work. The situation is often defined as one of 'would not' rather than 'could not', although why this is so is not always clear.

Financial considerations may be playing a large part, as may the psychological effects of acknowledging that a person will never work again. The implications for the family may be something on which they turn their back. In this instance the patient may be able to cope with the hopelessness of the situation more readily than his relatives, because the reality of the situation never leaves him. For most people, their work defines, at least in part, their role. It may be that the patient has resigned himself to another role in which work plays no part, while his relatives still use work to define themselves and others.

Many chronic patients will find employment difficult to both achieve and maintain. In the Atkinson study (1981) only 28 per cent of 166 patients under 60 years old were currently in employment. Floyd (1984), in a survey of 130 schizophrenic patients, found that in a 12-month follow-up period, over half were never employed. Of those who were employed, between 60 and 70 per cent were unemployed for part of the time, compared to less than 5 per cent for the general population in the area in which the patients were living.

Unemployment is not the only work-related problem to confront the patient. Even when employment is available, it may not be the end of the patient's problems. Maintaining a routine and concentration are frequent difficulties. Among other things, such difficulties can result in the patient having to lower his job expectations and take a job he feels is below his qualifications. This can, in turn, aggravate feelings of depression, low self-esteem and inadequacy. It can also exacerbate problems in communication with workmates if the patient feels he is doing a job 'below him'. What to tell people at work is also a problem: how does one explain residual odd behaviour, the grimacing or shaking of drug side-effects, and regular trips to the hospital? Such issues and how to handle them are discussed by Atkinson (1985). Floyd found that patients tended to leave jobs voluntarily rather than be dismissed, mainly because the patient found the situation too 'stressful'.

Trade unionists, among others, emphasise that one of man's basic rights is the 'right to work'. That society is organised around work is affirmed daily, not only in the rush hour but in the lack of other activities to fill this time, and the lack of opportunities for those who do not work to meet others. While some find hobbies or voluntary work to occupy their time, most people without jobs complain of boredom and isolation.

Housework.   Housework is a special category of its own. Problems in completing domestic chores may be similar to maintaining a routine job, or it may be even more difficult for some since there is no outside structure. Others find that the freedom to work at their own pace and to their own standards is a positive factor in completing the work.

Although the 'housewife' role is traditionally only ascribed to women, men who stay at home may find that it is a role they can fulfil. But where it is not the cultural norm for men to appear in this role, then assuming it can lead to further alienation for the male patient. Whether the patient should be encouraged to step outside the conventional roles of his or her peers will be discussed in Chapter 10, and the therapist should also examine their own assumptions: not all women are housewives or want to accept this as their 'natural' or only role, single women may be encouraged to seek paid employment as part of rehabilitation, but not married women. Anyone, married or single, male or female, who wants to work should be encouraged to do so, and they will face similar problems in both seeking work and remaining in work. A married woman who successfully maintains her home, cares for her family and who is seen as a success in rehabilitation terms, may still have unresolved problems if she really wants to work. Even where the 'housekeeper' role is accepted, whether by men or women, boredom and isolation may still present as problems.

Leisure

If work provides problems for the patient, leisure can present even more, possibly the most serious being what to do to fill the time. Leisure, just as much as work, shows the cultural and class differences in a society. Shorter working hours, the aim of many workers, brings with it increased leisure time, but some groups, notably the unemployed and the chronic sick or disabled, have this increased free time forced on them. The issue of choice may be important here. What is valued when chosen or worked for, may be a burden when imposed. That such groups are 'ill prepared to use it constructively or even to adapt to it without psychological ill effects for themselves as individuals and for society, as a whole' (Gussen 1967), is accepted by many, but little is done to alleviate this. Being in work does not guarantee that leisure time will not hang heavily. Ferenczi (1950) likens 'Sunday neurosis', or more commonly now 'weekend neurosis', to agoraphobia; instead of being a fear of wide-open spaces, it is a fear of 'wide-open time'.

Whether 'free time' and 'leisure time' differ only in terms of semantics or whether there are wider issues involved is a question which there is neither time nor space to debate here. One distinction frequently made, however, distinguishes free time as being time not spent in paid employment, but includes time spent on other duties such as chores, and describes leisure time as being time devoted to recreational pursuits. If this division is created by an individual for himself it can be helpful in structuring time and giving some purpose to the day, but it can be senseless if arbitrarily imposed from outside. Gardening may be a chore for one person, a pleasant hobby for another, and for a third person the prime reason for living.

All too often the concept of leisure and recreation take on middle-class values which centre around doing something 'useful' or 'creative'. The growth of interest in Eastern culture and religion during the 1960s and 1970s has lent emphasis to the concept and practice of 'being' and the need to not have to always 'fill time' but to allow relaxation and meditation in equal part, to concentrate on what one is, but this is still a minority viewpoint in the face of the 'work ethic' which seems to be gaining lost ground as the 1980s progress. Pressure to fill time 'meaningfully' is probably one of the greatest hinderances to filling time at all. Doing anything, whether 'creative' or not, is a great step forward for many patients, even if this only involves making a decision to turn the television on and then actually to watch and follow a programme. As Lamb (1971) points out, 'the price of being an intellectual snob is to be rendered ineffective in helping most people utilise their leisure time'.

Money.   A further complicating factor in the use of time, but one which should not be underestimated, is money. Many patients are living on social security payments of some kind, often with elderly parents on a retirement pension. If there is little money left over from necessities, then doing something that costs money may be out of the question. Even if relatives can afford to pay for things for the patient, the patient may not be happy about accepting them. The cost of activities should always be borne in mind when planning rehabilitation tasks and activities; this includes hidden costs such as travelling. Lack of money may influence interaction at a very basic level: one man described sitting in a pub with a half-pint but being asked to move on by the manager because he was so slow in drinking it. The manager seemed to think there was something sinister in his sitting for an hour and drinking so litle. He could not afford to buy any more. Another man reports making a pint last an evening, and enjoying watching the people in the pub and overhearing parts of conversation. When asked why he never joined in, or tried to talk to anybody, said that he would inevitably be in a situation where someone would buy him a drink and he could not afford to reciprocate. It was easier not to get into the situation in the first place than to try to explain to a stranger that he did not want a drink because he could not afford to return it.

Levels of Stimulation

That the schizophrenic individual is vulnerable to high environmental levels of stimulation has been considered in the preceding chapters. Whether this is a core psychological deficit of either peripheral or cognitive difficulties that makes patients vulnerable to stimulating environments, or whether it is some other process at work is, in the short term, less important than helping the patient cope with the problem.

Psychophysiological reactions have been monitored in response to 'stressful' situations in both home environments (Tarrier, Vaughn, Leff and Lader 1979) and laboratory environments (Sturgeon, Kuipers, Berkowitz, Turpin and Leff, 1981). Measurements included sweat gland activity and heart rate changes. These studies are important in terms of the effect on the patient of being with a high EE relative and have been discussed in Chapter 4. Again, the solution may have as much to do with changing the relative's behaviour as the patient's. How are these changes to be applied and implemented?

PART THREE

HELPING THE FAMILY

8 WORKING WITH THE FAMILY

Community care, in its guise of the 'revolving door' cycle of admission, discharge, relapse and readmission, has done little to confront the challenge of the continuing care of the chronically mentally ill. Parts One and Two of this book consider the various community and family factors which contribute to relapse and readmission. Involving the family in treatment and rehabilitation is one of the more recent ways of meeting this challenge. This chapter considers a number of issues which have to be confronted before deciding how the family is to be involved. Each method of involvement has its advantages and disadvantages and these need to be balanced against the purpose of the therapy and expectations of outcome, number of patients, number and expertise of staff, staff enthusiasm and all the other practical considerations which can so easily bedevil the introduction of change or innovation in a therapy programme or institution.

Working with the family involves different skills from working with individuals. What these are depends on how the family is employed. Skills for family therapy, as such, are detailed in various handbooks and textbooks on family therapy, but involving relatives as co-therapists or informing or educating them involves yet other perspectives.

To use 'family therapy' can become a goal in its own right and Gale (1979) strikes a warning note against this: 'The family therapy movement has become something of a social movement with a quasi-evangelical flavour. The frequent existence of social movements for the creation of change and reform is, of course, an historical and socio-psychological fact.' Such movements involve science, medicine and therapy as well as politics, social reform and religion. 'They have a common life cycle which begins with enthusiasm and ends with doubt and denial. The present fervour and financial and commercial commitment, to the transcendental meditation and biofeedback movements, in the absence of any scientific evidence of note in favour of their efficacy, stands as a warning to us all.'

Although especially useful in marital problems and non-psychotic disorders of children, the limitations of full family therapy as such in the treatment of schizophrenia are recognised. In 1972 Massie and Beels concluded that family therapy in its usual forms was unwarranted for schizophrenics and their families. McFarlane (1983) traces the decline of conventional family therapy with schizophrenics to a low in the middle-1970s and the resurgence of the newer forms of family therapy since then. Chapter 4 examines the ways in which the family can participate in therapy.

Who to Involve?

The number of relatives involved in rehabilitation and their kinship to the patient varies between and within studies. Whether this matters depends on both theoretical issues, in terms of the goals of therapy, and practical concerns. Who constitutes 'family' and how they are used varies enormously. One person may be all the immediate family a patient has, and can be contrasted with involving more than one relative or one family member from a larger household. Involving spouses will be different from involving parents or yet other relatives. Some of the studies, for example, Lurie and Ron (1971), Anderson (1983), and Mueller and Orfanidis (1976), state that the programme was for parental families only. Others are less specific. In some special circumstances a family member or friend who does not live with the patient may be usefully involved, either because they spend a lot of time with the patient or have particular influence over him. Parents of the patient, even if not living with him, may still be a powerful factor. Headley (1977) involves parents in both individual and marital therapy with their adult child, believing that 'positive changes can be achieved for independent adults through the involvement of older parents (super ego figures). A new family balance and different family rules evolve through restructuring the relationship of persons who are now peers.' Recognising that psychotherapy can change a person's relationship with their parents, Headley assumes that parents may often feel baffled, hurt or anxious when their relationship to their adult child changes. This would be particularly true either if 'their adult child severed the relationship, or if their bonds to him began to seem uncomfortably thin and strained'.

The advantages of involving more than one relative must be weighed against the disadvantages. Some problems may need everybody's co-operation; for example, everyone living in the house will probably need to be involved to deal with tension or 'atmosphere' within the family which is stressful to the patient. Differential tolerance of disruptive behaviours and different methods of coping with them may need family discussion, especially where one individual is particularly resistant to change. Likewise, various family members will provide different cues or reinforcement of behaviour, and this must be dealt with with each relative. This is not to say that one person cannot act as a 'go-between' between family and therapist, but that some things may be difficult to deal with at one remove. Even then the family need not be seen as a group, but individually if necessary. In the psycho-educational programme devised by Anderson the whole family is seen initially and then a 'family ombudsman' is appointed to liaise between the hospital and family.

On the debit side are the practical problems of trying to get a number of people together at one time, and to then agree on goals and the process of a therapy. This can be a particular problem in the family of the schizophrenic where the patient is an adult and clearly identified as a 'patient' with an illness; relatives may not see themselves or their behaviour as relevant to what they define as the problem. Several people might be in work where there are adult siblings also living in the home, and it is probably unrealistic to expect them to take time off for therapy sessions in which they see themselves as having only marginal involvement. This would be especially true of people who are in jobs where they would lose money through taking time off to attend sessions.

In practical terms, the most useful person to involve will be the relative who spends most time with the patient, who *can* attend sessions, and who *agrees* to attend sessions. It may be possible to add more people later once this base is established, if and when desirable.

Type of Family Involvement

There are four basic models, whether one or several relatives participate in the programmes. The relatives can meet with the therapist alone, either with or without the patient, or several families can meet with the therapist, in a group, again with or without the presence of the patients. Refinements and variations can be added to this, such as the use of more than one therapist. For example, Mueller and Orfanidis (1976) report the use of co-therapists with the family and patient.

Multiple family groups are popular, and are reported by Mass and Odaniell (1958), Lurie and Ron (1971), Atwood and Williams (1978), Leff, Berkowitz and their colleagues, Scharfstein and Libbey (1982), and McLean *et al.* (1982). Multiple groups have a number of advantages, not least of which is their efficient use of therapist time. Family groups enable relatives to share their problems with others. Most feel this to be useful as it helps relieve feelings of isolation and uniqueness with regard to the illness. Problems are shared, as are various approaches to their solution. Not only relatives learn from this sharing of coping strategies: professionals can also learn new, adaptive ways of management, as well as spot unhelpful or maladaptive coping patterns. Some of the research reports more 'plain speaking' from relatives in multi-family groups: they are more blunt and yet more accepting among themselves than with therapists.

These family groups can provide social support which is more far-reaching than simply within the group. Relatives may meet outside the group or after termination of formal group sessions. This may be important for families who have become socially isolated. Scharfstein and Libbey (1982) report the use of a 'social stage' at the beginning of their group: 'groups began with conversation' and 'coffee and cookies were served'. It has already been noted from the McLean *et al.* study (1982) that this group went on to form a pressure group, the Alliance for the Mentally Ill.

Some researchers prefer to work with one family at a time, for example, Mueller and Orfanidis (1976), Atkinson (1981), and Falloon *et al.* (e.g. 1982). Falloon, Liberman, Lillie and Vaughn (1981) do, however, also report using a multi-family group. Anderson's (1983) psycho-educational programme has both individual family elements and multifamily sessions. Clearly, each therapist can deal with a smaller number of families if they are seen separately, but this might be compensated for by a more intensive concentration on their problems requiring a shorter programme. This will not apply, of course, if 'long-term' support is one of the aims of the programme. It should be noted that both the Falloon and Atkinson studies report working in the family's home. The advantages and disadvantages of this will be discussed later in this chapter.

Should the Patient be Involved?

Most of the studies involve the patient with the family, although some of the multi-family groups are for relatives only, for example, Atwood and Williams (1978). This has the advantage for some relatives in that they feel freer and more able to express their feelings about their ill relative when he is not there to be hurt by the remarks, to disagree with comments or to retaliate with negative feelings of his own.

It also removes the patient from any anxiety which may be engendered by hearing how his problems cause the family distress and difficulties of their own. In some cases it is easier to concentrate on the family's problems when the patient and his apparently overwhelming and insuperable difficulties are not present. Relatives can feel that their problems are trivial compared to those of the patient, and be hesitant about voicing them. The very sharing of problems and emotions may be a release for the relatives and they are able to mourn the 'loss' of their ill relative without that person having to witness this. Feelings of guilt may be relieved when this is shared by others and relatives can see how others blame themselves senselessly. Also, the range of families involved may assuage guilt as relatives see families involved from all types of backgrounds and with all kinds of involvement with one another.

Against this must be weighed the possible creation or exacerbation of feelings of paranoia in susceptible patients, when they are excluded. In such cases the aim of the group meetings should be clearly explained to the patient: they are for the support and education of relatives, and it is the *relative's* problems and feelings that are being discussed and managed, not the patient's. It should be made clear to patients that the meetings are not to discuss them, and that staff members will not betray any confidences they have made. However, where the aim of the programme is to change the patient's behaviour, then it seems reasonable that the person most involved must be there.

The patient's involvement in multiple family groups can be especially useful in terms of interfamily communication. Patients sometimes find it easier to explain how they feel, or how schizophrenia affects them, to someone outside their family, even though their own parents may be in the group. Likewise, parents may find they can discuss issues with other patients more calmly than they can with their own ill relative. Where relatives have difficulty in coming to terms with the actual symptoms and reality of schizophrenia, then the confirmation of the information they are being given is sometimes easier to accept and assimilate when it comes from a patient other than their own ill relative. For example, relatives who persist in seeing the patient as lazy or stubbornly negative may interpret anything their relatives says as an 'excuse', but they may be more open to comments from other patients in similar circumstances about how difficult it is for them to do things. Seeing only the consequences of symptoms, relatives sometimes have difficulty in accepting the bizarre nature of schizophrenic symptoms and may reject the idea that their son hears voices or sees things, or feels controlled. To have this corroborated by another patient, especially one who does not seem to be manifesting the symptoms at the time, can encourage relatives to reassess their concept of schizophrenia.

When Should the Family be Involved?

As in all other areas there are a number of conflicting opinions about the best time to begin a family programme, ranging from on admission, to discharge, to any time at all. Scharfstein and Libbey (1982), for example, began on the day of admission, when relatives were told about the orientation programme and when the next meeting was. This was followed up by a telephone call one or two days later. The aim of the programme in starting at this time was to help patients and family adjust to the inpatient treatment and deal with the stress brought about by admission. Anderson (1977) also begins intervention during the inpatient phase, and suggests that the 'chances of involving a resistant family are better if the first family contact occurs at the time of admission or very close to it'. Rather than at admission, Leff and his colleagues and Lurie and Ron (1971) begin their family involvement at discharge. Hospital admission is almost certainly going to come at a time of crisis and relapse, and Scott (1973a, 1973b) suggests that hospital admission can be avoided by providing the family with help and support at this time.

The advantages of beginning a family programme in connection with inpatient treatment, whether at admission or discharge, include the dramatic nature of events which surround admission and the family's inability to cope with the problem. Change is indicated and the family may be more open to acknowledging their problems and their part in the wider problem.

The only real disadvantage of linking the programme to admission or inpatient status is that a number of patients and their families who might benefit from the programme will either be missed, or have to wait for a relapse (which might be prevented, or at least hospitalisation prevented, by the programme) until they are eligible. Since most of the schizophrenic population will be in contact with the hospital for medication, they should not be difficult to trace. Both Atkinson (1981) and Hudson (1978) take patients and their families into their programmes at any time and, although some are resistant to the idea of change, most accept the programme. Those who refuse it at such time, preferring the *status quo*, can be offered therapy again if and when the patient relapses.

Home- or Hospital-based Treatment?

Home-based treatment is obviously only a possibility for families who are being seen alone, and not for multiple groups. It has been used, therefore, less often than hospital-based programmes. However, it might be useful in some circumstances. Falloon, Boyd, McGill, Strang and Moss (1981) report five advantages of conducting sessions in the home: a greater attendance of family members; involvement with families' social networks; improved generalisation of new behaviour; reduced tension for those who become anxious in hospitals; and increased self-disclosure by family members.

Generalisation

As Falloon and Liberman (1983) remark, 'the major rationale for conducting the family intervention in the home concerned the issue of generalisation'. It is well known that skills learned in one setting do not always generalise to another. Both patients and relatives have to learn new patterns of behaviour and the relaxed, familiar setting of their own home may help the acceptance and assimilation of these. Rehearsal of new behaviours can seem more 'real' in the setting in which they are to occur, and the 'real setting' can provide more solutions to the problem than may occur in a more artificial setting.

Family and Patient Co-operation

Family resistance to involvement in programmes will be discussed later in this chapter, but one way to overcome this may be by taking the programme to them, rather than making them come to it. This is also true for patients who resist therapy or who are irregular attenders at clinics. It appears that both relatives and patients have to invest less time and energy in the programme because they do not have to visit the hospital. Of course they still need to put effort into the programme to achieve change, but the effort is directly related to the immediate problems and not to peripheral activities like travelling. This might be important where the family lives some distance from the hospital, and depends upon whether they have a car or whether public transport is being used, how convenient this is, and how expensive.

Patients who avoid hospital contact may be more willing to meet the therapist at home; at least avoidance is harder. The patient may not answer the door, but this ploy will not work if there is a relative who will let the therapist in. To avoid the therapist, then, the patient must make a special trip out of the house. For many patients the effort involved in this is greater than tolerating the visit, so they stay. Those who do 'disappear' have often done something they rarely do; made a decision, carried it out in a positive way and gone out. This in itself may be seen as an advance!

The family may be willing to co-operate more if they believe the therapist to be fully committed to the programme, and to them. Such a commitment is demonstrated by a willingness to visit the family at home, on a regular basis, which is seen to take more time and effort than usual. Indeed, many of these families are unused to any regular contact with, or commitment from, one individual. This in itself is important to people used to constantly changing staff and superficial contact with many people. It does mean, however, that any promises made and not kept may assume increased significance for the family, as they are added to a series of dashed hopes. These unfulfilled promises from the past may themselves contribute to the unwillingness of either families or patients to become involved in yet another new programme.

Often, visits to the home result in a freer atmosphere where other family members can 'drop in' when they are available, or when they or the patient see the need. This can expand the nature of the programme, if this is seen as appropriate, to include more areas of the patient's life and further aid generalisation.

Therapist's Assessment

By visiting the patient and family at home the therapist has an opportunity to assess behaviour in its natural setting, and to learn more about the patient's lifestyle and the family norms. It also gives both patient and family the freedom, in a more open atmosphere, to raise problems which might not seem directly relevant in the hospital office. Such issues may range from financial problems to an inability to deal with bureaucracy, or to behavioural problems in other family members.

For example, in a home meeting one woman patient was able to raise the problems she was having in dealing with her youngest daughter. She admitted that she had been worried about the girl for some time, but had been unable to raise the matter at the hospital because 'it didn't seem relevant to anything I was asked'. Another patient's unwillingness to spend time with his father was made more understandable when the father came home unexpectedly one afternoon drunk, and his alcohol abuse and violent tendencies were revealed. Seemingly trivial incidents which have emotional significance for the patient can be revealed. Some problems need referral to other agencies and a clear understanding of the role and scope of other professionals is needed for this. For example, social workers are not necessarily the best people to whom to refer a patient for welfare rights assistance, although the assumption for many is that this is their main function.

Goals of Treatment

For any family programme to work successfully, the goals of treatment must be agreed between the therapist, the patient and the family. As several of the studies point out, this is not always straightforward. Most relatives and patients can be clear about the type of behaviour they want removed, for example, 'voices' or 'depression', 'being unco-operative' or 'sullenness'. Often relatives have more idea of what they would like to see added to the patient's behavioural repertoire than does the patient himself. Typically, relatives want the patient to 'do more around the house', 'get out more', 'talk more', 'have friends', 'get a girl/boyfriend', 'get a job'. Relatives often express such wishes negatively at first: 'I'm fed up with him sitting there, why doesn't he do something?' Goals often differ between the three involved parties, not only in terms of priority, but also in terms of acceptability of a particular goal or whether a goal is seen as relevant. A number of issues, discussed here briefly, relate to the setting and agreeing of goals.

Different Families, Different Problems

The research outlined in Chapters 5 and 6 indicates quite clearly that different families have different problems, and therefore the goals of treatment will be different between families. For some families objective burden will be high, but with little expressed subjective burden; for other families the reverse, or some other pattern, will occur. It is important in starting a programme, either in a group or with an individual family, that the therapist does not hold such preconceived notions about what does or does not constitute a programme, and that the family's individual needs are fully understood or taken into account. It is easier to plan fully around a family seen individually, but even in multi-family groups there can be consensus decisions about problems and priorities without these being imposed by the therapist or leader.

Factors that affect the family's perception or definition of a problem include not only symptoms and bizarre behaviour, but also the type of family, marital or parental relationships, the patient's role in that family, how many other family members there are, the space in the house, financial considerations, family attitudes, appreciation and knowledge of mental illness, and so forth, as described earlier.

Whose Problem?

Not only do families differ in their perception of what constitutes a problem, but so do patients and their families. A difficulty encountered almost immediately in many families centres around the concept of what behaviour is 'a problem' or 'unacceptable'. Some behaviours defined as unacceptable by the family do not come into the category 'ill': for example, getting up late and staying in bed too long, playing a radio/record player too loud, too often or too late, wearing too much make-up or bizarre clothes, or having friends of whom the parents do not approve.

Relatives will often be looking to the therapist for confirmation that these are 'problems' and that the programme will do something about them. If the therapist categorises such behaviour as being unacceptable or a problem, it is often then equated with being 'ill' in the minds of the relative, and becomes a legitimate cause for concern. It might be useful to have a category of behaviour defined as 'normal, but possibly unreasonable' over which relative and patient must compromise to find a solution, in the same way they would if the behaviour occurred without the patient being ill. Families should be encouraged to see this as a normal part of family decision-making, and not part of therapy as such. Falloon and Liberman (1983) in their reports of behavioural family interventions stress the problem-solving training that follows on from communication training.

Appropriate Goals

Therapists as well as relatives can mislabel behaviour, set unrealistic or inappropriate goals, and make unwarranted assumptions about procedure, outcome and norms. Olshansky (1972) discusses eleven of these assumptions, or 'myths' as they apply to vocational rehabilitation, but they can usefully be considered in terms of all rehabilitation. Some of these have been discussed earlier, but deserve reiteration.

Deserving special attention when setting goals, particularly long-term goals, are the myths that every patient can be, or wants to be, rehabilitated back to work, that the labour market can employ them, and that once 'rehabilitated' an individual stays 'rehabilitated' and does not need either continuing or intermittent help. The 'whole man' myth, by suggesting that individuals should always be seen as 'wholes', may prevent small changes being achieved with parts of a larger problem, when the 'whole' problem has parts which are insurmountable.

Hospital or other staff are likely to concentrate, at least initially, on behaviours related to the illness. In many instances these are either less stressful or more easily tolerated by relatives than other, seemingly more trivial, problems. Since many of the behaviours related to the schizophrenia itself will be difficult to change, family goodwill and co-operation can be gained by dealing with what they consider priorities, and which also may have a higher chance of success.

It is easy to fall into the trap of legitimising or medicalising problems unnecessarily. Many patients who complain of poor sleep and who receive sedatives for this are trying to sleep for long periods of time. What to do with their time is the problem, not the ease with which they sleep. Before goals are set or norms decided upon, care should be taken to ensure that the norms are the right ones and not just those of the therapists. What does the family agree is normal? What do other people in the area do? There is no point in trying to teach or encourage a patient to plan and carry out a week's shopping in one go, if everyone else in the street shops on a day-to-day basis. If parents complain that a patient spends half the morning in bed, then an appropriate comparison group might be other unemployed men of his age, rather than his employed father. For any therapy to be successful, the specific goals must be acceptable to the patient and his family and the environment in which they live. Care should always be given that assumptions about what is 'normal' are not made too freely or without checking the appropriate culture or family.

Goals should not focus only on the identified patient. One benefit of relatives' groups and family programmes is the support they give to the relatives in a variety of ways. Atwood and Williams (1978) speak specifically of families receiving 'permission from the group to take their own needs into account'. This includes to have a social life of their own, to make use of 'the public system for financial support' and to help themselves by 'exploiting all existing mental health resources for their relative'. Many families are uncomfortable in pushing for their own rights, whether from the family, the hospital or the state; having models in the group who do this, plus permission and support so to do, can be extremely helpful. Spaniol, Zipple and Fitzgerald (1984) suggest that permission may need to be given for families to put 'greater time and energy into themselves' and to 'create a greater balance within their own lives'.

What Can the Programme Do?

The limitations of treatment, or even a therapist, are rarely acknowledged, and may only surface in relation to an individual having unrealistic expectations of a programme, or unrealistic goals. It is important to be honest with families over the complexity of the problem and the limitations both in terms of knowledge and resources for treating it. It can help families and patients to come to terms with the situation if they have an understanding of the illness, its treatment method and research and to know, for example, that the most up-to-date medication is being used, or has been tried. They should also know that to keep seeking second opinions in the hope of turning up some new 'wonder drug' will not be successful. Relatives sometimes hear of new treatments, often from the United States, and often of dubious efficacy. These include megavitamin therapy or allergy-testing. Careful explanation needs to be given regarding these and their general lack of availability in the National Health Service.

The 'myth of adequate knowledge' (Olshansky, 1972) leads to unfulfilled expectations, dissatisfaction and even depression in therapists as well as patients and relatives. It is important to recognise that just because therapists can state a problem, it does not mean that they have a solution. Some problems cannot be solved (at least in the present) no matter how much time, money, effort, staff or resources are poured into them. The therapist, as well as the family, needs to recognise that no one individual has all the answers. There are times when it is right to refer an individual or a problem to another person or agency, and this should not be seen as a sign of defeat. As Olshansky (1972) comments: 'The myth of the romantic and heroic counsellor struggling in isolation against overwhelming odds dies slowly.'

Family Roles

Family roles is an important area, both in terms of setting goals and gaining family co-operation. Most of the research studies report, either directly or indirectly, that giving support to the family in their role as care-giver was an important part of the programme. In some instances it may be necessary or desirable to go beyond simply giving support to this role, but to 'legitimise' it in terms of everyone (patient, family, and hospital and other staff) acknowledging that a particular relative is the primary care agent and deserves the recognition due to this role. Family co-operation can be enhanced by acknowledging family roles and norms in other ways. Even if family members are not being asked to change their behaviour directly, changes in the patient's behaviour will undoubtedly affect them.

Unless such changes are foreseen and planned they may have unwanted consequences and lead to further dissatisfaction within the family or even to sabotage of the programme. For example, in a family where the mother (or wife) either has the primary role of 'housewife' or defines herself as such, to encourage the patient to take on household chores without discussing how this might be done with the mother could lead to her feeling that her role in the family was being eroded, which may further cause anxiety or depression. Even on a practical level it will mean that the mother will have to revise habits, often of many years' standing, to accommodate the patient's help. It may also mean that she has free time to which she is unused, and in some instances may need support to both accept this and make use of it.

The family's rights must be protected as well as the patient's. This includes the right to privacy and to do things without the patient. Sometimes, this can be overlooked in an effort to integrate the patient into the family. One mother finally reported after several weeks of difficulties with the programme that, although she had initially agreed to take her son shopping with her, she wanted to change her mind. She was used to doing the shopping slowly, had a set pattern and talked to both shopkeepers and various friends and neighbours she met on the way. Thus shopping fulfilled a social function as well as its more obvious one. When her son accompanied her she found that not only did he become impatient and start shuffling and suggesting they move on, but she felt inhibited in her conversations in front of him. Consequently, she started to make excuses not to take him. A solution was found when it was agreed that there would be specific shopping trips with her son to enable him to cope with the task, plus some purely 'social trips' together, but that she could also have her usual shopping trips on her own.

The difficulties of the adult-child role and interaction with parents has already been discussed and should be borne in mind throughout all aspects of a family programme.

How Long Should Programmes Last?

As in all other areas, there is wide variation between the reported studies. Atwood (1983) reports a relatives' group lasting between eight to twelve sessions; Atkinson (1981) notes weekly family sessions of one hour for six months; Anderson reports four overlapping treatment phases, but once the patient has left hospital there are sessions every two to three weeks for one to two years; Falloon and Liberman (1983) cite 40 sessions over two years; Leff and colleagues report a variable number of family sessions (in addition to four lectures and the relatives' group) ranging from a minimum of one to a maximum of 25 sessions.

One advantage in having a time-limited programme is that relatives who are cautious about committing themselves may agree to a limited period of intervention when they might not to an open-ended programme. A short timespan may also help relatives to focus on the task in hand (Weinberger, 1971). Fathers, who are often harder to get to commit to a programme, may be more willing to do so and less likely to withdraw, if they know when the group or programme will end (Donner and Gamson, 1971).

How short is 'short' in a time-limited programme is open to debate: although some relatives may feel security in knowing that a therapist is prepared to commit himself or herself to the family for two years, others might find this a daunting prospect initially. It is not clear in many of the studies whether families were told a time scale, or whether the intervention was seen as fairly 'open-ended', but happened to last about two years.

Closed or Open Groups?

Whether groups should be closed, that is, one group of people staying together and usually for a fixed period, or open, where new members can be added at any time, applies to both multi-family and relative-only groups. Closed groups have their advantages in that they foster group cohesiveness in which members come to know and trust one another and can, therefore, be more open in their revelations. It also allows for a set programme to be followed, which might be useful in terms of education and the presentation of information in an ordered, structured way. Group cohesiveness can be fostered by emphasising commitment to the group and its norms. Thus attendance would be expected at every meeting, and meetings are held at the same time and place and for the same duration. Commitment, consistency and, above all, confidentiality are stressed.

On the other hand, open groups may be more practical, in that members can attend either when they feel the need, or at any time. If a family programme is to begin at the time of the patient's hospitalisation, for example, then there may not be enough new patients to make a group feasible at any one time, but they could join an already existing group. In such a case, following through a clear, cohesive educational package may not be so straightforward.

Families will have to be seen individually, and possibly given written material, or use could be made of periodic seminars to review topics such as 'symptoms', 'treatment', 'management', 'drugs' and so on. Although support should be given to members joining an existing group for the first time to prevent isolation, many relatives find it less threatening as they feel they can take time to see what happens, watch others and generally 'learn the ropes'.

Working in the Home Setting

In the hospital setting the tendency is for everyone — patient, relative and therapist — to look to the professional for answers. The therapist is in his setting, in a role of authority and, often unintentionally, dominates the proceedings. The balance of 'power' shifts by transferring these discussions to the family's living room. This requires adjustment by all parties. The therapist suddenly finds himself in the position of 'guest' rather than 'host'. While this might cause anxiety and loss of role definition for some, it also allows a broadening of perspective through increased knowledge of the situation and thus gives greater freedom in initiating therapeutic strategies. The relative and/or patient, now in the role of host, can experience some anxiety, but more usually gains in confidence and feels freer to discuss problems and complaints, offer suggestions and confess their ignorance. Since this will be an unusual approach to therapy for the families, care should be taken that they do not see this as an invasion of their privacy and that they are given explanations for why it is happening.

The hospital provides security and restriction for both the therapist and patient. Both know what will happen at the hospital and the rules rarely change; but interviews at home are not necessarily so formal, or played to the same rules. There are not the interruptions to the therapist that are possible at the hospital, nor is there a queue of other patients waiting to be seen. The family may have interruptions, however, and although these must be dealt with, they should not become ways of avoiding issues or of changing the subject. The patient cannot get up and walk out so easily as he might do in a hospital setting; he certainly cannot escape to go home, and so might find the sessions more pressurised. So, too, might the therapist, who is faced with reality and cannot escape so readily or hide behind a 'white coat' or his desk.

Other problems in practical arrangements can arise. Seating, for example, is arranged by the family and the therapist may be shown to a particular chair. This may well be someone's 'seat', often a powerful family figure, and the family may expect the therapist to take on this role, or behave like this person. Arranging seating to suit the needs of the situation rather than the family's usual pattern (which will tend to be around the television) needs care and tact, but will be important. Barriers, such as the desk, that both family and therapist are used to are missing. If this makes people feel uncomfortable then it must be acknowledged, otherwise seating plans will tend to reflect this uncomfortableness, with, for example, the family arranged on one side of a coffee table and the therapist on the other. Likewise, behaviour such as being offered a cup of tea or coffee can be both time-consuming and distracting, but can occasionally reveal interesting insights into the family system. For example, the mother poured tea for everybody in one family, but the patient was left to pour her own.

As in any therapy it needs to be made clear from the outset that the therapist is not there to take 'sides'. Involving the relatives means that he will not collude with them to change the patient, particularly against his wishes. This is especially important when the home is primarily the relatives' rather than the patient's, as is the case for example, when an adult child has moved back to live with his or her parents, or when the relative has welcomed the visits and 'persuaded' the patient to accept them. Some patients are living with family they do not really want to be involved with, or who do not really want them, because there is nowhere else for them to go, or because they could not cope living on their own. All of this will affect therapy and the degree to which patients and relatives feel comfortable with both the programme and the setting.

Compliance With and Resistance To Programmes

The research studies cited vary in their reporting of drop-out from programmes or the resistance some families have to change. It is unlikely that there will be any programmes which do not lose some families or where they are not overtly or subtly sabotaging the programme. Why might this be so, and how might such problems be overcome? One possible answer, i.e. taking the programme to the family in their own home, has already been discussed. Hudson (1978) worked with chronic schizophrenic patients and found that 'setting up a behavioural programme in the home setting for this patient group proved even more problematic than the literature had suggested'. Of twelve families she found difficulty in reaching agreement over goals in six, four patients refused to co-operate, three families feared the patient enough not to want to change 'their present policy of "humouring" the patient', four families were concerned about the effects of the programme, either in it leading to disappointment and depression or relapse, and in three families the 'relatives themselves were not well enough to co-operate'. These obstacles were overcome in only five cases.

Not all studies have such difficulties: for example Kanter and Lin (1980) report that 'difficulty in securing initial co-operation of relatives is rare'. They use, however, the sanction of refusing treatment if the relatives do not co-operate. Maintaining co-operation of relatives is a separate issue from initial co-operation. Scarpitti, Lefton, Dimitz and Pasamanick (1964) found that a major block to maintaining a treatment programme with schizophrenics living with their families was that both the patient and his family tended to lose interest in the programme once they believed he was 'cured' or even when he had shown some improvement. It seemed that the families did not accept that the patients needed continuing care. This is a common finding and also affects patients who may want to discontinue medication. Education about the illness and its course may help with this problem.

Atkinson (1981, 1982) found that even though it was not always easy to get relatives involved in the programme, a large majority agreed willingly. It was also much easier to get both the patient's involvement and co-operation and to maintain this when the family was involved, than when the patient was invited to accept a behavioural programme alone.

There has not been a clear study of whether some families of schizophrenics are more likely to drop out of therapy than others, or even whether some benefit more than others. Some conclusions come from other areas, however. McMahon, Forehand, Griest and Wells (1981) found that parents who dropped out of a parent behavioural training programme were more likely to be of lower socioeconomic status than those who completed, and the mother was more likely to be depressed and to issue commands. It would be useful to have some more objective data on family drop-outs or resistance to programmes in families of schizophrenics.

Family Expectations of Treatment

It may be that one of the reasons for resistance to or non-co-operation with programmes is that the therapy offered is not in line with relatives' expectations and goals. This is clearly shown in Hudson's study (1975) when half the client group did not agree with goals. Other studies hint at this, although some are clearly goal-free at the beginning and define the group/programme in terms of the relatives' expressed wishes. What relatives actually want will be taken up in detail in Chapter 11, but there are some general points to be made here.

Few studies even try to look at family or patient's expectations of therapy or satisfaction with it. Atkinson (1981) tried to look at expectations of perceived change during, and satisfaction with, a behavioural programme for patients and relatives. The findings from this were confused and difficult to interpret. All that can be said is that relatives tend to have slightly higher expectations than the patients and that nearly 40 per cent of patient-relative pairs disagreed in their rating of expectations. Relatives and patients both report little perception of change, even when more objective target data shows considerable improvements in specific areas.

In terms of satisfaction with the programme, there is again disagreement between relative-patient pairs, the direction of such disagreement being evenly divided. The relationship between expectations, perceived change and satisfaction seems to be complex and confusing, and is probably idiosyncratic. Some of the patterns produced seem both logically and psychologically unlikely, and probably relate to expectations changing as the programme progresses, or to fears of expressing real dissatisfaction.

Although research in the area of expectancy and improvement has suggested that a link might exist between expectancy and outcome, the precise nature of this link is uncertain. Martin, Fried-meyer, Moore and Claveaux (1977) found 'evidence of a significant linear relationship between patients' expectancies and their clinical improvement through hospitalisation, but no convincing evidence of a curvilinear component to the relationship'. They take this as supporting the hypothesis that expectancy may predict clinical improvement, but not cause it. Wilkins (1973) in a litera-ture review, concludes that 'the construct "expectancy of therapeutic gain" emerged prematurely and without the empirical support necessary to establish its validity'. Lebow (1982), review-ing literature on consumer satisfaction with mental health treatment, reports that, despite this type of assessment now being quite common, researchers have been 'insufficiently concerned with methodology', and that little has been done to assess the reliability or validity of such studies. From the studies it seems that the nature and interaction of expectancy, satisfaction and outcome is complex and far from understood, but merits further attention.

The other studies do not consider expectations and satisfaction formally, but the concepts do creep into the work. Anderson (1983) makes specific reference to decreasing 'family frustration, concern and criticism': one of the three issues emphasised is the decreasing and modifying of family expectations, at least temporarily, to make the family 'less likely to be surprised' or 'let down' by the patient's behaviour.

An important part of both relatives' and patients' education about schizophrenia may be the part it plays in decreasing expect-ations and making them more realistic, and is an area for further investigation. What is a realistic expectation of such therapy programmes is open to question. In view of both the patient's and family's past learning history in connection with rehabilitation programmes, the most realistic expectation of all may be to expect *no* change.

Working With Voluntary Groups

A further way of working with relatives can be achieved by becom-ing involved in a self-help group. The National Schizophrenia Fellowship, for example, has local groups throughout the country. One of its primary aims is to provide support for relatives and this also involves education. As well as offering the group advice or expertise, involvement with such groups — even on a limited basis — can be useful for the professional in terms of learning more about how the illness affects families. Relatives are often more open in their comments and revelations in such circumstances, and thus new insights can be gained. Difficulties in providing treatment or inadequacies in provision of services can be discussed, and relatives helped to understand the professionals' position, and vice versa. Such a dialogue can help to break down barriers, and may establish better working relationships between relatives and professionals. The importance of such groups is, however, that they are *self-help* and organised by relatives or patients; care should be taken not to intrude on this. A recent publication by Richardson (1984) offers advice on working with such groups.

9 COMMUNICATION IN THE FAMILY

Most of the family theories of schizophrenia emphasise communication as the central issue, whether the problems lie in communication between parents and thus affects the child only indirectly, or whether the difficulty is directly between the child and a parent. Both Lidz and Wynne support the notion of problems between parents (see Chapter 4), of which communication plays a part, whereas Bateson's double-bind affects the child more directly. Searles' theory (1959) is interesting because his is the only theory to directly confront the possibility that the child may drive the parent mad. These theories and their inadequacies have been explored in Chapter 3. However, one area of research bears further consideration, namely the work on expressed emotion in the family.

Expressed Emotion in the Family

Emotionality in the family was first researched in the early 1960s by Brown *et al.* in London (Brown, Monck, Carstairs and Wing, 1962). The term 'expressed emotion' (EE) and its measurement as high or low in families came into being in the early 1970s (Brown, Birley and Wing, 1972). But what exactly is expressed emotion? Brown's study described it as being composed of three parts, namely, critical comments, hostility and over-involvement. It is worth noting that it was the interview with the relative alone which produced the significant finding; if emotion in the family is to be assessed (whether formally or informally) the relative should be seen alone by the therapist at least once. Also, if critical comments are to occur, they are likely to be made early, the majority appearing in the first hour of the interview. Whether or not time is the crucial factor is uncertain, as in some interviews the relative was allowed a period of free expression until questioning could begin in a more systematic fashion.

The first three areas covered in the interview dealt with psychiatric history, irritability and quarrelling, and clinical symptoms, and accounted for 67 per cent of all critical comments over the 15

146

interviews. Vaughn and Leff (1976a, 1976b; Leff, 1976) replicate this study using a shorter interview. They again find that critical comments are made in the first hour of the interview and have only a low correlation with the length of interview. This is in contrast to relatives of depressed patients who show no lowering of criticism after the first hour and a highly significant correlation between number of critical comments and length of interview.

Two other variables of reported prognostic significance in the Brown study (1962) were again found to be important. Maintenance drug therapy was defined as taking medication for eight out of nine months of follow-up; of the 37 patients in the trial, 21 were on regular maintenance therapy. Face-to-face contact with relatives was also measured. In both cases significant interactions were found with the high EE group. Drugs did not seem to have a protective effect in the low EE group, but did in the high EE group; low face-to-face contact had no effect in the low EE group, but was significantly related to lower relapse rates in the high EE group.

A further replication study, this time in California (Vaughn, Snyder, Freeman, Jones, Falloon and Liberman, 1982) showed strikingly similar results. During the nine-month follow-up period, 56 per cent of patients in the high EE homes relapsed, compared to 17 per cent in low EE homes. One notable difference, however, was that in London most families fell into the low EE group, whereas in California only one-third of the families were rated as being low on expressed emotion. Hostility was also rated as being more common in California than London. The authors conclude that 'while cultural differences may produce differing distributions of high vs low EE in families containing a schizophrenic member, the pattern of high EE retains its predictive importance cross-culturally'.

So far the studies have used the shortened Camberwell family interview to rate expressed emotion, which rates both content of speech and vocal aspects of spontaneous comments and thus requires rigorous training for a rater to become reliable. Ratings of criticism depend not only on content but also on vocal factors and changes in these, particularly tone, pitch and speed of voice. Thus a statement that appears neutral in its content can be given a variety of different emotional meanings. It is to rate such meaning accurately (or at least in a previously agreed way) that training is required, since the distinctions may be subtle. As Kuipers (1979) indicates 'a critical remark can be defined as a comment that shows that the respondent dislikes, resents or disapproves of the patient or his behaviour; to qualify as *critical*, it must have a vocal component more intense than mere *dissatisfaction* (which itself is not predictive of relapse)'.

This is not very practical in a clinical setting. A more general and easily applied rating would be useful, for example, if characteristics of families which show high EE could be identified and distinguished from those that do not. Vaughn and Leff (1981) suggest that there are four such characteristics. First, there is a difference in actual emotional response, as would be expected. High EE relatives express anger, acute distress, or both, in response to the patient's illness; low EE relatives show behaviour which is 'cool, controlled and concerned but not overly anxious' in response to the patient's illness. The studies by Tarrier *et al.* (1979) and Sturgeon *et al.* (1981) demonstrate the psychophysiological changes in patients in both home and experimental settings in the presence of their high EE relatives, and not in patients with low EE relatives.

The second characteristic is the 'relative's level of intrusiveness'. Relatives high on expressed emotion do not allow patients personal space or autonomy and disregard the common need of the schizophrenic patient for social distance. In contrast, low EE relatives allow such social distance. The third factor concerns the relative's attitude towards the illness itself. Whereas low EE relatives believe that the patient is suffering from a 'legitimate illness', the high EE relatives were doubtful that the patient has a genuine illness. They believe the patient has, or should have, control over his symptoms, and can be held responsible for his condition.

The last characteristic that distinguishes the two groups concerns the relative's level of tolerance of the illness and their expectations. These feelings inter-relate with their attitudes towards the illness, so low EE relatives are able to tolerate both disturbed behaviour and long-term social problems and impairments better than high EE relatives, who are more likely to be impatient and intolerant, both regarding symptoms and low performance. Few allowances are made for the patient's condition and his inability to control all of his behaviour, and such relatives may put considerable pressure on a patient to behave in a manner they consider normal.

The intrusive nature of high EE relatives has been indicated in a further study (Kuipers, Sturgeon, Berkowitz and Leff, 1983). Although the link between high expressed emotion, relapse and psychophysiological correlates is known, it is still not known exactly how the relatives affect the patients when they return home, except to say that the circumstances of the home environment are 'stressful'. Although the studies measuring psychophysiological changes involved both relatives and patients, studies measuring the expressed emotion itself were with relatives only. Kuipers *et al.* (1983) set out to 'examine behavioural aspects which might characterise high EE relatives by direct observation' with the dual hope that this would both 'aid recognition in the clinical setting and to discover more about the process of relapse'.

A video recording of an interview with relative and patient was made at the hospital during the first month of the patient's admission when the patient was still acutely ill. All patients lived with and spent at least 35 hours a week in contact with a relative who had previously been assessed for expressed emotion. Although there are a number of problems with this type of interview, and behaviour may not be the same as in the home setting, it is nevertheless a useful place to start such research.

Kuipers *et al.* (1983) 'hypothesised that acutely ill schizophrenic patients would show social behaviours characteristic of avoidance in interaction with high but not low EE relatives'. These avoidance behaviours were to be measured by looking at speaking behaviours, both separately and together. No significant differences at all were found between patients with high and low EE relatives. Why there should not be any differences is unclear. As Kuipers *et al.* (1982) point out, it may be that the measurements used were 'inappropriate' or 'that the hypotheses were ill-conceived'. Although the assumption is made that the behaviour of relatives rated as high EE is socially intrusive and aversive and it was expected that patients would avoid this, they may not actually do so because they do not have the appropriate skills. They may not perceive their relatives' behaviour as being aversive or may even feel that the behaviour is not aversive.

One difference was found in the interviews, and that was in the amount of time relatives spent talking: high EE relatives spend significantly more time talking than low EE relatives. They also looked less at the patient than did low EE relatives. This could be a useful clinical measure, since if 'a relative who spent more than two minutes speaking in the five-minute sample is defined as high EE, then over 80 per cent of relatives in this experiment are placed in the correct EE category. Similarly, a cut-off point of less than 14 seconds' silence classifies over 75 per cent correctly.' Kuipers *et al.* suggest that high EE relatives found pauses and silences uncomfortable, and that by speaking so much they tended to dominate the interview as well as expressing their 'anxiety and upset'. Much of the information they gave was irrelevant and they tended to ignore questions or comments from the patient and often answered for him. In contrast, low EE relatives spend more time listening to the patient, to pause before replying, to wait for the patient to reply and not to speak for him, and to consider and answer the patient's questions.

From these studies a picture of the high EE relative can be built up but as Kuipers *et al.* conclude: 'EE has been defined operationally and remains a predictively accurate but esoteric measure which is not easily transferred to the clinical setting.' How useful, then, is the concept of expressed emotion?

Vaughn and Leff's original study (1976b) made two basic and important assumptions. First, that the index of relative's expressed emotion is a reasonable indicator of family relations and, second, that the attitude shown by the relative towards the patient during the interview is representative of an enduring relationship over time. The results of the research linking high EE to relapse cause it to be considered as aversive. Although two studies show that patients in interaction with their high EE relatives are more physiologically aroused than those patients with low EE relatives, the Kuipers *et al.* study indicates that patients do not respond behaviourally to this. It might be useful, therefore, to consider expressed emotion in the wider concept of the family and the patient's perception of family communication.

In families with more than one relative, is the relative with whom the patient spends the most time the one with the highest expressed emotion? Even in low expressed emotion homes (as defined by one relative), there may be another relative whose interaction could be described as high on expressed emotion. A further factor could be the amount of expressed emotion generally in the household, not only that expressed to or about the patient. This could be affected by the number of people in the family, although how emotional levels could be measured in this sense is difficult to imagine. For instance, would it be possible, or sensible, to conceive of two people producing twice the expressed emotion of one? The number of comments may be greater, but is this true of the level of emotional intensity? Variations could produce highly emotional families with high or low expressed emotion towards the patient, or fairly unemotional families which show high or low expressed emotion to the patient. How much of the family interaction that is defined as critical may be crucial? Does embedding criticism within a framework of neutral or positive criticism dilute the effect of criticism at all? In addition, does a highly critical or over-involved atmosphere affect the patient, even when such behaviours are directed at other family members?

The patient's perception of the interaction may well be a key variable and there seems to be, if not contradictory, at least variable data on this. Do patients see the criticism or over-involvement directed at them as aversive? In some cases it might be necessary to ask whether it is seen at all, since over-involvement might characterise highly dependent relationships. A patient's perception of the situation will be influenced by a variety of variables, one of which might be the relative's general style of interaction. Someone who is openly hostile or critical to everyone, or over-involved in the lives of all family members, may have a different effect on the patient than one who only directs this type of interaction to the patient. In such circumstances what may be crucial is whether or not the patient sees himself as discriminated against within the family's communication system, by receiving more or a different quality of emotional interactions from his relatives. It is sometimes possible that low expressed emotion may seem to be a discrimination by some patients if this differs from the general mode of a relative's interaction. It does not, however, seem likely that this would be a very common pattern.

Changing Expressed Emotion

Having established that high expressed emotion is somehow linked to relapse rates and that intervention with such families can reduce relapse rates (e.g. Leff, Kuipers, Berkowitz, Eberlein-Fries and Sturgeon, 1982), the specifics of how this might be achieved can be considered.

Identifying Emotional Families

Reviewing the research on expressed emotion, Kuipers (1979) suggests that the 'most immediately practical use of EE would be as a clinical screening device; to determine which families might be most likely to benefit from intervention to reduce relapse rates'. It will not be possible, however, for most therapists to measure expressed emotion in the same way as in these research investigations, and it should be remembered that the interview is a research tool. Not only is a rigorous three-month training period required, but the interview procedure itself is lengthy, requiring at least four hours per patient. A simplified assessment scale needs to be used if high expressed emotion is to be a really useful clinical tool. Until this is available, are there other ways of identifying such families? Using the research findings it is probably possible to categorise families in a fairly rough-and-ready fashion: those where patients are likely to remain reasonably well after discharge, and those who are at greatest risk of relapse, and who are most in need of maintenance, medication and support. What, then, are the indicators?

Critical Comments.   Two-thirds of relatives make some critical comments, and Vaughn and Leff (1976a) rated as high EE relatives who made six or more critical comments. For practical purposes these can be rated on a common-sense approach using content, voice tone and other nonverbal behaviours. For example, the statement 'He has a bath every day when he gets home from the day centre' has a different emphasis when spoken as 'He *has* to have a bath every day when he gets home from the day centre', or, as it was actually spoken, 'He has a bloody bath every bloody day when he gets home from the bloody day centre', the 'bloody' getting more forceful each time. Without training it is likely that more will be rated as critical than otherwise, but this might not be a bad thing. A content analysis of the criticial remarks (Vaughn, 1977) indicates that two-thirds relate to longstanding characteristics and attributes of the patient rather than to more recent changes in behaviour. Thus the relatives are seen to be criticising the patient before the illness started, or at least before the present acute episode. Such statements are characterised by the use of absolute terms such as 'always' and 'never'; for example 'He always was a lazy so-and-so' or 'She never made any attempt to do anything'. Thus it seems that present behaviour is seen as an intensification of, or a result of, previously noted faults or traits. This leads into the next category.

Blaming the Patient.   The patient is blamed or held responsible for his present behaviour and circumstances. The presence of illness may not be recognised or may even be actively denied. Relatives will make statements such as 'He could stop if he really wanted to', 'If she made an *effort ...*', or 'He's just stubborn, he always has been'. This should be contrasted with low EE relatives who are more likely to note change and to assume some, possibly external, reason for this. 'He's never been like this before, so I knew something must have happened', or 'There must be something wrong with her to make her say things like this'. This is closely related to the next category.

Relative's Attitude Toward the Illness.   High EE relatives tend not to see the patient as ill, and believe that he is malingering, or responsible, or in control of the situation. In marked contrast, low EE relatives accept the fact that the patient has an illness, and cannot be blamed for either his condition or what he does. Statements made tend to be similar to those in the above category.

Relative's Emotional Response.   High EE relatives show their emotions during the interview, particularly anger and acute distress, but also fear, anxiety, resentment and related feelings. These feelings are in response to the patient's behaviour, their response to it, their inability to cope with the situation and the effect the patient has on them and their lives. This last response is particularly characteristic of high rather than low EE families. For example, a high EE relative is likely to say: 'I get really fed-up with him hanging around the house all day, under my feet. I can't get on with anything,' or 'I get so anxious wondering what he's going to do next'. Low EE relatives either do not experience such emotions, or are better at masking them to present a cool, controlled and calm front. Their concern for the patient shows, but is not overly anxious. They generally take a more pragmatic approach to the problem and assume that they will be able to cope somehow.

Relative's Level of Tolerance.   Acceptance of the patient's condition as an illness means that low EE relatives are usually more tolerant of the patient's disturbed behaviour, and of the more long-term consequences of the illness in terms of social impairment. They may have fairly low expectations of the patient, both in the present and for the future, and do not exert undue pressure on him to control his symptoms or to behave 'normally'. In contrast, high EE relatives are intolerant of disturbed behaviour, which often shows itself as impatience and a demand for the patient to behave normally. Few, if any, allowances are made for the patient's illness and the fact that he cannot always control his behaviour.

Over-involvement and Intrusiveness.   This can take two forms in high EE relatives. First, they can make repeated attempts to establish contact by offering unsolicited and unwelcome advice or opinions which are usually of a critical nature. Either the patient does not want to make any contact at all, or he may prefer a more limited contact.

A second form of contact can be established when the relative gives over-protective help, which may or may not be welcome. Although the behaviour may be seen on the surface as positive (being 'helpful', 'concerned', 'caring'), it often implies criticism, with the unspoken assumptions that the patient cannot deal with this himself. Overprotectiveness may not always show itself in speech unless questions are carefully phrased to elicit exactly how much the relative does for the patient, the types of decisions they make for the patient, or what they allow him to do.

In behavioural terms it may mean that the family does not leave the patient alone in the house, or does not allow him out on his own, even though the medical team thinks it is safe to do so. Such relatives may not take holidays so as to be with the patient and may arrange their life entirely around the patient. Patients faced with such an over-involved and overprotective relative may feel that their privacy has been invaded, that they are not allowed to be responsible for themselves, and consequently feel highly stressed. However, some patients accept this overprotectiveness and enter into a mutually highly dependant relationship with the over-involved relative.

On the other hand, low EE relatives allow the patient to maintain a degree of social distance and to make decisions for himself. The difference can be seen in two mothers who remarked that the patient was, at best, unreliable in taking his medication. One said, 'But it's his choice, isn't it?', whereas the other said, 'I try to insist he takes his tablets. I give them to him with a drink, right on time, and stand over him until he's swallowed them'. She also admitted to crushing them up and mixing them with his food on occasions.

In Vaughn and Leff's (1976) study, marked emotional over-involvement alone only added 5 per cent to the total in the high EE category. In most cases it was linked to criticism. It is, however, an important category, because some of the relative's burden and consequent intolerance may stem from their over-involvement. Such relatives present themselves as being self-sacrificing, and their situation in dramatised and exaggerated ways.

Intervention

Chapter 4 outlines the intervention programme designed to alter and minimise expressed emotion. Elements of this and other programmes, which could be used independently or recombined in various ways, bear further discussion.

Education. Since high EE relatives are either unaware that the patient is ill or reject this notion, education about the nature of schizophrenia, its symptoms, cause, prognosis and treatment may help change this stance. Although simply giving information is not, in itself, usually enough to change either attitudes or behaviour, it is a useful starting point where there is ignorance. Since the research shows that many relatives and patients have little understanding of the illness, are told little about it, and are not encouraged to discuss it with professionals, simply having the opportunity to be given information, and to discuss openly the issues, may help relatives reassess their views.

Although educating relatives and patients about the problem with which they are so closely involved seems straightforward, it is not entirely without controversy. The two main issues raised are whether relatives and patients should be educated and whether this helps them to be more positive to the patient, and if so, what they should be told. The objection to the former is that it is a form of labelling, which either relatives or patients might find distressing (this argument is often used for not giving patients their diagnosis), or that labelling may lead to an 'over-medicalisation' of the problems. Some of the issues surrounding labelling have been discussed in Chapter 7.

Other research has suggested, for example, that relatives may feel they have no control over the patient if his behaviour is labelled 'ill' (Armstrong, 1978), or that such labelling may cause relatives to reject the patient (Bott, 1977) or that a sick role, as defined by the patient being labelled ill, reduces the contact and social interaction between the patient and relative (Golding, Becker, Sherman and Rappaport, 1975). On the other hand, it is pointed out that to understand and cope with the illness, relatives need to know what the symptoms are (Kint, 1977); relatives find it easier to feel and express sympathy for the patient if they realise that he is ill (Hatfield, 1979b). Most importantly, relatives themselves want to know. As the National Schizophrenia Fellowship (1974) points out, 'First and above all, they (*the relatives*) need to understand how and why the sufferer is "different" from other people; that is, to understand what schizophrenia is'.

The second issue of what relatives should be told is, for many, even more controversial. Throughout this chapter (indeed, throughout the book) schizophrenia has been referred to as an illness, but not everyone would agree with this. This topic requires a book in its own right and will not be discussed here. A biochemical model of schizophrenia was presented by Berkowitz and her colleagues (Berkowitz, 1984; Berkowitz, Eberlein-Fries, Kuipers and Leff, 1984) in their educational programme and would seem to be a fairly standard approach. It might be useful, however, to mention other viewpoints even if they are to be dismissed, since relatives may come across them or they may be presented by different professional groups. Agreement and consistency among professionals may be an important gain from the education programme both for the relatives and for the professionals themselves. If there is disagreement then it should be confronted openly, and dealt with both in the professional team and with the families. Being given contradictory information and advice may prove as problematic for relatives as not having any at all.

If it is assumed that relatives should be educated about schizophrenia then probably the best way to do this is in groups, with both a didactic presentation and discussion. Handouts could be used or any of the books written for relatives and patients recommended (e.g. Atkinson, 1985). The studies by both the Vaughn, Leff and colleagues team, and Anderson and colleagues discussed in Chapter 4 describe how such education might be organised.

In presenting information to relatives it must be remembered that many will have only a basic education. They may know little about schizophrenia and about mental illness in general. Jargon and technical terms must be explained. It is useful to use such terms rather than try to eliminate them, as relatives will come across them with other professional staff or in their reading. Every term should be checked in terms of what the relatives understand by it: even a word such as 'diagnosis', which is known and used, is often not understood in terms of why one is made, what use is made of it and, most important, how it is made. For example, it may be useful to explain that physical tests may be carried out to *exclude* the possibility of other illnesses rather than to *confirm* schizophrenia. Words that might need explanation include diagnosis, prognosis, symptoms and aetiology.

The symptoms need to be explained clearly and carefully to the relatives whose understanding of the illness is usually only from their own perspective. They often do not understand or see the patient's behaviour in terms of thought disorder, disturbances of perception of volition, or the other classic symptoms. Relatives often concentrate more on the social aspects of the illness that they can see readily, and need a description of how these fit into the wider picture. The variations in symptoms and the course of the illness need explanation. In discussing aetiology, the multifactorial nature of schizophrenia's cause should be emphasised; the contributory factors of genetics, stress and the family's influence on relapse and the general course of the illness should also be discussed.

When dealing with treatment it is again important to start the discussion at a very basic level. It may be that a description of the following night be necessary: what happens on admission as a part of hospital routine; a description of drug therapy, its pros and cons and its expected or potential side-effects; how patients are treated; other therapies such as industrial, occupational and social. The role of various professionals should be explained, including psychiatrists, psychologists and social workers. The relationship between these groups and their responsibilities are very confused for many people. For example, understanding that psychologists and social workers cannot prescribe drugs may save the frustration of applying to these people for changes in drugs.

Changing Communication.   Explaining to relatives the concept of expressed emotion and its relationship with relapse may be the first step in dealing with this problem. Relatives need to be helped to assess for themselves their own pattern of communication, to establish when they are being critical, overprotective or over-intrusive. Relatives may assert that the patient cannot be left, but this requires a complete examination of exactly what happens if the patient is left alone, how often there is trouble when the patient is alone, and how serious this is. It might be that the relatives are using an isolated incident as the rationale for all their behaviour. There are no guarantees in terms of behaviour or patient's response, and it might be that relatives need to be encouraged to take risks, for example, to go out and see how the patient copes at home without them, rather than to assume he will not cope and never give him the opportunity to prove he can.

It is easiest to assess the family's interaction patterns if they are seen alone, and multi-family therapy may not be possible at this stage. Intervention will need to be tailored to each family and their specific problems and deficits in communication skills. Some aspects of communication will be appropriate to all families. Non-verbal behaviour such as voice tone, eye contact and body posture may need examining, particularly for any negative aspects they may have. Being clear and specific can be practised, and the setting of realistic goals achieved, rather than being vague or only complaining: for example, learning to say, 'I would like you to make your own bed' rather than, 'You never do anything to help in the house' or even 'You're a slob'. Giving unasked-for advice or making demands can be avoided by making 'I' statements and explaining feelings. For example, rather than saying 'You never tell me where you're going. You should know by now we expect you to tell us when you're going out', it might be more acceptable to say, 'I worry when you disappear and no one knows where you are or when you'll be back. It would help me if you would just tell me you're going out'.

All of the various techniques used in social skills training should be employed, including instruction, shaping and coaching, modeling, reinforcement, feedback, rehearsal and homework. Teaching families to express their positive feelings towards one another is also part of the communication skills programme. Again, families should be taught to be clear and specific, rather than vague and global. By communicating positive feelings frequently the general atmosphere in the family can be improved and tension lowered. This is not to suggest that negative feelings should never be communicated, but they can be communicated in a manner (e.g. specific, with request for behavioural changes) that makes them useful, rather than simply adding to the problem.

The more passive part of communication should not be neglected and families can be taught 'active listening'. Relatives who showed high expressed emotion in the interview studies were poor listeners. They tended to ignore what the patient said in particular, but many professionals would recognise these relatives as poor listeners with them as well. Low expressed emotion relatives paused before replying, waiting for the patient to respond. Since some schizophrenic patients seem to have slow reaction time, often all that is needed is to give them longer than 'normal' to respond. Using the previously mentioned techniques, relatives can learn to listen more appropriately and attentively. Two important listening skills are asking questions which clarify the situation and checking that the interpretation relatives put on statements are correct.

Communicating Outside the Family

The research on burden in the family indicates that a number of families experience some degree of shame or embarrassment through their relative's illness and that this might go as far as their feeling socially isolated. Although learning more about the illness may help improve the relative's attitude to both the illness and the patient, more can be done to help relatives and patients tell people outside the immediate family about the patients' illness. Using the same techniques of modelling, coaching, rehearsal, reinforcement feedback and homework, relatives can practise telling people what they need to know. Multi-family groups to discuss this problem are useful, as those relatives who have successfully dealt with this problem can give help, advice and encouragement to others. Discussion about who should be told what and how includes considering various groups of people, such as close relatives and friends, more distant relatives, neighbours and acquaintances, and, in the work situation, workmates, superiors and how to deal with the issue of mental illness in job applications. Not everybody needs to be told everything; individual families can make their own decisions about this. It is often useful to practise deflecting particularly intrusive questions from others which go beyond what the family (including the patient) wants to divulge.

Communicating with Children

A neglected group in research on families with a schizophrenic member are the children, be they younger siblings of the patient, his own offspring, or nephews or nieces. They need to be told in terms that they can understand why the patient behaves as he does. The impact of the patient's behaviour on their life can be discussed with them, and they should be allowed to express their feelings freely as well as to consider how the situation can best be managed to everyone's satisfaction. Some children come in for teasing at school about their 'mad' or 'funny' relative and this can lead to a number of behavioural problems at school, including poor work, truancy and fighting. The child's parent should be encouraged to explain family circumstances to the child's teacher so that he can deal most effectively and appropriately with the situation. In some circumstances the child may need someone of their own to talk to about their problems and feelings and how they cope with them.

An area of particular importance that should be discussed with every child is what they should do if the patient behaves in a way which frightens them. Specific instructions need to be given about who to go to if the child's parents are not there; not just 'another grown-up' but 'go and tell Auntie Mary next door'. Children should be encouraged *always* to tell someone if the patient does anything which frightens them. Once the problem has been handled with the patient, time must then be spent with the child to allow him to express his feelings and to reassure him and explain what has happened.

10 PROBLEM SOLVING AND REDUCING STRESS

Dealing with the specific problems and issues a family raises is one of the most difficult areas to confront the therapist. Relatives are asking for concrete help with clearly defined issues, ranging from wanting to know what to do if the patient will not take medication, to how to deal with bizarre behaviour or ideas. They want to know how to cope with aggressive outbursts and how to help the patient find a job or friends or to be generally more social. Usually, the relatives will have tried many solutions and, although wanting help, will view new solutions with pessimism and suspicion. If they are involved in some form of educational programme, then the information they are getting about the illness and its treatment may encourage them to reassess their methods of coping and to approach new methods of management with more optimism.

It helps if relatives are aware of the part stress plays in schizophrenia and of the vicious circle of pressure from relatives or the environment that can lead to an exacerbation of symptoms or problems. This in turn puts more burden on relatives which means they deal with the situation less well and thus put more pressure on the patients, and so on and so forth. Once this circle is understood, relatives may be more open to the idea that it can be broken at several points, only one of which involves changing the patient's behaviour directly. More indirect methods have to do with changing the stress levels put upon the patient; one of these, the expressed emotion in the family, has been dealt with in the preceding chapter.

Relatives may also come to appreciate that although they may seek, and get, specific advice for dealing with immediate problems, it would be of more help to them to learn a global approach to dealing with the continuing situation, which they can use whenever necessary in the future. These general and sometimes more indirect solutions offer the most to families in terms of managing the ongoing nature of schizophrenia. The solutions centre around reducing stress in any way available and learning how to solve problems as constructively and with as little stress as possible.

Problem-solving Skills

Learning the skills to solve problems is a first step to dealing with all the specific difficulties a family has. Falloon *et al.* (e.g. 1981) describe problem-solving as 'the core of family management training' because it 'improves families' ability to cope with major crises as well as lesser problems of day-to-day living'. Learning to solve problems as a family is related to communication in that relatives need to have good communication skills to be able to discuss problems and their solutions. Falloon *et al.* outline six stages in the problem-solving sequence: (1) identify a specific problem, (2) list alternative solutions, (3) discuss pros and cons, (4) choose the best solution, (5) plan how to implement the solution, and (6) review efforts. These form the basis of any training in problem-solving, and can be expanded or extended as necessary. It would be possible to deal with the basic principles and examples in a multi-family group, but each family will require time to work on their problems alone.

1. Identifying Problems.   This stage involves all the members of the family and the patient, if he is present, listing problems, airing grievances and generally bringing up for discussion any issues they feel should be dealt with or changed. At this stage all problems need to be identified and/or recorded. The therapist is involved in noting the problems, eliciting information and classifying issues where necessary. It is important at this stage that the therapist does not make premature judgements about what is or is not a problem, or priorities, nor offers advice or reassurance. This is likely to be inappropriate if all the facts or opinions are not yet known. It may also stop further discussion.

2. Identifying Priorities and Goals.   A consensus agreement must be reached between relatives, patient and therapist about which problems are the most pressing and require priority. It is important that all members of the family (or at least those involved in therapy) are given a chance to air their views on what constitutes the greatest problem for *them* as well as for the family as a whole. At each stage it is important to ensure that the discussion is not dominated by one person and that everyone has an opportunity to speak. The therapist should avoid commenting on problems or priorities early in the discussion, as this may prevent further open discussion. However, the therapist should help the family to come to an agreement about priorities, pointing out where necessary that certain skills are needed to solve some problems or that other changes may have to be made. This begins to move into the next stage, but before solutions are discussed the family can begin to consider the problem in terms of specific goals to be achieved rather than broad global areas, and to see goals in positive rather than negative terms. This aids the identification of solutions if the problem is stated as 'the patient should do more' rather than just 'he doesn't do anything'.

3. Identifying Solutions.   The family is encouraged to identify and list as many solutions to the problem as they can. 'Brainstorming' methods are useful, which means suggestions are merely recorded as they occur, with no discussion allowed of the suggestion at this stage. Again, all members should be encouraged to make at least one suggestion and the family should be told they must come up with at least five or six different solutions to prevent them considering the first one as the 'best' or most 'obvious', and to stop one person stating that his (or another) solution is clearly 'the best'. The therapist should encourage the family to approach the problem from all angles and to consider their own expectations and behaviour as well as the patient's.

4. Discussion.   Every solution is discussed separately in terms of its advantages and disadvantages, which should be recorded. Skills needed to carry out each solution should be considered, as should other changes that might need to be made. The family should question whether or not these relate to any other problem areas. In some intances at this stage, the specific problems made need to be reviewed in terms of breaking them down into stages. It is not always possible to do this without also discussing solutions to problems. On the other hand, solutions may suggest different aspects of a problem, although most of this should occur at the planning stage. For example, travelling on public transport may not have been considered a real problem until a solution requires this to take place.

The financial cost of a solution is often neglected (particularly by the therapist!) and this can cause some families severe problems. Being unable to afford to carry out a solution may well be something they are loathe to mention to the therapist.

5. Preferred Solution.   Again, a consensus agreement must be reached within the family on what is seen as the 'best' or preferred solution following the discussion. It may be that a combination of suggestions provides the best solution.

6. Planning.   This can be a fairly lengthy stage as every aspect of the preferred solution has to be considered and planned. At this stage it might become clear that a solution requires a number of different subgoals or stages. Clear and careful planning is vital as it is often neglect of the small details that leads to failure. Planning for alternatives is also necessary, in case something goes wrong or does not happen as anticipated.

7. Rehearsal.   A normal behavioural programme will follow where skills need to be learnt. This may include modelling, coaching, feedback and the usual techniques. A rehearsal or practice session is helpful even if this is not necesary. Areas of potential difficulty may come to light and these can be referred back for further planning. Both relatives and patients can gain in confidence through knowing they coped in a practice session. This need not always be a full behavioural rehearsal but can be simply a talking-through of the procedure step by step.

8. Homework.   The family engage in the planned activities.

9. Feedback.   The family, with the therapist, review how effective the solution was 'in real life'. The family should be reinforced for any real attempts to carry out the solution, even if it was not entirely successful. During this discussion the family should be encouraged to review the solution itself, as well as their implementation of it. If things went wrong, why did this happen? What can they do about it? Is the solution itself not the answer? Or do they need new skills? Or better planning? It is to be hoped that families will realise that their first attempts are unlikely to be wholly successful or to solve a problem immediately, and that repeated efforts are needed.

10. Future Sessions and Homework.   The family may need to go through this sequence a number of times to deal with one problem. They may require therapist input to deal with the first few problems. Gradually, however, they should be encouraged to go through this process themselves at home and to use therapy sessions to outline plans to the therapist and to review how the plans worked.

The family should be encouraged to use this format in their approach to problem-solving even if, at first, they find some overlap between stages or find they have to retrace their steps because something they thought was clear and specific turns out not to be at a later stage. When problems are seen to inter-relate, the family can more easily appreciate that there is not one simple answer to their difficulties, and that their attitudes and expectations are brought into question as they discuss problems and solutions.

For example, a family may firmly believe the main problem is 'tension in the family' which can best be solved by spending more time apart. However, it is only when they come to discuss where the patient can go that other problems surface. The patient, for example, will not — or cannot — go out during the day, and will only go out for a walk at night. This then raises other questions. Is this to do with daylight and darkness, or being seen by other people, or something else? At this stage the family realise there is little point in planning where the patient might go if, for whatever reason, the primary problem is that he cannot leave the house. Clearly, this should have come out in the early discussions about problems, but often such difficulties do not surface until the family reach the stage of discussing solutions. Once this has happened once or twice the family learn to be more open, objective and far-reaching in their approach to problems. They are able to analyse the situation more carefully in order to reach the primary problem, before they start planning solutions.

Advantages of Teaching Problem Solving

The first advantage is that the family learn a strategy they can use on their own and will not always be dependent on therapist input. It is something they can apply in many family situations and not just those to do with the patient. This in turn may improve the family atmosphere and be of benefit to the patient. The structured approach to problem-solving dissipates much of the emotion that would otherwise be engendered by many of the issues raised, and which would normally raise the level of family tension and prevent rational discussion.

The interaction between problems and their overlap becomes

obvious in these sessions. This often helps the family to accept that they all play a part, both in the development of the problem and in its solution. It also becomes clear that only rarely does a problem, or its solution, lie with one person. Members of a family realise that they often feel the same way about something, even if they have not been able to discuss it openly before. Even where an issue is a real problem for only one person, rather than for the family as a whole, sharing it within the family can relieve the emotional burden on the individual and also help the family appreciate that point of view. It also means that the entire family resources can be used in dealing with that problem, including emotional support. A collective approach to dealing with the family's difficulties means that if a solution fails to resolve a problem completely or if a solution cannot be found, then this failure is the responsibility of the whole family; blame cannot be placed on one person alone. This also aids family unity and prevents individuals feeling isolated with the problem or with failure in its resolution.

Reducing Face-to-face Contact

Much emphasis is placed on dealing with the expressed emotion of families. This is an important issue but it is easy to overlook the other side of the Vaughn and Leff study (1976a); that is, in families with high expressed emotion, of the group of patients who spent less than 35 hours a week with their relatives, fewer relapsed than the group who spent more than 35 hours a week in face-to-face contact (Vaughn and Leff, 1976a). Where families are highly involved with one another, reducing the amount of time they spend together is as important as dealing with the emotional over-involvement, although in many instances the two will be inter-related.

Reducing face-to-face contact is not always as easy as it sounds. It may be that relatives, or the patient, or both, need persuading that they *do* spend too much time together. Where a relationship is highly mutually dependent, both sides may be resistant to spending more time apart, possibly because they have no one else with whom to spend time and no outside interests.

In a problem-solving session on reducing contact, the family will usually start by making the suggestion that the patient should go out more, and then consider where he can go. They may need prompting to view the problem from the other side, that relatives could go out and allow the patient some time in the house on his own. This is likely to raise the issue of whether the patient *can* be left on his own. A common problem is that relatives are unhappy about leaving a patient alone in the house, occasionally with good reason, but more often not. Various solutions to this problem must then be considered. If the patient really cannot be left, is there anyone else who can stay with him and allow his parents, for example, to go out together?

Both patients and relatives may need encouragement to go out, and suggestions for places to go and things to do. Day care facilities may seem an obvious solution to getting the patient out of the house for part of the day, and is often the family's favoured course. Sometimes this is not possible and the reasons will have to be discussed with the relatives. Their response to this news will also need discussion: simply venting their anger or disappointment may not be enough and more positive alternatives to dealing with this issue may be needed. A different approach may be to look for a long-term, less personal solution. Relatives might write to their local MP and councillors regarding the lack of facilities for the mentally ill in the area. That done, it may be easier to look for alternatives for the immediate future without the weight of unexpressed emotions or frustration at having the first choice blocked. Arranging to spend time apart should be accomplished in the most positive way possible, and neither party should feel they are being forcibly excluded from the house. The feeling of 'punishment' can be reduced if it can be combined with solving other problems.

It is not easy to find places for the patient to spend time. This is particularly so when there are other problems with the patient such as lack of interests, a difficulty in dealing with people, and withdrawal. It is important to acknowledge that a lack of things to do is not just a problem for the mentally ill, but for many who are unemployed. It is unrealistic to expect a hobby to take the place of a job for most people. When this problem is compounded by a lack of money (a problem for many families), filling time becomes even more difficult.

Medication

Medication is the third protective factor for lowering relapse rates. Where the family has low expressed emotion there is some indication that medication may be of little benefit, whereas it may be extremely important in families with high expressed emotion. Although the use of maintenance medication is a clinical decision, it should be discussed thoroughly both with the patient and, where necessary, the relatives. It is in areas such as this that problems with confidentiality can arise. Although medication is a matter between patient and doctor, relatives with whom the patient lives will usually expect to know what drugs the patient is taking, why, and if they are changed. It is reasonable for the relative to have the relevant information if he is responsible for seeing that the patient takes his medication. Whether a relative *should* be in this position is a debatable issue itself and should be discussed in the family group. Some relatives do not want the task of supervision and feel it is not something which can be expected of them; others assume that the task naturally falls to them. Conflict will tend to arise only where a patient refuses to take medication and the relative insists that he does, particularly if the latter then resorts to subterfuge.

Intervention Strategies and Coping Skills

It is the day-to-day management of schizophrenia that concerns relatives the most, and few have the necessary skills to cope effectively with the many problems this involves. In addition to teaching families new communication skills and problem-solving skills, there is a case for discussing the other behavioural techniques that might be used to change behaviour.

Instructions

Many patients find concentrating difficult, complicated or long series of instructions hard to remember, and the actual language used difficult to interpret at times. Relatives can learn how to be specific in their instructions and to avoid ambiguity and generalities. This is particularly important where patients are over-literal in their interpretation of remarks and misunderstand humour. If necessary the relative or patient can write instructions down and refer to them when necessary.

Reinforcement

The use of reinforcement to change and maintain behaviour is useful when clearly explained to relatives. It should be sincere, without negative signals (either non-verbal or in the use of qualifying statements, e.g. 'that was good *but* ...'), close to the desired behaviour and given for specific behaviour. That is, the patient should be told why he is being reinforced in terms of particular problems; thus, he should not just be told 'you look nice today', but an explanation given, with reference to clean clothes, or the fact that the patient has had a bath or a shave, or whatever else the desirable behaviour is that has been successfully carried out. In some instances rewards can be made contingent upon specific behaviour, for example, the patient only gets breakfast if he gets up for it by a certain time; it is not taken to him in bed or made specially to suit him.

The consistent nature of responses and their effect on behaviour should be explained, so that once a decision has been made about how the family will respond to a certain behaviour, everyone does this and on each occasion. If one person does not agree then it should be discussed, since subtle, or not-so-subtle, sabotage will prevent any change in the patient's behaviour.

Setting Limits and Taking Risks

As part of their problem-solving tasks, the family and the patient should examine what they consider to be acceptable and unacceptable behaviour and try to set limits. Doing this when a patient is well can sometimes be used to help control behaviour when he is not, and previously agreed limits can be reiterated. Although many patients will not be able to respond rationally at such a time, some can and find these known and accepted limits a form of security.

While discussing limits relatives can also begin to explore, with the patient and therapist, the extent to which they are prepared to take risks that might lead to relapse. Where there is a difference of opinion between relatives and patient, causing tension, conflict and stress which may contribute to relapse, these must be weighed against the relatives' insistence with what they believe to be the right course of action. There are no rules for when risks should be taken and when relatives should give way, but opening up this area for debate can help both relatives and patients to appreciate the other's point of view. Such restrictions apply both to the patient's and the relative's behaviour. The limits may include how much pressure can be brought to bear on a patient to take part in activities he does not want to be involved in, criticism of the patient, over-involvement and so on.

Contracts

A contract can be formal in terms of a written and signed agreement or it can be a more informal, verbal agreement made in the presence of other family members as witnesses. Two family members negotiate (using problem-solving skills) changes in their behaviour contingent upon the other person behaving in a certain way. This is especially useful when neither person is likely to perform the behaviour spontaneously or without some form of persuasion. Both sides agree to carry out a behaviour they otherwise would not, which the other person wants. Thus the patient might agree to get up at a specified time for breakfast, in return having the breakfast of his choice provided. As in goal-setting, it is better to have positive behaviour rather than negative; that is, something will be done rather than something will not, although often it is negative behaviour on the part of relatives that patients want stopped, for example, a stop to nagging or pressurising.

Time Out

Both family and patient should be allowed to say when they feel a situation is getting more than they can deal with, and request time away from the situation. This can range from a patient saying he can spend only 30 minutes with visitors after which he wants to be on his own, to a relative saying he can only listen to the patient's problems for a certain length of time. It is especially important when someone (relative or patient) is too emotional to discuss a situation or problem at a particular time. They can then ask for 'time out' and resume the discussion at a later time. However, care should be taken that this procedure is not used to avoid ever discussing a topic.

Independence

In using all these techniques, the goal of the patient's independence should be borne in mind. It is all too easy to maintain the patient in the child role by the use of instructions, rewards and so forth. A frequent check should be made where such techniques are used explicitly to ensure whether they are still necessary. The aim should be to return to the normal rules and regulations that govern everyday behaviour as quickly as practicable.

Discharge

The way in which a patient is discharged from hospital and returned to the care of his family is an occasion on which either good relations can be established and cemented between relatives and professionals, or when they can break down completely. Relatives' complaints surrounding this procedure cover every aspect. 'Discharge often happens casually, without warning or prior consultation with the relatives with whom the patient is going to live, and regardless of home circumstances' (Silbertson, 1985). Relatives are particularly concerned to know details of medication and continuing treatment, including hospital appointments, and will ask for advice or management on a day-to-day basis. They may want to know why the patient is being discharged at that time especially if, as far as they know, it occurs '*before* any treatment has been given, with the sufferer as bad as he was when admitted, or because of disruptive behaviour' (Silbertson, 1985).

The National Schizophrenia Fellowship (1983) suggests 'there is evidence of a great deal of practical difficulty in the area of discharge from hospital'. It has devised a code of practice which outlines the procedure it would like to see followed when a patient is to be discharged. Seven areas of concern are identified:

1. The caring or concerned relative or friend should be appointed;
2. Information should be given to the relative or friend;
3. Changes of responsibility should be notified;
4. The family should be warned of the possibility of self-discharge by the patient;
5. Relatives should be involved in the plans for discharge;
6. The relative should be allowed access to the consultant;
7. Relatives should be allowed access to a second opinion.

When identifying the 'concerned relative', it is to be remembered that this is not necessarily the nearest relative as defined in the Mental Health Act. On discharge it should be checked that this person is both able and willing to provide a home for the patient, and that the patient is prepared to live there. As well as providing information about discharge in terms of date, time, travel arrangements and all arrangements for aftercare, the NSF emphasises the importance of being told the 'procedure to be adopted in case of relapse', a much-neglected area of advice.

Relatives' Emotions and Problems

Most of these issues will be discovered and discussed throughout the therapeutic programme, but often only as they come to light in connection with the patient's problems and his response to them. A number of themes occur and re-occur in reports of relatives' groups that may require dealing with explicitly with relatives, if not dealt with elsewhere. Such themes include intolerance of the illness and the handicaps it causes, an inability to be separated from the patient, reducing guilt, fear and isolation, reducing fears of relinquishing control, accepting the individual needs of family members to have privacy and to socialise without the patient, and the power the patient has over the family.

This latter issue is often neglected and although it sometimes stems from ignorance about schizophrenia and a misunderstanding of how the patient might behave in some instances, the patient does exert a considerable control over the family. This can be the result of suspiciousness causing misinterpretation of what is said and done, or of more conscious forms of 'telling tales' or even blackmail regarding possible violence. In such cases relatives may not express such difficulties in front of the patient and, although they can be dealt with only by involving the patient, sessions alone with relatives may be needed to bring the problems to light.

Patients as Parents

A neglected group in discussing family programmes are the children of a schizophrenic parent. Some reference has been made to them, but there are areas to which special attention should be paid. There are a number of psychophysiological and neurological variables on which children of schizophrenics show problems, including delayed and deficient motor development, auditory-visual integration, deficiencies in right-left orientation, and they are hyperlabile and hypersensitive in automatic functioning (Marcus 1974a, 1974b). While parents' mental illness has no effect on the intelligence of very young children, school grades are likely to be lower than in a control group (Rolfe, 1972) Such children may also have problems with sustained attention (Erlenmeyer-Kimling, Marcuse, Cornblatt, Friedman, Ranier and Rutschmann, 1981).

In such families children themselves can be the direct recipients of help, or the parent can be given help and advice on the skills involved in being a patient. Goodman (1984) describes 'Project PACT (Parents and Children Together)' which involves both aspects, including building support networks between an aide and the mother, parenting skills training, and child socialisation.

11 WHAT DOES THE FAMILY REALLY WANT?

This is a formidable question to answer, and the only way to come close to it is to ask the relatives themselves. A number of studies have tried this, but with varying results. A professional finds it difficult to understand the full meaning of some of the answers given, as the information is received and dealt with intellectually, with the emotional intensity behind the answer being ignored. An insight into this dichotomy is given by Wasow (1983): 'As a clinical professor of social work working in the area of chronic mental illness, I try to write in the spirit of collegial friendship, armed with a review of the literature and properly documented footnotes. As a parent of a chronic schizophrenic, with a ten-year background in dealing with the mental health and legal systems, I write with unmitigated rage and pain!'

Talking to relatives is the first obvious step towards understanding the relative's position, and their thoughts and feelings about the service they are receiving. Reading some of the case histories written by relatives of schizophrenic patients also gives insight into the families' experiences, and shows how deeply their lives are affected by the condition (e.g. Reed, 1976; McDonald, 1980; Ogdon and Kerr, 1981). The research on 'what relatives want' is scarce.

Hatfield (1979a, 1979b) used a questionnaire to investigate from what resources the family had sought help, how helpful these had been, and what help the family would like. The families were all members of the Schizophrenia Association of Greater Washington (SAGW), 'the only self-help group related to this disease in the area'. The relatives were given checklists of nine professional and informal supports or resources and eight 'services' which the family might like. Eighty-five per cent of the respondents were parents, and each relative was the one most responsible for the patient's care.

The resource which was acknowledged as being used the most often, and as being of greatest value, was 'lectures and books'. In terms of being sought out for help, friends came next, followed by relatives and individual therapy (group therapy and family therapy being just behind). Friends were also reported as being of the most value, with relatives not far behind. It is interesting to note that about half of those seeking therapy report it to be of no value. Parents of other schizophrenics were valued highly, and also SAGW staff, although fewer relatives sought help from them.

Of the eight choices given for 'assistance desired by caregivers', three could be chosen. Only two were chosen by over 50 per cent of relatives, namely 'knowledge and understanding of patient's symptoms' and 'specific suggestions for coping with patient's behaviour'. Over 40 per cent wanted 'people to talk to who have known the experience'; almost one-third wanted 'substitute care to relieve the family' and slightly less than this wanted the patient to 'change place of living'. The last three options, 'more understanding from friends and relatives', 'relief from financial stress' and 'therapy for self' were chosen by comparatively few relatives.

Looking at these results together, the importance of books to the families seems clearer than it otherwise might. It is from books and lectures that the family have been able to learn about schizophrenia and possibly also to have had some suggestions for management. Although it is useful to know that information about the illness and its management are what relatives want most, in this study they were given only a limited number of choices. How do relatives respond if they are given an open choice?

The author looked at this question in a survey of members of the National Schizophrenia Fellowship in Scotland. Relatives were asked open-ended questions, including 'What do you think can be done about it (schizophrenia)?' 'What is your biggest problem?' and 'What would help you most?' This generated a wide range of answers, with little agreement. The two problems which the greatest number of relatives mentioned were 'the future' and 'getting help when it's needed'. These were followed by the social problems of the patient, family friction and supervision. The three areas of help which relatives reported wanting most were: day care of some kind; changes in the 'professional approach'; direct help for relatives. Letting the relatives speak for themselves highlights the meaning for those involved of these 'simple' categories.

What is Your Biggest Problem?

'Not knowing when my mum is experiencing a delusion' (son, 17 years).

'Worrying about what will happen in later years when he will not have his parents at his side. Apart from smoking, watching TV and playing records, his days pass' (father, 71 years).

'Coping day to day with the terrible terrifying behaviour patterns of my son' (mother, 54 years).

'The disturbance it causes within the family' (wife).

'My biggest problem is a personal one, concerning anxiety over the children, with regard to the hereditary aspect of the illness, as there is a very strong hereditary incidence of the illness within my husband's family (father and grandmother). I feel it has made us a "disunited" family — two younger children do not quite know how to treat the patient — as he has never really fulfilled the interested, steady father role. Eldest daughter has no contact with her father on any personal level' (wife, 46 years).

'The biggest problem is the fact that my son refuses all medication. He had an allergy to an early treatment and that finished pills of any kind. The problem in a crisis is to know where to turn for help' (adoptive mother, 76 years).

'How to understand my son's illness, how best to handle him, as sometimes I think he is a bit irresponsible, and I tend to row with him which I know isn't good for him. My son has now refused to take any medication and has stopped attending the hospital as an outpatient. His GP made arrangements for him to have his injections at the surgery, which he has also stopped. He now only calls at the doctor for his sick line. At present he is very well, but tends to stay in bed some days for most of the day. I can't get him to take up any constructive hobby, though he reads all the time ... What can be done about his awkwardness?' (mother, 46 years).

'Watching my son and wondering what the future holds for him' (mother, 46 years).

'The future' (father, 50 years).

'Over the past 17 years I've had numerous problems and each one as big as the other. The most consistent one I would say has been over my husband's medication, no matter what type of drug has been prescribed to him (and outwith him not continually taking dosages as per instructions), there has never been a prolonged state of levelness and in relationship to this over the years it appears to me — what and if anyone can do to help him?' (wife, 48 years).

'Meeting old school friends or other acquaintances and listening to all their families' successes then having to "skate" round their enquiries about him' (mother).

'Coming to terms with the apparent lack of concern for this type of patient. I have observed this myself on fairly regular visits, particularly to my brother's ward ... I know that it is easy to criticise as a visitor to the ward but it does appear that the staff keep to themselves a lot in their office and that the patients are left to fend for themselves' (brother, 43 years).

'Finding something which will interest my son, to keep him from becoming bored or frustrated each day, e.g. odd jobs which don't require a lot of concentration' (father, 62 years).

'Anxiety about the future of my two sons when I am no longer around to provide a safety net' (mother, 68 years).

'Where our daughter is concerned, having somewhere for her to go, to occupy her day and to prevent the illness recurring. By making a compulsory order for her such as to attend at a centre which would be for her benefit, this should be a priority for such sufferers. Various governments have promised all kinds of help and amenities for as far back as I can remember, *but* for 30 years now, conditions are just the same as they always were' (mother, 66 years).

'I think my biggest problem is having a grandchild (son of daughter) (sufferer) in my house also, and having to be responsible for him. Especially when his mother is present and I feel she should take more interest. Her interest seems childlike and not responsible' (mother, 54 years).

'Who is to care and nurse my sister properly on the death of my mother? Because I have to work I am unable to care for her properly' (sister, 44 years).

'The future for my sister. Will she have to spend her life in hospital?' (sister, 28 years).

'Trying to get my son tested for allergies — in case there is a chance that this might be the answer. Perhaps there are bigger problems, such as the future' (mother, 58 years).

'After-hospital treatment, care and rehabilitation of our daughter. Trying to ensure that finances are kept in order' (parents, 63 years).

What Would Help You Most?

'An informative booklet on schizophrenia, with clear definitions of the difficulties encountered by relatives of sufferer' (son, 17 years).

'If somewhere employers who understand this illness could have jobs available, even part-time' (father).

'Not living with my son' (mother, 54 years).

'When the illness is first diagnosed more information should be given to patient and sufferer about the nature of the illness. It was only several years later after seeing an article in a magazine that I was made aware of the NSF and was able to get hold of leaflets explaining all the aspects of the illness to me. No information is forthcoming from GP, psychiatrist or hospital by way of explaining the symptoms and when help may be required for the sufferer' (sister, 34 years).

'At present, I feel the public has a "cultural" antipathy towards the word "schizophrenia". Only time and education will erode this. Until this happens there will be inadequate money for research. Personally, I consider this research to be the only thing which will help sufferers. Practically speaking, some form of accommodation with expert supervision which would take some of the tension away from the children — also give them a holiday and myself on our own (wife, 46 years).

'Someone able to listen to endless problems and able to make his advice acceptable' (adoptive mother, 76 years).

'To know more about the illness, to have more time with the doctors to discuss in detail what could have caused the illness and what symptoms to look for in case of relapse. To have somewhere or someone to turn to if any problems were to arise suddenly' (mother, 46 years).

'To see my son in an occupation which would use his talents almost to the full without stretching him unduly and causing stress (father, 57 years).

'If more people knew and understood the illness' (mother, 46 years).

'If I understood what was happening' (father, 50 years).

'1. Hospital administration: there is a lacking in urgent procedure; relatives are left with far too much responsibility while attempting to receive instant needed help for the sufferer. I also feel there is an inadequate hospital communication system especially with the hospital psychiatrist, also to have liaison measures promoted which should involve the psychiatrist, patient and nearest relative, enabling all to discuss and hear valid points so that there is no "doubt or mistrust" formed on singular feedbacks.
2. Certainly a provision within the Mental Health Act geared to give more help and some protection for the relatives. The relatives are the least thought of — yet so much depends on them in handling the person with a mental disability.
3. I would like to see an independent structure formed under the mental welfare "organisation" whereupon a relative can set out grievances, problems and concerns, etc., related not to the patient and the relative(s) but all others involved over the situation of the mentally disturbed.
4. In principal that this "organisation" could be the "go between" for the relative(s) "rights"(?) (As far as I am aware the relative has very few legal "rights" under the present Mental Health Act), and

be a supportive network which the relative(s) can rely upon and be treated as a person who has responsibilities and a life of their own. (By "organization" I mean a legal government set-up (with updated views)' (mother, 48 years).

'More understanding and *care* for sufferers and *relatives* also, outside and within mental hospitals. Closer contact with both as people rather than as patient and relative, with more trust and friendship along with the medical needs, such as drugs etc., rather than a number on a file with a label on it' (mother, 50 years).

'If my husband could realise (patient) cannot stand up and "be a man" on occasions when he has a "down" period and life looks black and dismal even in the happiest situation at home with his twin sister and brothers e.g. at Christmas time' (mother, 56 years).

'A *day centre* where young sufferers could go (which is) nearer than 50 miles (away)' (mother, 56 years).

'To know our son had a place of his own and someone to turn to for support and encouragement outside the family — someone trained to give practical help and support' (mother, 53 years)

'Obviously a "breakthrough" in research so that we might see our sons well again and a tremendous load lifted from us' (mother, 60 years).

'Some sort of laundry service would help enormously — a very mundane answer. Also some domestic help — not affordable on pension' (mother, 60 years).

'To find some vigorous young professionals with open minds, prepared to step out of the wellworn paths of their predecessors, which have led to nowhere, to come into the field with us, instead of waiting in consulting rooms for us to bring our broken children, too late' (father, 70 years).

'Apart from a cure — more readiness from the medical profession to discuss, at regular intervals, day-to-day progress (if any) and problems' (father, 70 years).

'More aftercare, day centres, a type of hostel where they could have a tempoary change of environment' (father, 62 years).

'A simplification of the present "benefits" system, so that they were entitled to a "disability" benefit without the present complicated system of assessment which is difficult to follow unless one is an expert in the field' (mother, 68 years).

'Financial. I had to give up work when crisis was at peak' (mother, 54 years).

'I think if I could discuss the situation more openly, without it affecting my daughter, as it still is a stigma' (mother, 54 years).

'A workshop or meeting place to attend afternoons or evenings. Sufferer has great difficulty getting up and is far from his best in mornings' (mother, 68 years).

'A sheltered housing scheme near or within the grounds of a hospital with nursing supervision 24 hours a day (if needed) — but with private accommodation for single people to live as near normal lives as possible' (sister, 44 years).

'Doctors who are willing to try any avenue to find help for the patient' (mother, 58 years).

'To hear that a cure had been found for this dreadful illness, and someone to talk to, in the same situation as myself' (mother, 57 years).

'Talking with someone who really understood the problem' (mother, 59 years).

What Do You Think Can Be Done?

'More understanding through publicity as this may solve some of the problems created by way entertainment media uses mental illness, especially schizophrenia (son).

'Nothing' (mother, 54 years).

'More research into finding out exactly what causes it' (sister, 34 years).

'In my opinion, the only *real* constructive work is *research*. While being very grateful for modern drugs, we should not be discouraged from stressing their limited value in terms of "real care" or in allowing the public to assume that they are the *panacea*, simply because the patient is discharged from hospital. Ironically it is the "tranquillising" drugs which have acted as a spur to relatives to press for more research, *better education of the public* and which have given relatives an opportunity to observe patients closely on a long-term basis' (wife, 46 years).

'My experience has left me in the belief that very little can be done' (adoptive mother, 76 years).

'Apart from drugs and understanding, I do not know. I keep hoping there will be a breakthrough and a cure will be found' (mother, 46 years).

'I wish more research could be done' (mother, 59 years).

'More research, better monitor on drugs, higher grade in mental nursing' (mother, 50 years).

'Society in general could be educated as with first-aid classes not to be scared of unusual behaviour' (mother, 56 years).

'GPs better trained to recognise the symptoms. Early diagnosis so that the patient gets help quickly' (mother, 53 years).

'As the mind is not immutable, all things are possible; even in deepest insanity there are beach-heads of sanity — we can learn to understand and widen them. The myths and fear of mental illness can be greatly reduced by education and information. The place of the people we are concerned about is in an understanding community not in herds of instability' (father, 70 years).

'I don't think that the medical people should ever despair and that as new drugs/pills become available then they should be tried on long-term patients; if the medical staff have given up hope of a cure then this rubs off adversely on the patient' (brother, 43 years).

'Much more research into causes which should lead to more knowledge about treatment' (mother).

'More professional support when patient no longer requires hospital treatment (sister, 45 years).

'Society would have to be trained to have more feeling and understanding' (mother, 60 years).

'Where treatment is concerned, a lot has been done to keep the illness under control. What concerns me more is the lack of practical help for sufferers living alone. Instead of social workers or the community nurses calling for a short period, I think money would be better spent by home helps calling twice a week and helping with household tasks, for those patients whose concentration is not so good. They also might feel more secure by having a home help calling' (mother, 66 years).

'I wish I knew. I would like to see more research into subject and a more open approach to discussing it as an illness, and not being afraid to mention it in case of discrimination. People are afraid so are not informed' (mother, 54 years).

'Acceptance and education of general public' (mother, 65 years).

'More money channelled into biochemical drug research' (sister, 44 years).

'More provision of facilities requiring more money from government. Public awareness to create more pressure on government' (sister, 28 years).

'Medication can be used to alleviate but not cure in most cases. I think all patients should be tested for food and chemical allergies, and treated accordingly. If possible they should be desensitized' (mother, 58 years).

'Set up an organization which is operated with the same zeal as the RSPCA but concerned with humans' (brother).

'Use less drugs and encourage the patients by therapy to regain self-confidence' (mother, 57 years).

'Various drugs seem to control the condition. If the sufferer could be enabled to have enough trust to allow himself to feel his emotions and not suppress them, he would be able to relate to others more easily' (mother, 59 years).

'More provision is needed in the period of transition between hospital and return to normal living' (father, 63 years).

How Do You Feel About the Treatment and Care That You Have Experienced?

'My son's treatment and care was standard. At the beginning of his treatment in 1976 I was not aware there was no cure and was misled by doctors' (mother, 54 years).

'I dislike the use of ECT and wish the medication to control the illness was in drug form only and that injections were not necessary' (sister, 34 years).

'Referrals from GP to psychiatrists are usually speedy, which is a good thing' (sister).

'I have no complaints' (wife).

'Medical, hospital treatment in the early stages very satisfactory ... After-care appears to be so low key as to be almost non-existent as far as the official medical service is concerned. In this field the NSF has been very much more helpful than any government sources' (father, 63 years).

'My son has been on drugs for three years. That's about all the treatment he's had' (mother).

'We are grateful for it, over all' (mother).

'All that can be done has been done for our sons, but the final responsibility rests with basically me, the mother. I wish someone could help me, but there is no way for this except a breakthrough' (mother, 60 years).

'I feel there is room for improvement' (brother, 43 years).

'The family should be advised when treatment changes' (brother).

'In the medical sense my son's treatment has been good. In the social sense (or rehabilitation sense), pretty mediocre' (mother).

'Mixed feelings — more time from psychiatric consultants spent with relatives or parents required' (father, 64 years).

'Very little help from social services, DHSS' (father).

'Very good in (city). The medical personnel with whom I have been in contact personally have been caring and helpful' (mother, 68 years).

'Well pleased' (mother, 76 years).

'I have no fault with the treatment she received at (hospital), but on some of the admissions she should have remained longer as she was no sooner home than she was as ill as ever. Schizophrenics can be very cunning and doctors and nurses may get an impression that they are fit for discharge, but it is the parents and relatives who are on the receiving end, then they are discharged before they are fit' (mother, 66 years).

'I have been especially pleased with our GP's treatment. Psychiatrist was very kind but I did get a shock when my daughter came home from hospital and I expected her to be fully recovered. It took them some time to sit down and explain the situation to me. This is *wrong*' (mother, 54 years).

'Hospital care for patient adequate in 1959 to quite good latterly. Most of the time my daughter has been out of hospital, and then the care has been basic or non-existent till 1978 when a team, including psychiatric community nurse, has treated her which has been an improvement. Hospital beds are now far too hard to obtain, so admission is difficult' (mother, 65 years).

'Doctors have done all they can' (mother, 68 years).

'The care she has received is good. But there has been very little communication with the family. No real support when we needed it — no explanations about the illness, etc. We are never informed of progress, etc' (sister, 28 years).

'In the past, frustrated and sometimes humiliated and made to feel guilty' (mother, 58 years).

'I feel my son has been having really good treatment at (state hospital) whereas in (hospital) I am not so sure. My son was allowed home at weekend while his drugs were being cut down. One weekend he stabbed me and I know it was cutting out of drugs to blame' (mother, 57 years).

'As a parent I experienced a frustrating lack of information from the psychiatrists, especially when our son was discharged from hospital. There was no factual advice given to deal with the everyday dilemmas, e.g. about lying in bed for most of the day — no one has given any sort of advice about this' (mother, 59 years).

'Much more should be explained to parents. OK, the "big boys" of psychiatry know their job and we know and appreciate this but it is difficult to see reasons for lots of *their* behaviour, e.g. shutting up patients in solitary for their own good, not getting outside is bound to be detrimental to physical health as well as mental, or so it seemed to me before realising (that) to face outside can be terrifying' (mother, 56 years).

'It has left a lot to be desired. Lack of continuity and communication caused so many problems, making it quite impossible for the patient's family to "let go". One is also aware that the treatment may be "crude" and that the side-effects of medication make life even more difficult for the patient' (mother, 53 years).

'First initial care was inadequate — a wait of 22 hours before help arrived — could have been a dangerous situation — I could not go for help as I was frightened to leave the children alone with him. The elderly GP never seemed to consider the possibility of this illness. He just wanted to "keep away". Here in all honesty I cannot blame him. Probably the best is being done, within the limits of resources, space, beds, hostels, finance and knowledge' (wife, 46 years).

'Doctors do not have sufficient time to give to the individual and the same applies to hospitals' (mother, 76 years).

'Although hospital has been very kind, I believe the drugs administered have a robot effect and cause sufferer to sleep too much' (mother, 46 years).

'At the beginning of their illness I am afraid not much help; also hospitalization left a lot to be desired' (mother, 50 years).

'I feel that the care in hospital was good, but the treatment is hit-and-miss' (father, 50 years).

'I am disappointed with the treatment prescribed to my husband and more than disappointed over hospital and certainly so-called after-care service. The after-care has been practically non-existent, only coming into "being" on few occasions over a 17-year period' (wife, 48 years).

'*Angry* at the inadequate after-care. *Frustrated* at impersonal attitude of most of the nursing staff in mental hospitals. *Depressed* at lack of information from professional bodies regarding the illness when first diagnosed' (mother, 50 years).

'One cannot expect much from establishments that are under-staffed and over-worked in extremely wearing circumstances and relatively badly paid. There must be little energy left to think of better ways of doing things. The pressures to run the patients to suit the hospitals, and drugs used to this end, must at times be difficult to avoid. We like to keep out of mental hospitals' (father, 70 years).

REFERENCES

Alanen, Y.O., Hagglund, V., Harkonen, P., Kinnunen, P. (1968) 'On Psychodynamics and Conjoint Psychotherapy of Schizophrenic Men and their Wives', *Psychotherapy and Psychosomatics, 16*, 299-300
——Kinnunen, P. (1974), 'Marriage and the Development of Schizophrenia', *Psychiatrica Fennica*, 121-143
Allodi, F.A. (1973) 'The Vanishing Chronic: The Reduction of the Resident Patient Population of a Large Urban Ontario Mental Hospital From 1950 to 1970 with an Analysis of Associated Administrative and Therapeutic Changes', *Canadian Journal of Public Health*, May/June, 279-289
Allon, R. (1971) 'Sex, Race, Socioeconomic Status, Social Mobility and Process-Reactive Ratings of Schizophrenics', *Journal of Nervous and Mental Disease, 15*, 343-350
American Psychiatric Association (1980) *Diagnostic and Statistical Manual of Mental Disease*, 3rd edn., American Psychiatric Association, New York.
Anderson, C.M. (1977) 'Family Invervention with Severely Disturbed Inpatients', *Archives of General Psychiatry, 34*, 697-702
——(1983) 'A Psychoeducational Program for Families of Patients with Schizophrenia', in W. McFarlane (ed.), *Family Therapy in Schizophrenia*, Guilford Press, New York
——Hogarty, G.E., Reiss, D.J. (1980) 'Family Treatment of Adult Schizophrenic Patients: A Psychoeducational Approach', *Schizophrenia Bulletin, 6*, 490-505
——Hogarty, G.E., Reiss, D.J. (1981) 'The Psychoeducational Family Treatment of Schizophrenia', in M. Goldstein (ed.), *New Directions for Mental Health Services: New Developments in Interventions with Families of Schizophrenics*, no. 12, Jossey-Bass, San Francisco
Anthony, E.J. (1972) 'The Contagious Subculture of Psychosis', in C.J. Sagger, H.S. Kaplan (eds.), *Progress in Group and Family Therapy*, Brunner/Mazel, New York
Appleton, W.S. (1974) 'Mistreatment of Patients' Families by Psychiatrists', *American Journal of Psychiatry, 131*, 655-657
Apte, R. (1968) 'Halfway House: A New Dimension in Institutional Care', *LSE Occasional Papers on Social Administration No. 27*, George Bell, London
Armstrong, B. (1978) 'Society v. the Mentally Ill: Exploring the Roots of Prejudice', *Hospital and Community Psychiatry, 29*, 602-607
Astrup, C., Ødegaard, O. (1960) 'The Influence of Hospital Facilities and Other Local Factors upon Admissions to Psychiatric Hospitals', *Acta Psychiatica et Neurologica Scandinavica, 35*, 289-301
Atkinson, J. (1969) 'An Experiment in Group Work with Schizophrenics and their Families', *Case Conference, 16*, 300-305
Atkinson, J.M. (1981) 'Behaviour Modification with Chronic Schizophrenic Patients Living with their Families', unpublished PhD thesis, University of Hull
——(1982) 'The Effect of Involving a Relative in Behavioural Programmes with Chronic Schizophrenic Patients in the Home Setting', *International Journal of Behavioural Social Work and Abstracts, 2*, 33-40
——(1985) *Schizophrenia. A Guide for Sufferers, and their Families*, Turnstone Press, Wellingborough, Northants
Atwood, N. (1983) 'Supportive Group Counselling for the Relatives of Schizophrenic Patients' in W.R. McFarlane (ed.), *Family Therapy in*

Schizophrenia, Guilford Press, New York
——Williams, M.E.D. (1978) 'Group Support for the Families of the Mentally Ill', *Schizophrenia Bulletin*, 4, 415-425
Bateson, G., Jackson, D.D., Haley, J., Weakland, J. (1956) 'Towards a Theory of Schizophrenia', *Behavioural Science*, 1, 251-264
Becker, H.S. (1963) *Outsiders: Studies in the Sociology of Deviance*, Free Press, Glencoe, Illinois
Beels, C.C. (1975) 'Family and Social Management of Schizophrenia', *Schizophrenia Bulletin*, no. 13, 97-118
——(1979) 'Social Networks and Schizophrenia', *Psychiatric Quarterly*, 51, 209-215
——McFarlane, W.R. (1982) 'Family Treatments of Schizophrenia: Background State of the Art', *Hospital and Community Psychiatry*, 33, 541-550
Berkowitz, R. (1984) 'Therapeutic Intervention with Schizophrenic Patients and their Families: A Description of a Clinical Research Project', *Journal of Family Therapy*, 6, 211-233
——Eberlein-Fries, R., Kuipers, L., Leff, J. (1984) 'Educating Relatives About Schizophrenia', *Schizophrenia Bulletin*, 10, 418-429
——Kuipers, L., Eberlein-Fries, R., Leff, J.P. (1981) 'Lowering Expressed Emotion in Relatives of Schizophrenics', in M. Goldstein (ed.), *New Directions for Mental Health Services: New Developments in Interventions with Families of Schizophrenics*, no. 12, Jossey-Bass, San Francisco.
——Kuipers, L., Leff, J. (1981) 'Keeping the Patient Well: Drug and Social Treatment of Schizophrenic Patients', *Psychopharmacology Bulletin*, 17, 89-90
Birley, J.T.L., Brown, G.W. (1970) 'Crises and Life Changes Preceding the Onset or Relapse of Acute Schizophrenia', *British Journal of Psychiatry*, 116, 327-333
Bleuler, M. (1978) *The Schizophrenic Disorders: Long-term Patient and Family Studies*, trans. S.M. Clemens, Yale University Press, New Haven
Bott, E. (1977) 'Hospital and Society', *British Journal of Medical Psychology*, 49, 97-140
Brooke, E. (1959) *Second International Congress for Psychiatry 1957. Congress Report Vol. 3*
Brown, G.W. (1959) 'Experiences of Discharged Chronic Schizophrenic Patients in Various Types of Living Group', *Millbank Memorial Fund Quarterly*, 37, 105-131
——(1966) 'Comment on Paper by Vaillant, G., The Prediction of Recovery in Schizophrenia', *International Journal of Psychiatry*, 2, 617
——(1974) 'Meaning, Measurement and Stressful Life Events', in B.S. Dohrenwend, B.P. Dohrenwend (eds.), *Stressful Life Events: Their Nature and Effects*, John Wiley and Sons, London
——Birley, J.L.T. (1968) 'Crises and Life Changes and the Onset of Schizophrenia', *Journal of Health and Social Behaviour*, 9, 203-214
——Birley, J.L.T., Wing, J.K. (1972) 'Influence of Family Life on the Course of Schizophrenic Disorders: A Replication', *British Journal of Psychiatry*, 121, 241-258
——Bone, M., Dalison, B., Wing, J.K. (1966) *Schizophrenia and Social Care*, Maudsley Monograph No. 17, Oxford University Press, London
——Carstairs, G.M., Topping, G.C. (1958) 'Post Hospital Adjustment of Chronic Mental Patients', *Lancet*, 2, 685-689
——Harris, T.O., Peto, J. (1973) 'Life Events and Psychiatric Disorders. Part 2: Nature of the Causal Link', *Psychological Medicine*, 3, 159-176
——Monck, E.M., Carstairs, G.M., Wing, J.K. (1962) 'Influence of Family Life in the Course of Schizophrenic Illness', *British Journal of Social and Preventive Medicine*, 16, 55-68
——Rutter, M. (1966) 'The Measurement of Family Activities and Relationships. A

Methodological Study', *Human Relations, 19,* 241-265

Burton, A. (1974) 'The Alchemy of Schizophrenia', in A. Burton, J.J. Lopez-Ibor, W.M. Mendel (eds), *Schizophrenia as A Life Style,* Springer, New York

Byrne, L., O'Connor, T., Fahy, J.T. (1974) 'The Home Behaviour of Schizophrenic Patients Living in the Community and Attending a Day Centre', *British Journal of Psychiatry, 125,* 20-24

Carstairs, G.M., Tange, W.I., O'Connor, N., Barber, L.E.D. (1955) 'Changing Population of Mental Hospitals', *British Journal of Preventive and Social Medicine, 9,* 187-190

Caputo, D.U. (1963) 'The Parents of Schizophrenics', *Family Process, 2,* 339-356

Carpenter, W.T., Strauss, J.S. (1974) 'Cross-cultural Evaluation of Schneider's First-rank Symptoms of Schizophrenia. A Report from the International Pilot Study of Schizophrenia', *American Journal of Psychiatry, 131,* 682-687

Carter, M.J. (1975) 'The Double-bind: Therapeutic Interventions', in S. Smoyack (ed.), *The Psychiatric Nurse as a Family Therapist,* John Wiley and Sons, New York

Cheek, F.E. (1965) 'The Father of the Schizophrenic: The Function of a Peripheral Role', *Archives of General Psychiatry, 13,* 336-345

——(1967) 'Parental Social Control Mechanisms in the Family of the Schizophrenic — A New Look at the Family Environment of the Schizophrenic', *Journal of Schizophrenia, 1,* 18-53

——Laucius, J., Matincke, M., Beck, R. (1971) 'A Behaviour Modification Training Programme for Parents of Convalescent Schizophrenics', in R.D. Rubin, H. Fensterheim, A.A. Lazarus, C.M. Franks (eds), *Advances in Behaviour Therapy: Proceedings of the Third Conference of the Association for the Advancement of Behaviour Therapy,* Academic Press, New York

Civrezu, T. (1975) 'The Reintegration of the Schizophrenic into the Community', in M. Lader (ed.), *Studies in Schizophrenia,* Headley Bros, London

Clark, R.E. (1948) 'The Relationship of Schizophrenia to Occupational Income and Occupational Prestige', *American Sociological Review, 13,* 325-330

——(1949) 'Psychosis, Income and Social Prestige', *American Journal of Sociology, 54,* 433-440

Clausen, J.H., Kohn, M.L. (1959) 'Relation of Schizophrenia to the Social Structure of a Small City', in B. Pasamanick (ed.), *Epidemiology of Mental Disorder,* American Association for the Assessment of Science, Washington DC

Cohen, C.L., Sokolovsky, J. (1978) 'Schizophrenia and Social Networks: Ex-patients in the Inner City', *Schizophrenia Bulletin, 4,* 546-560

Cooper, B. (1961a) 'Social Class and Prognosis in Schizophrenia — Part I', *British Journal of Preventive and Social Medicine, 15,* 17-30

——(1961b) 'Social Class and Schizophrenia — Part II', *British Journal of Preventive and Social Medicine, 15,* 31-40

——(1978) 'Epidemiology' in J.K. Wing (ed.), *Schizophrenia. Towards a New Synthesis,* Academic Press, London

Cooper, J.E. (1975) 'Concepts of Schizophrenia in the United States of America and in Great Britain: A Summary of Some Studies by the US-UK Diagnostic Project', in M.H. Lader (ed.) *Studies in Schizophrenia,* Headley Brothers, London

Creer, C., Sturt, E., Wykes, T. (1982) 'The Role of Relatives', in J.K. Wing (ed.), *Long Term Community Care: Experience in a London Borough,* Psychological Medicine Monograph Supplement 2

Cumming, J., Cumming, E. (1957) *Closed Ranks,* Harvard University Press, Cambridge

Davison, G.C. (1969) 'Appraisal of Behaviour Modification Techniques with Adults in Institutional Settings', in C.M. Franks (ed.), *Behaviour Therapy — Appraisal and Status,* McGraw-Hill, New York

Dawson, M.E., Nuechterlein, K.H. (1984) 'Psychophysiological Dysfunctions in the

Developmental Course of Schizophrenic Disorders', *Schizophrenia Bulletin, 10,* 204-232

Dincin, J., Selleck, F., Streicker, S. (1978) 'Restructuring Parental Attitudes — Working with Parents of the Adult Mentally Ill', *Schizophrenia Bulletin, 4,* 497-508

Dohrenwend, B.P., Egri, G. (1981) 'Recent Stressful Life Events and Episodes of Schizophrenia', *Schizophrenia Bulletin, 7,* 12-23

Doll, W. (1976) 'Family Coping with the Mentally Ill: An Unanticipated Problem of Deinstitutionalisation', *Hospital and Community Psychiatry, 27,* 183-185

——Thompson, E.H. Jr, Lefton, M. (1976a) 'Beneath Acceptance: Dimensions of Family Affect Towards Former Mental Patients', *Social Science and Medicine, 10,* 307-313

——Thompson, E.H. Jr., Lefton, M. (1976b) 'An Invisible Crisis: The Burden of the Family Coping with the Mentally Ill as an Unintended Consequence of De-institutionalisation', Paper presented at 53rd Annual Meeting of the American Orthopyschiatry Association, Atlanta

Donner, J., Gamson, A. (1971) 'Experience with Multi-family, Time-limited, Outpatient Groups at a Community Psychiatry Clinic', in H.H. Barton (ed.), *Brief Therapies,* Behavioural Publications, New York

Dunham, H.W. (1944) 'The Social Personality of the Catatonic Schizophrenic', *American Journal of Sociology., 49,* 508-518

——(1965) *Community and Schizophrenia: An Epidemiological Analysis,* Wayne State University Press, Detroit

Dush, D.M., Brodsky, M. (1981) 'Effects and Implications of the Experimental Double-bind', *Psychological Reports, 48,* 895-900

Duval, M. (1979) 'First Person Account: Giving Love and Schizophrenia', *Schizophrenia Bulletin, 5,* 631-636

Early, D.F., Magnus, R.V. (1966) 'Population Trends in a Mental Hospital', *British Journal of Psychiatry, 112,* 595-601

——Nicholas, M. (1971) 'The Developing Scene. Ten-year Review of a Psychiatric Hospital Population', *British Medical Journal,* 25th December, 793-795

Emery, A.E.H., Pullen, I. (1984) *Psychological Aspects of Genetic Counselling,* Academic Press, London

Erlenmeyer-Kimling, L. (1968) 'Studies on the Offspring of Two Schizophrenic Parents', in D. Rosenthal, S.S. Kety (eds), *The Transmission of Schizophrenia,* Pergamor Press, Oxford

——Marcuse, Y., Cornblatt, B., Friedman, D., Ranier, J., Rutschmann, J. (1981) 'The New York High-Risk Project', in N.F. Watt, E.J. Anthony, L.C. Wynne, J. Rolf (eds), *Children at Risk for Schizophrenia: A Longitudinal Perspective,* Cambridge University Press, New York

Esterson, A., Cooper, D.C., Laing, R.D. (1965) 'Results of Family-Orientated Therapy with Hospitalised Schizophrenics', *British Medical Journal,* 8th December, 1462-1465

Falloon, I.R.H. (1984) 'Relapse: A Reappraisal of Assessment of Outcome in Schizophrenia', *Schizophrenia Bulletin, 10,* 293-299

——Boyd, J.L., McGill, C.W. (1982) 'Behavioural Family Therapy for Schizophrenia' in J.P. Curan, P.M. Monti (eds), *Social Skills Training A Practical Handbook for Assessment and Treatment,* Guilford Press, New York

——Boyd, J.L., McGill, C.W., Razain, J., Moss, H.B., Gilderman, A.M. (1982) 'Family Management in the Prevention of Exacerbation of Schizophrenia, A Controlled Study', *New England Journal of Medicine, 306,* 1437-1440

——Boyd, J.L., McGill, C.W., Strang, J.S., Moss, M.B. (1981) 'Family Management Training in the Community Care of Schizophrenia', in M. Goldstein (ed.), *New Directions for Mental Health Services: New Developments in Interventions with Families of Schizophrenics,* no. 12, Jossey-Bass, San Francisco

——Liberman, R.P. (1983) 'Behavioural Family Interventions in the Management of Chronic Schizophrenia', in W.R. McFarlane (ed.), *Family Therapy in Schizophrenia*, Guilford Press, New York

——Liberman, R.P., Lillie, F.J., Vaughn, C.E. (1981) 'Family Therapy of Schizophrenics with High Risk of Relapse', *Family Process, 20*, 211-221

Farina, A., Garmezy, N., Barry, H. (1963) 'Relationship of Marital Status to Incidence and Prognosis of Schizophrenia', *Journal of Abnormal and Social Psychology, 67*, 624-630

Faris, R.E.L. (1934) 'Cultural Isolation of the Schizophrenic Personality, *American Sociological Review, 40*, 155-164

——Dunham, H.W. (1939) *Mental Disorders in Urban Areas: An Ecological Study of Schizophrenia and Other Psychoses*, University of Chicago Press, Chicago

Feldman, J.J. (1960) 'The Household Interview Survey as a Technique for the Collection of Morbidity Data', *Journal of Chronic Disease, 11*, 535-537

Fenton, F.R., Tessier, L., Struening, E.L. (1979) 'A Comparative Trial of Home and Hospital Psychiatric Care', *Archives of General Psychiatry, 36*, 1073-1079

Ferenczi, S. (1950) *Further Contributions to the Theory and Technique of Psycho-Analysis*, Hogarth Press, London

Ferreira, A.J., Winter, W.D. (1965) 'Family Interactions and Decision Making', *Archives of General Psychiatry, 13*, 214-223

——Winter, W.D., Poindexter, E. (1966) 'Some Interactional Variables in Normal and Abnormal Families', *Family Process, 5*, 60-75

Fleck, S. (1979) 'The Family in the Treatment of Schizophrenics' *Journal National Association of Private Psychiatric Hospitals, 10*, 22-30

——Lidz, T., Cornelison, A. (1963) 'Comparisons of Parent-Child Relationships of Male and Female Schizophrenic Patients', *Archives of General Psychiatry, 8*, 1-7

Floyd, M. (1984) 'The Employment Problems of People Disabled by Schizophrenia, *Journal of Occupational Medicine, 34*, 93-95

Freeman, H.E., Simmons, O.G. (1958a) 'The Social Integration of Former Mental Patients', *International Journal of Social Psychiatry, 4*, 264-271

——Simmons, O.G. (1958b) 'Mental Patients in the Community: Family Settings and Performance Levels', *American Sociological Review, 23*, 147-154

——Simmons, O.G. (1963) *The Mental Patient Comes Home*, John Wiley and Sons, London

Freud, S. (1914) 'On Narcissism: An Introduction', in *Freud's Collected Papers*, vol. 4, Hogarth Press (1925), London

Fromm-Reichmann, F. (1948) 'Notes on the Development of Treatment of Schizophrenics by Psychoanalytic Psychotherapy', *Psychiatry, 11*, 263-273

Frumkin, R.M. (1955) 'Occupation and Major Mental Disorders', in A.M. Rose (ed.), *Mental Health and Mental Disorder*, Morton, New York

Gale, A. (1979) 'Problems of Outcome Research in Family Therapy', in S. Walrond-Skinner (ed.), *Family and Marital Psychotherapy: A Critical Approach*', Routledge and Kegan Paul, London

Gardner, E.A., Babigan, H.M. (1966) 'A Longitudinal Comparison of Psychiatric Services to Selected Socio-economic Areas of Monroe County, New York', *American Journal of Orthopsychiatry, 36*, 818-828

Gentry, D.L. (1981) 'Brief Therapy I', in R.J. Corsin (ed.), *Handbook of Innovative Psychotherapies*, John Wiley and Sons, New York

Gerard, D.L., Houston, L.G. (1953) 'Family Setting and the Social Ecology of Schizophrenia', *Psychiatric Quarterly, 27*, 90-101

Getzels, J.W. (1954) 'The Question Answer Process: A Conceptualisation and Some Derived Hypotheses for Empirical Examination', *Public Opinion Quarterly, 18*, 80-91

Gittelman-Klein, R., Klein, D.F. (1969) 'Premorbid Asocial Adjustment and

Prognosis in Schizophrenia', *Journal of Psychiatric Research*, 7, 35-53
Goldberg, E.M. (1967) *The Families of Schizophrenic Patients*, Pergamon Press, London
——Morrison, S.L. (1963) 'Schizophrenia and Social Class', *British Journal of Psychiatry*, 109, 785-902
Goldberg, S.C., Schooler, N.R., Hogarty, G.C., Roper, M. (1977) 'Prediction of Relapse in Schizophrenic Outpatients Treated by Drug and Sociotherapy', *American Journal of Psychiatry*, 134, 171-184
Golding, S.L., Becker, G., Sherman, A., Rappaport, J. (1975) 'The Behaviour Expectations Scale. Assessment of Interaction with the Mentally Ill', *Journal of Consulting and Clinical Psychology*, 43, 109
Goldstein, M.J., Kopeikin, H.S. (1981) 'Short and Long Term Effects of Combining Drug and Family Therapy', in M. Goldstein (ed.), *New Directions for Mental Health Services: New Developments in Interventions with Families of Schizophrenics*, no. 12, Jossey-Bass, San Francisco
——Rodnick, E.H., Evans, J.R., May, P.R.A., Steinberg, M.R. (1978) 'Drug and Family Therapy in the Aftercare Treatment of Acute Schizophrenics', *Archives of General Psychiatry*, 35, 1169-1179
Goodman, S.H. (1984) 'Children of Disturbed Parents: A Research-Based Model for Intervention', in B. Cohler, J. Musick, (eds), *Intervention with Psychiatrically Disabled Parents and their Young Children, New Directions for Mental Health Services*, No. 24, Jossey-Bass, San Francisco
Gottesmann, I.I., Shields, J. (1972) *Schizophrenia and Genetics: A Twin Study Vantage Point*, Academic Press, New York
——Shields, J. (1976) 'A Critical Review of Recent Adoption, Twin and Family Studies in Schizophrenia. Behavioural Genetics Perspective', *Schizophrenia Bulletin*, 2, 360-401
——Shields, J., Hanson, D.R. (1982) *Schizophrenia: The Epigenetic Puzzle*, Cambridge University Press, Cambridge
Gould, E., Glick, I.R. (1977) 'The Effects of Family Presence and Brief Family Intervention on Global Outcome for Hospitalised Schizophrenic Patients', *Family Process*, 16, 503-510
Grad, J., Sainsbury, P. (1963) 'Mental Illness and the Family', *Lancet*, 544-547
——Sainsbury, P. (1966) 'Evaluating the Community Psychiatric Service in Chichester: Results', in E.M. Gruenberg (ed.), *Evaluating the Effectiveness of Mental Health Services*,
Gussen, J. (1967) 'The Psychodynamics of Leisure' in P.H. Martin (ed.), *Leisure and Mental Health: A Psychiatric Viewpoint*, American Psychiatric Association, Washington DC
Häfner, H., Reiman, H. (1970) 'Spatial Distribution of Mental Disorders in Mannheim, 1965', in E.H. Hare, J.K. Wing (eds), *Psychiatric Epidemiology*, Oxford University Press, London
Hajdu-Gimes, L. (1940) 'Contributions to the Etiology of Schizophrenia', *Psychoanalytic Review*, 27, 421-438
Haley, J. (1959a) 'An Interactional Description of Schizophrenia', *Psychiatry*, 22, 321-322
——(1959b) 'The Family of the Schizophrenic: A Model System', *Journal of Nervous and Mental Diseases*, 129, 357-374
——(1960) 'Direct Study of Child-Parent Interactions. Workshop 1959. 3. Observations of the Family of the Schizophrenic', *American Journal of Orthopsychiatry*, 30, 460-467
——(1968) 'Testing Parental Instructions to Schizophrenic and Normal Children: A Pilot Study', *Journal of Abnormal Psychology*, 73, 559-565
——(1970) 'Family Therapy', *International Journal of Psychiatry*, 9, 233-242
Hamilton, M.W., Hoenig, J. (1966) 'The Impact of an Extra-Mural Service on

Social Isolation', *Social Psychiatry*, 1, 97-102

Hammer, M., Makiesky-Brown, S., Gutwirth, L. (1978) 'Social Networks and Schizophrenia', *Schizophrenia Bulletin*, 4, 533-545

Hare, H.E. (1955) 'Mental Illness and Social Class in Britain', *British Journal of Preventive and Social Medicine*, 9, 191-195

——(1956a) 'Mental Illness and Social Conditions in Bristol', *Journal of Mental Science*, 102, 349-357

——(1956b) 'Family Setting and Urban Distribution of Schizophrenia', *Journal of Mental Science*, 102, 753-760

Harris, A., Linker, I., Norris, V., Shepherd, M. (1956) 'Schizophrenia: A Prognostic and Social Study', *British Journal of Social and Preventive Medicine*, 10, 107-114

Hatfield, A.B. (1978) 'Psychological Costs of Schizophrenia to the Family', *Social Work*, 23, 355-359

——(1979a) 'Help-Seeking Behaviour in Families of Schizophrenics', *American Journal of Community Psychology*, 7, 563-569

——(1979b) 'The Family as Partner in the Treatment of Mental Illness', *Hospital and Community Psychiatry*, 30, 338-340

——(1981) 'Coping Effectiveness in Families of the Mentally Ill: An Exploratory Study', *Journal of Psychiatric Treatment and Evaluation*, 3, 11-19

——(1982) 'Therapists and Families: Worlds Apart', *Hospital and Community Psychiatry*, 33, 513

Headley, L. (1977) *Adults and Their Parents in Family Therapy. A New Direction in Treatment*, Plenum Press, New York

Heston, L.L. (1966) 'Psychiatric Disorders in Foster Home Reared Children of Schizophrenic Mothers', *British Journal of Psychiatry*, 112, 819-825

Hirsch, S.R., Leff, J.P. (1971) 'Parental Abnormalities of Verbal Communication in the Transmission of Schizophrenia', *Pyschological Medicine*, 1, 118-127

——Leff, J.P. (1975) *Abnormalities in Parents of Schizophrenics*, Institute of Psychiatry Maudsley Monograph No. 22, Oxford University Press, London

Hoenig, J., Hamilton, M.E. (1967) 'The Burden on the Household in an Extra-Mural Psychiatric Service', in H. Freeman, J. Farndale (eds), *New Aspects of the Mental Health Services*, Pergamon Press, London

——Hamilton, M.W. (1969) *The Desegregation of the Mentally Ill*, Routledge and Kegan Paul, London

Hoffman, L.W., Lippitt, R. (1960) 'The Measurement of Family Life Variables', in P.H. Mussen (ed.), *Handbook of Research Methods in Child Development*, John Wiley and Sons, New York

Holden, D.F., Levine, R.R.J. (1982) 'How Families Evaluate Mental Health Professionals, Resources and Effects of Illness', *Schizophrenia Bulletin*, 8, 626-633

Hollingshead, A.B., Redlich, F.C. (1953) 'Social Stratification and Psychiatric Disorders', *American Sociological Review*, 18, 163-169

——Redlich, F.C. (1954) 'Schizophrenia and Social Structure', *American Journal of Psychiatry*, 110, 695-701

——Redlich, F.C. (1958) *Social Class and Mental Illness*, John Wiley and Sons, New York

Holzman, P.S. (1977) 'The Modesty of Nature: A Social Perspective on Schizophrenia', *Social Science Review*, 51, 588-603

Hoover, C.F., Franz, J.D. (1972) 'Siblings in the Families of Schizophrenics', *Archives of General Psychiatry*, 26, 334-342

Hudson, B.L. (1975) 'A Behaviour Modification Project with Chronic Schizophrenics in the Community', *Behaviour Research and Therapy*, 13, 239-341

—— (1978) 'Behavioural Social Work with Schizophrenic Patients in the

Community', *British Journal of Social Work, 8,* 159-170

Jaco, E.G. (1954) 'The Social Isolation Hypothesis and Schizophrenia', *American Sociological Review, 19,* 565-577

——(1960) *The Social Epidemiology of Mental Disorders,* Russell Sage, New York

Jacobs, S., Myers, J. (1976) 'Recent Life Events and Acute Schizophrenic Psychosis: A Controlled Study', *Journal of Nervous and Mental Disease, 162,* 75-87

——Pinsoff, B.A., Paykel, E.S. (1974) 'Recent Life Events in Schizophrenia and Depression', *Psychological Medicine, 4,* 444-453

Jung, C.G. (1906) *The Psychology of Dementia Pracox,* trans. A.A. Britt (1936) *Nervous and Mental Disease Monographs,* New York

Juni, S. (1980) 'The Stigma of Mental Illness as a Cultural Phenomenon: A Study of Schizophrenia in the Orthodox Jewish Family', *Family Therapy, 7,* 224-235

Kallmann, F.J. (1938) *The Genetics of Schizophrenia,* Augustin, New York

——(1946) 'The Genetic Theory of Schizophrenia. An Analysis of 691 Schizophrenic Twin Index Families', *American Journal of Psychiatry, 103,* 309-322

Kanter, J., Lin, A. (1980) 'Facilitating a Therapeutic Milieu in the Families of Schizophrenics', *Psychiatry, 43,* 106-119

Kaufer, F.H., Phillips, J.S. (1970) *Learning Foundations of Behaviour Therapy,* John Wiley and Sons, New York

Kelley, F.E. (1964) 'Attitudes and Outcome in Schizophrenia', *Archives of General Psychiatry, 10,* 389-394

Kennard, D., Clemmy, R., Mandlebrote, B. (1977) 'Aspects of Outcome in a Therapeutic Community Setting', *British Journal of Psychiatry, 120,* 475-480

Kessler, S.S. (1976) 'Progress and Regress in the Research on the Genetics of Schizophrenia', *Schizophrenia Bulletin, 2,* 434-439

Kety, S.S., Rosenthal, D., Wender, P.H., Schulsinger, F. (1968) 'The Types and Prevalence of Mental Illness in the Biological and Adoptive Families of Adopted Schizophrenics', in D. Rosenthal, S.S. Kety (eds), *The Transmission of Schizophrenia',* Pergamon Press, Oxford

——Rosenthal, D., Wender, P.H., Schlusinger, F., Jacobsen, B. (1978) 'The Biological and Adoptive Families of Adopted Individuals Who Become Schizophrenic: Prevalence of Mental Illness and Other Characteristics', in L.C. Wynne, R.L. Cromwell, S. Matthysses (eds), *The Nature of Schizophrenia: New Approaches to Research and Treatment,* John Wiley and Sons, New York

Kint, M.G. (1977) 'Problems for Families vs Problem Families', *Schizophrenia Bulletin, 3,* 355-356

Kirk, S.A. (1974) 'The Impact of Labeling on Rejection of the Mentally Ill: An Experimental Study', *Journal of Health and Social Behaviour, 15,* 108-117

——(1975) 'The Psychiatric Sick Role and Rejection', *Journal of Nervous and Mental Disease, 161,* 318-325

Klee, G.D., Spiro, E., Balin, A.K., Gorwitz, K. (1967) 'An Ecological Analysis of Diagnosed Mental Illness in Baltimore', in R.R. Monroe, *et al.* (eds), *Psychiatric Epidemiology and Mental Health Planning,* Psychiatric Research Report No. 22, The American Psychiatric Research Association, April,

Klein, H., Person, T., Itil, T. (1972) 'Family and Environmental Variables as Predictors of Social Outcome in Chronic Schizophrenia', *Comprehensive Psychiatry, 13,* 317-334

Kohn, Mc.L. (1968) 'Social Class and Schizophrenia: A Critical Review', *Journal of Psychiatric Research, 6,* 155-173

——(1973) 'Social Class and Schizophrenia: A Critical Review and Reformulation', *Schizophrenia Bulletin, No. 7,* 60-71

——Clausen, J.A. (1955) 'Social Isolation and Schizophrenia', *American Sociological Review, 20,* 265-273

Korer, J.R., Freeman, H.L, Cheadle, A.J. (1978) 'The Social Situation of Schizophrenic Patients Living in the Community', *International Journal of Mental Health*, 6, 45-65

Kramer, M., Van Korff, M., Kessler, L. (1980) 'The Lifetime Prevalence of Mental Disorders: Estimation, Uses and Limitations', *Psychological Medicine*, 10, 429-435

Kringlen, E. (1967) *Heredity and Environment in the Functional Psychosis*, Heinemann, London

Kuipers, L. (1979) 'Expressed Emotion: A Review', *British Journal of Social and Clinical Psychology*, 18, 237-243

——Sturgeon, D., Berkowitz, R., Leff, J. (1983) 'Characteristics of Expressed Emotion: Its Relationship to Speech and Looking in Schizophrenic Patients and their Relatives', *British Journal of Clinical Psychology*, 22, 257-264

Laqueur, P., LaBurt, H., Morang, E. (1964) 'Multiple Family Therapy', in J. Masserman (ed.), *Current Psychiatric Therapies, IV*, Grune and Stratton, New York

Laing, R.D. (1960) *The Divided Self: A Study of Sanity, Madness and the Family*, Tavistock Publications, London

——(1961) *The Self and Others*, Tavistock Publications, London

——(1967) *The Politics of Experience*, Penguin, Harmondsworth

Lamb, H.R. (1971) *Rehabilitation in Community Mental Health*, Jossey-Bass, San Francisco

——Goertzel, V. (1971) 'Discharged Mental Patients: Are They Really in the Community?', *Archives of General Psychiatry*, 24, 29-34

Lane, E. (1968) 'The Influence of Sex and Race on Process-Reactive Ratings of Schizophrenics', *Journal of Psychology*, 31, 15-20

Lapouse, R., Monk, M.A., Terris, M. (1956) 'The Drift Hypothesis and Socio-economic Differentials in Schizophrenia', *American Journal of Public Health*, 46, 978-986

Lazarus, T., Locke, B.Z., Thomas, D.S. (1963) 'Migration Differentials in Mental Disease', *Millbank Memorial Fund Quarterly*, 41, 25-42

Lebow, J. (1982) 'Consumer Satisfaction with Mental Health Treatment', *Psychological Bulletin*, 91, 244-259

Lee, E.S. (1963) 'Socio-economic and Migration Differentials in Mental Disease: New York State 1949-1951, *Millbank Memorial Fund Quarterly*, 41, 249-268

Leff, J.P. (1976) 'Schizophrenia and Sensitivity to the Family Environment', *Schizophrenia Bulletin*, 2, 566-574

——(1979) 'Developments in the Family Treatment of Schizophrenia', *Psychiatric Quarterly*, 51, 216-232

——(1983) 'The Management of the Family of the Chronic Psychiatric Patient', in I. Barofsky, R.D. Budson (eds), *The Chronic Psychiatric Patient in the Community: Principles of Treatment*, SP Medical and Scientific Books, New York

——Hirsch, S.R., Gaind, R., Rhodes, P.D., Stevens, B. (1973) 'Life Events and Maintenance Therapy in Schizophrenic Relapse', *British Journal of Psychiatry*, 123, 659-660

——Kuipers, L., Berkowitz, R. (1983) 'Interventions in Families of Schizophrenics and its Effect on Relapse Rate', in W.R. McFarlane (ed.), *Family Therapy in Schizophrenia*, Guilford Press, New York

——Kuipers, L., Berkowitz, R., Eberlein-Fries, R., Sturgeon, D. (1982) 'A Controlled Trial of Social Intervention in the Families of Schizophrenic Patients', *British Journal of Psychiatry*, 141, 121-134

Lenikan, P., Crocetti, G. (1962) 'An Urban Population's Opinion and Knowledge About Mental Illness', *American Journal of Psychiatry*, 118, 692-700

Levy, S.M. (1976) 'Schizophrenic Symptomatology: Reaction or Strategy? A Study of Antecedents', *Journal of Abnormal Psychology, 85*, 435-445

Liberman, R.P. (1970) 'Behavioural Approaches to Couple and Family Therapy', *American Journal of Orthopsychiatry, 40*, 106-118

——Falloon, I.R.H. Aitchison, R.A. (1984) 'Multiple Family Therapy for Schizophrenia, A Behavioural, Problem-Solving Approach', *Psychosocial Rehabilitation Journal, 7*, 60-77

——Neutchterlein, K.H., Wallace, C.J. (1982) 'Social Skills, Training and the Nature of Schizophrenia' in J.P. Curran, P.M. Monti (eds), *Social Skills Training — A Practical Handbook for Assessment and Treatment*, Guilford Press, New York

——Wallace, C.J., Falloon, I.R.H., Vaughn, C.E. (1981) 'Interpersonal Problem Solving Therapy for Schizophrenics and Their Families', *Comprehensive Psychiatry, 22*, 627-630

Lidz, R.W., Lidz, T. (1949) 'The Family Environment of Schizophrenic Patients', *American Journal of Psychiatry, 106*, 332-345

Lidz, T. (1972) 'The Nature and Origins of Schizophrenic Disorders', *Annals of Internal Medicine, 77*, 639-645

——(1975) *The Origin and Treatment of Schizophrenic Disorders*, Hutchinson, London

——(1976) 'Commentary on "A Critical Review of Recent Adoption, Twin and Family Studies of Schizophrenia: Behaviour Genetic Perspectives"', *Schizophrenia Bulletin, 2*, 402-412

——Cornelison, A., Fleck, S., Terry, D. (1957) 'The Intrafamilial Environment of the Schizophrenic Patient: II. Marital Schism and Marital Skew', *American Journal of Psychiatry, 114*, 241-248

——Cornelison, A., Terry, D., Fleck, S. (1958) 'Intrafamilial Environment of the Schizophrenic Patient: VI. The Transmission of Irrationality', *Archives Neurologica Psychiatrica, 79*, 305-316

Lukoff, D., Snyder, K., Ventura, J., Neuchterlein, K.H. (1984) 'Life Events, Familial Stress and Coping in the Developmental Course of Schizophrenia', *Schizophrenia Bulletin, 10*, 258-292

Lurie, A., Ron, H. (1971) 'Multiple Family Group Counselling of Discharged Schizophrenic Young Adults and Their Parents', *Social Psychiatry, 6*, 88-92

Lystad, M.H. (1957) 'Social Mobility Among Selected Groups of Schizophrenic Patients', *American Sociological Review, 22*, 283-292

McDonald, F. (1980) *A Tragedy of Schizophrenia: The Wife's Tale*, in H. Rollin (ed.), National Schizophrenia Fellowship, Surbiton

McFarlane, W. (1983) 'Introduction' in W. McFarlane (ed.), *Family Therapy in Schizophrenia*, Guilford Press, New York

McGill, C.W., Falloon, I.R.H., Boyd, J.L., Wood-Silverio, C. (1983) 'Family Educational Intervention in the Treatment of Schizophrenia', *Hospital and Community Psychiatry, 34*, 934-938

Mackie, L., Pattullo, P. (1977) *Women at Work*, Tavistock, London

McLean, C.S., Greer, K., Scott, J., Beck, J.C. (1982) 'Group Treatment for Parents of the Adult Mentally Ill', *Hospital and Community Psychiatry, 33*, 564-568

McMahon, R.J., Forehand, R., Griest, D.L., Wells, K.C. (1981) 'Who Drops Out of Treatment During Parent Behaviour Training?', *Behaviour Counseling Quarterly, 1*, 79-85

Malzberg, B., Lee, E.S. (1956) *Migration and Mental Disease: A Study of First Admission to Hospitals for Mental Disease, NY, 1939-1941*, Social Service Research Council, New York

Marcus, J. (1974a) 'Neurological Findings in Children of Schizophrenic Parents', in E.J. Anthony (ed.), *The Child in His Family: Children at Psychiatric Risk*, vol. 3, John Wiley and Sons, New York

——(1974b) 'Cerebral Function in Offspring of Schizophrenics: Possible Genetic Factors', *International Journal of Mental Health, 3,* 57-73

Marsella, A.J., Snyder, K.K. (1981) 'Stress, Social Supports and Schizophrenic Disorders: Towards an Interactional Model', *Schizophrenia Bulletin, 7,* 152-163

Marshall, J.R. (1984) 'The Genetics of Schizophrenia Revisited', *Bulletin of the British Psychological Society, 37,* 177-181

Martin, P.J., Friedmeyer, M.H., Moore, J.G., Claveaux, R.A. (1977) 'Patients' Expectations and Improvements in Treatment: The Shape of the Link', *Journal of Clinical Psychology, 33,* 827-833

Mass, P., Odaniell, J. (1958) 'Group Casework with Relatives of Adult Schizophrenic Patients', *Mental Hygiene, 62,* 504-520

Massie, H.N., Beels, C.C. (1972) 'The Outcome of the Family Treatment of Schizophrenia', *Schizophrenic Bulletin No. 6,* 24-36

Mednick, S.A., Baert, A.E. (1981) *Prospective Longitudinal Research: An Empirical Basis for the Primary Prevention of Psychosocial Disorders,* Oxford University Press, Oxford

Mellor, D.A. (1970) 'The First-Rank Symptoms of Schizophrenia', *British Journal of Psychiatry, 117,* 15-23

Meyers, J.K., Roberts, B.A. (1959) *Family and Class Dynamics in Mental Illness,* John Wiley and Sons, New York

Miller, N.B., Cantwell, D.P. (1976) 'Siblings as Therapists: A Behavioural Approach', *American Journal of Psychiatry, 133,* 447-450

Mischler, E.G., Scotch, N.A. (1963) 'Sociocultural Factors in the Epidemiology of Schizophrenia', *Psychiatry, 26,* 315-343

Moore, R.A., Benedcke, P., Wallace, J.G. (1963) 'Social Class, Schizophrenia and the Psychiatrist', *American Journal of Psychiatry, 120,* 149-154

Morrison, S.L. (1959) 'Principles and Methods of Epidemiological Research and their Application to Psychiatric Illness', *Journal of Mental Science, 105,* 999-1007

Mosher, L.R. (1969) 'Schizophrenogenic Communication and Family Therapy', *Family Process, 8,* 43-63

Moss, H.B., Falloon, I.R.H., Boyd, J.L., McGill, C.W. (1982) 'Strategies of Behavioural Family Therapy in the Community Treatment of Schizophrenia', *International Journal of Family Psychiatry, 3,* 289-299

Mueller, P.S., Orfanidis, M.McG. (1976) 'A Method of Co-therapy for Schizophrenic Families', *Family Process, 15,* 179-191

Murphy, H.B.M., Raman, A.C. (1971) 'The Chronicity of Schizophrenia in Indigenous Tropical Peoples. Results of a Twelve Year Follow-up Survey in Maritius', *British Journal of Psychiatry, 118,* 439-497

Murphy, J.M. (1976) 'Psychiatric Labeling in Cross Cultural Perspective', *Science, 191,* 1019-1028

National Schizophrenia Fellowship (1974) *Social Provision for Sufferers From Chronic Schizophrenia,* NSF, Surbiton

——(1947a) *Living with Schizophrenia — by the Relatives,* NSF, Surbiton

——(1975) *Schizophrenia — The Family Burden,* NSF, Surbiton

——(1983) *Good Relations. A Code of Practice for those Discharging Patients,* NSF, Surbiton

Neale, J.M., Oltmans, T.F. (1980) *Schizophrenia,* John Wiley and Sons, New York

Nuechterlein, K.M., Dawson, M.E. (1984) 'A Heuristic Vulnerability Stress Model of Schizophrenic Episodes', *Schizophrenia Bulletin, 10,* 300-312

Niskanen, P., Pitikanen, T.A. (1972) 'Attitudes of the Relatives of Schizophrenic Patients: A Comparative Study Between Home Based Treatment and Hospital Care', *Acta Psychiatrica Scandinavia, 48,* 174-178

Nolan, W.J. (1917) 'Occupation and Dementia Praecox', *New York State Hospital*

Quarterly, 3, 127-154

Nunnally, J., (1961) *Popular Conceptions of Mental Health,* Holt, New York

O'Brien, F., Azrin, N.H. (1973) 'Interaction-Priming: A Method of Reinstating Patient Family Relationships', *Behaviour Research and Therapy, 11,* 133-136

Ødegaard, Ø. (1956) 'The Incidence of Psychoses in Various Occupations', *International Journal of Social Psychiatry, 12,* 85-104

Ogdon, B.L., Kerr, M. (1981) *Virtuoso — The Story of John Ogdon,* Hamish Hamilton, London

Olshanksy, S. (1972) 'Eleven Myths of Vocational Rehabilitation', *Journal of Applied Rehabilitation and Counselling, 3,* 229-236

Olson, D.H. (1972) 'Empirically Unbinding the Double Bind: Review of Research and Conceptual Reformulations', *Family Process, 11,* 69-94

Orrill, R., Boyers, R. (1972) 'Schizophrenia, R.D. Laing and the Contemporary Treatment of Psychosis: An Interview with Dr Theodore Lidz', in R. Boyers, R. Orrill (eds), *Laing and Anti-Psychiatry,* Penguin, Harmondsworth

Parker, D., Kenning, P., Welder, J. (1971) *Mental Illness in a Modern City,* P.R. Association, London

Pasamanick, B., Scarpitti, F.K. Dimitz, S. (1967) *Schizophrenia in the Community,* Appleton Century Crofts, New York

Rabkin, J.G. (1980) 'Stressful Life Events and Schizophrenia. A Review of the Research Literature', *Psychological Bulletin, 87,* 408-425

Rawnsley, K., London, J.B., Miles, H.L. (1962) 'Attitudes of Relatives to Patients in Mental Hospitals', *British Journal of Preventive and Social Medicine, 16,* 1-15

Reade, W.K., Wertheimer, M. (1976) 'A Basis for the Diagnosis of Schizophrenia', *Journal of Consulting and Clinical Psychology, 44,* 878-880

Reed, D. (1976) *Anna,* Secker and Warburg, London

Reich, W. (1971) 'The Spectrum Concept of Schizophrenia: Problems for Diagnostic Practice', *Archives of General Psychiatry, 32,* 489-498

——(1976) 'The Schizophrenic Spectrum: A Genetic Concept', *Journal of Nervous and Mental Disease, 162,* 372

Richardson, A. (1984) *Working with Self-Help Groups. A Guide for Local Professionals,* Bedford Square Press, London

Ringuette, E., Kennedy, T. (1966) 'An Experimental Study of the Double Bind Hypothesis', *Journal of Abnormal Psychology, 71,* 136-144

Rolfe, J.E. (1972) 'The Social and Academic Competence of Children Vulnerable to Schizophrenia and Other Behaviour Pathologies', *Journal of Abnormal Psychology, 80,* 225-243

Rosenthal, D. (1968) 'The Heredity-Environment Issue in Schizophrenia: Summary of the Conference and Present Status of Our Knowledge', in D. Rosenthal, S.S. Kety (eds), *The Transmission of Schizophrenia,* Pergamon Press, Oxford

Rotenberg, M. (1974) 'Self-Labelling: A Missing Link in the Societal Reaction Theory of Deviance', *Sociological Review, 22,* 335-355

——(1975) 'Self Labelling Theory: Preliminary Findings Among Mental Patients', *British Journal of Criminology, 15,* 360-376

Rowitz, L., Levy, L. (1968) 'Ecological Analysis of Treated Mental Disorders in Chicago', *Archives of General Psychiatry, 19,* 571-579

Roy-Byrne, P., Gross, P., Marder, S.R. (1982) 'Financial Exploitation of Schizophrenic Patients by their Families', *Hospital and Community Psychiatry, 33,* 576-577

Rubinstein, D. (1974) 'Techniques in Family Psychotherapy of Schizophrenia', in R. Cancro, N. Fox, L.E. Shapiro (eds), *Strategic Intervention in Schizophrenia. Current Developments in Treatment,* Behavioural Publications, New York

Rutter, M. (1966) *Children of Sick Parents: An Environmental and Psychiatric*

Study, Maudsley Monograph No. 16, Oxford University Press, London
——Brown, G.W. (1966) 'The Reliability and Validity of Measures of Family Life and Relationships in Families Containing a Psychiatric Patient', *Social Psychiatry*, *1*, 38-53
——Hersov, L. (1977) *Child Psychiatry*, Blackwell, Oxford
Salokangas, R.K.R. (1983) 'Prognostic Implications of the Sex of Schizophrenic Patients', *British Journal of Psychiatry*, *142*, 145-151
Sartorius, N., Jablensky, A., Stromgen, E., Shapiro, R. (1977) 'Validity of Diagnostic Concepts Across Cultures: A Preliminary Report from the International Pilot Study of Schizophrenia', in L.C. Wynne, R.L. Cromwell, S. Matthysse (eds), *The Nature of Schizophrenia*, John Wiley, New York
——Shapiro, R., Kimura, M. (1975) 'Towards an International Definition of Schizophrenia: A Report from the International Pilot Study of Schizophrenia', in M.H. Lader (ed.), *Studies in Schizophrenia. Papers Read at the World Psychiatric Association Symposium "Current Concepts of Schizophrenia", London, November 1972*. Headley Brothers, London
Scarpitti, F.R., Lefton, M., Dimitz, S., Pasamanick, B. (1964) 'Problems in a Home Care Study for Schizophrenics', *Archives of General Psychiatry*, *10*, 143-154
Scharfstein, B., Libbey, M. (1982) 'Family Orientation: Initiating Patients and their Families to Psychiatric Hospitalsation', *Hospital and Community Psychiatry*, *33*, 560-563
Scheff, T.J. (1966) *Being Mentally Ill: A Sociological Theory*, Aldine, Chicago
Schneider, K. (1957) 'Primary and Secondary Symptoms in Schizophrenia', in S. Hirsch, M. Shepherd (eds), *Themes and Variations in European Psychiatry*, John Wright, Bristol
Schroeder, C.W. (1942) 'Mental Disorders in Cities', *American Journal of Sociology*, *48*, 40-48
Schulz, P.M., Schulz, S.C., Dibble, E., Targum, S.D., van Kammen, D.P., Gershon, C.S. (1982) 'Patient and Family Attitudes About Schizophrenia: Implications for Genetic Counselling', *Schizophrenia Bulletin*, *8*, 504-513
Schwartz, C., Myers, J.K. (1977a) 'Life Events and Schizophrenia, I. Comparison with a Community Sample', *Archives of General Psychiatry*, *34*, 1238-1241
——Myers, J.K. (1977b) 'Life Events and Schizophrenia, II. Impact of Life Events on Symptom Configuration', *Archives of General Psychiatry*, *34*, 1242-1245
Scott, R.D. (1973a) 'The Treatment Barrier: Part I', *British Journal of Medical Psychology*, *46*, 45-55
——(1973b) 'The Treatment Barrier: Part II. The Patient as an Unrecognised Agent', *British Journal of Medical Psychology*, *46*, 57-67
——(1976) 'Comments on Tenability and its Meaning', unpublished manuscript
——Montanez, A. (1971) 'The Nature of Tenable and Untenable Patient-Parent Relationships and their Connection with Hospital Outcome', in Y. Alanen (ed.), *Proceedings of the Fourth International Symposium on Psychotherapy of Schizophrenia*, Excerpta Medica, Amsterdam
Searles, H.F. (1959) 'The Effort to Drive the Other Person Crazy — An Element in the Aetiology and Psychotherapy of Schizophrenia', *British Journal of Medical Psychology*, *32*, 1-18
Seeman, M.V. (1983) 'Schizophrenic Men and Women Require Different Treatment Programs, *Journal of Psychiatric Treatment and Evaluation*, *5*, 143-148
Segal, S.P., Aviram, V. (1978) *The Mentally Ill in Community-Based Sheltered Care — A Study of Community Care and Social Integration*, John Wiley and Sons, New York
Selye, H. (1956) *The Stress of Life*, McGraw-Hill, New York
Serban, G. (1975) 'Parental Stress in the Development of Schizophrenic Offspring', *Comprehensive Psychiatry*, *16*, 23-36

Silbertson, D. (1985) 'Mental Health Act Commission 1983 Report' *National Schizophrenia Fellowship News*, March, 2-3

Singer, M.T., Wynne, L.C. (1966a) 'Principles for Scoring Communication Defects and Deviances in Parents of Schizophrenics: Rorschach and TAT Scoring Manuals', *Psychiatry, 29*, 260-288

——Wynne, L.C. (1966b) 'Communication Styles in Parents of Abnormals, Neurotics and Schizophrenics', in I.M. Cohen (ed.), *Family Structure, Dynamics and Therapy*, Psychiatric Research Reports of the American Psychiatric Association, no. 20, New York

Smets, A.C. (1982) 'Family and Staff Attitudes Toward Family Involvement in the Treatment of Hospitalised Chronic Patients', *Hospital and Community Psychiatry, 33*, 573-575

Smith, E.K. (1976) 'Effect of the Double-Bind Communication on the Anxiety Level of Normals', *Journal of Abnormal Psychology, 85*, 358-363

Snyder, K.S., Liberman, R.P. (1981) 'Family Assessment and Intervention with Schizophrenics at Risk for Relapse', in M. Goldstein (ed.), *New Directions for Mental Health Services: New Developments in Interventions with Families of Schizophrenics*, no. 12, Jossey-Bass, San Francisco

Sojit, C.H. (1971) 'The Double-bind Hypothesis and the Parents of Schizophrenics; *Family Process*, 10, 53-74

Sokolovsky, J., Cohen, C., Berger, D., Geiger, J. (1978) 'Personal Networks of Ex-mental Patients in a Manhattan SRO Hostel', *Human Organisation, 37*, 5-15

Soskis, D.A. (1972) 'Aetiological Models of Schizophrenia: Relationships to Diagnosis and Treatment', *British Journal of Psychiatry, 120*, 367-373

Spaniol, L., Zipple, A., Fitzgerald, S. (1984) 'How Professionals can Share Power with Families: Practical Approaches to Working with Families of the Mentally Ill', *Psychosocial Rehabilitation Journal, 8*, 77-84

Spring, B. (1981) 'Stress and Schizophrenia: Some Definitional Issues', *Schizophrenia Bulletin, 7*, 24-33

Stevens, B.C. (1972) 'Dependence of Schizophrenics on Elderly Relatives', *Psychological Medicine, 2*, 17-32

Streiner, D.L., Norman, G.R., McFarlane, A.H., Roy, R.G. (1981) 'Quality of Life Events and their Relationship to Strain', *Schizophrenia Bulletin, 7*, 34-42

Sturgeon, D. Kuipers, L., Berkowitz, R., Turpin, G., Leff, J. (1981) 'Psychological Responses to Schizophrenic Patients to High and Low Expressed Emotion Relatives', *British Journal of Psychiatry, 138*, 40-45

Sturt, E., Wykes, T., Creer, C. (1982) 'Demographic, Social and Clinical Characteristics of the Sample', in J.K. Wing (ed.), *Long Term Community Care: Experience in a London Borough*, Psychological Medicine Monograph Supplement 2

Sundby, P., Nyhus, P. (1963) 'Major and Minor Psychiatric Disorders in Males in Oslo: An Epidemiological Study', *Acta Psychiatrica Scandinavia, 39*, 519-547

Szasz, T. (1962) *The Myth of Mental Illness*, Secker and Warburg, London

——(1970) *The Manufacture of Madness*, Routledge and Kegan Paul, London

——(1979) *Schizophrenia*, Oxford University Press, Oxford

Tarrier, N., Vaughn, C., Leff, J.P., Lader, M.H. (1979) 'Bodily Reactions to People and Events in Schizophrenia', *Archives of General Psychiatry, 36*, 311-315

Taylor, M.A. (1972) 'Schneiderian First-Rank Symptoms and Clinical Prognostic Features in Schizophrenia', *Archives of General Psychiatry, 26*, 64-67

Thomas, D.S., Locke, B. (1963) 'Marital Status, Education and Occupational Differences in Mental Disease', *Millbank Memorial Fund Quarterly, 41*, 145-161

Tienari, P. (1975) 'Schizophrenia in Finnish Male Twins', in M.H. Lader (ed.),

Studies of Schizophrenia, Headley Bros, Ashford

Times, The (1970) 'A Case of Schizophrenia', 9th May

Todd, N.A. (1974) 'Patterns of Admission in Schizophrenia', *British Journal of Psychiatry, 125*, 588-592

——Bennie, E.H., Carlisle, J.M. (1976) 'Some Features of "New Longstay" Male Schizophrenics', *British Journal of Psychiatry, 129*, 424-427

Trute, B., Segal, S.P. (1976) 'Census Tract Predictors and the Social Integration of Structured Care Residents', *Social Psychiatry, 11*, 153-161

Turner, R.J., Wagenfeld, M.O. (1967) 'Occupational Mobility and Schizophrenia: An Assessment of the Social Causation and Social Selection Hypothesis', *American Sociological Review, 32*, 104-113

Vaughn, C.E. (1977) 'Patterns of Interactions in Families of Schizophrenics', in H. Katschnig (ed.), *Schizophrenia: The Other Side*, Urban and Schwarzenberg, Vienna

——Leff, J.P. (1976a) 'The Influence of Family and Social Factors on the Course of Psychiatric Illness', *British Journal of Psychiatry, 129*, 125-137

——Leff, J.P. (1976b) 'The Measurement of Expressed Emotion in the Families of Psychiatric Patients', *British Journal of Social and Clinical Psychology, 15*, 157-166

——Leff, J.P. (1981) 'Patterns of Emotional Response in the Relatives of Schizophrenic Patients', *Schizophrenia Bulletin, 7*, 43-44

——Snyder, K.S., Freeman, W., Jones, S., Falloon, I.R.H., Liberman, R.P. (1982) 'Family Factors in Schizophrenic Relapse — A Replication', *Schizophrenia Bulletin, 8*, 425-426

Venables, P.H., Wing, J.K. (1962) 'Levels of Arousal and the Sub-Classes of Schizophrenia', *Archives of General Psychiatry, 7*, 114-119

Wagner, J., Hartsaugh, D.M. (1974) 'Social Competence as a Process-Reactive Dimension in Schizophrenics, Alcoholics and Normals', *Journal of Abnormal Psychology, 83*, 112-116

Wallace, C.J. (1982) 'The Social Skills Training Project of the Mental Health Clinical Research Centre for the Study of Schizophrenia', in J.P. Curran, P.M. Monti (eds), *Social Skills Training. A Practical Handbook for Assessment and Treatment*, Guilford Press, New York

Wallis, G.C. (1972) 'Stress as a Predictor in Schizophrenia', *British Journal of Psychiatry, 102*, 375-384

Walsh, D. (1969) 'Mental Illness in Dublin — First Admissions', *British Journal of Psychiatry, 115*, 449-456

Waring, E.M. (1981) 'Cognitive Family Therapy in the Treatment of Schizophrenia', *Psychiatric Journal of the University of Ottawa, 6*, 229-233

Wasow, M. (1983) 'Parental Perspectives on Chronic Schizophrenia', *Journal of Chronic Diseases, 36*, 337-343

Watt, D.C. (1975) 'The Outpatient Treatment of Schizophrenics with Long-Acting Neuroleptics', in M. Lader (ed.), *Studies in Schizophrenia*, Headley Bros, London

Watts, N., Anthony, E.J., Wynne, L. and Rolf, J. (1982) *Schizophrenia: Children At Risk*, Cambridge University Press, Cambridge

Watzlawick, P., Beavin, J.H., Jackson, D.D. (1968) *Pragmatics of Human Communication*, Faber, London

Weinberger, G., (1971) 'Brief Therapy with Children and Their Parents', in H.H. Barton (ed.), *Brief Therapies*, Behavioural Publications, New York

Wender, P.H., Rosenthal, D., Kety, S.S., Schulsinger, F., Welner, J. (1974) 'Cross-Fostering: A Research Strategy for Clarifying the Role of Genetic and Experimental Factors in the Etiology of Schizophrenia', *Archives of General Psychiatry, 30*, 121-128

Wild, C.M., Shapiro, L.N., Abelin, T., (1977) 'Communication Patterns and Role

Structure in Families of Male Schizophrenics — A Study Using Automated Techniques', *Archives of General Psychiatry, 34*, 58-70

Wilkins, W. (1973) 'Expectancy of Therapeutic Gain: An Empirical and Conceptual Critique', *Journal of Consulting and Clinical Psychology, 40*, 69-77

Will, D.A., Jr (1959) 'Human Relatedness and Schizophrenic Reaction', *Psychiatry, 22*, 205-255

Williams, E. (1970) 'The Reaction of Schizophrenic Patients to "Double Bind" Type Communications'; paper presented at the British Psychological Society Conference, London

Willis, M.J. (1982) 'The Impact of Schizophrenia on Families: One Mother's View', *Schizophrenia Bulletin, 8*, 617-619

Wing, J.K. (1982) *Long Term Community Care: Experience in a London Borough,* Psychological Medicine Monograph Supplement 2

——Bennett, D.H., Denham, J. (1964) *The Industrial Rehabilitation of Long-Stay Schizophrenic Patients,* Medical Research Council Memo No. 42, HMSO, London

——Brown, G.W. (1970) *Institutionalisation and Schizophrenia,* Cambridge University Press, London

——Denham, J., Munro, A.B. (1959) 'Duration of Stay in Hospital of Patients Suffering from Schizophrenia', *British Journal of Preventive and Social Medicine, 13*, 145-198

——Freudenberg, R.K. (1961) 'The Response of Severly Ill Chronic Schizophrenic Patients to Social Stimulation', *American Journal of Psychiatry, 118*, 311-322

——Fryers, T. (1976) *Psychiatric Services in Camberwell and Salford,* Medical Research Council Social Psychiatry Unit, Institute of Psychiatry, London

——Leff, J., Hirsch, S., Gaind, R. (1972) 'Preventive Treatment of Schizophrenia: Some Theoretical and Methodological Issues'; paper presented at American Psychiatric Association Meeting, New York

Winter, W., Feirreira, A. (1967) 'Interaction Process Analysis of Family Decision Making', *Family Process, 6*, 155-172

World Health Organization (1975) *Schizophrenia: A Multi-Dimensional Study. A Summary of the Initial Evaluation Phase of the International Pilot Study of Schizophrenia,* WHO, Geneva

——(1979) *Schizophrenia. An International Follow-up Study,* John Wiley and Sons, Chichester

Wynne, L.C. (1970) 'Communication Disorder and the Quest for Relatedness in Families of Schizophrenics', *American Journal of Psychoanalysis, 20*, 100-114

——(1972) 'Family Research on the Pathogenesis of Schizophrenia: Intermediate Variables in the Study of Families at High Risk', in C.J. Sagger, H.S. Kaplan (eds), *Progress in Group and Family Therapy,* Brunner/Mazel, New York

——Ryckoff, I., Day, J., Hirsch, S. (1958) 'Pseudo-mutuality in the Family Relations of Schizophrenics', *Psychiatry, 21*, 205-220

Zubin, J., Spring, B. (1977) 'Vulnerability. A New View of Schizophrenia', *Journal of Abnormal Psychology, 86*, 103-126

Zusman, J. (1967) 'Some Explanations of the Changing Appearance of Psychotic Patients: Social Breakdown Syndrome Concept', *International Journal of Psychiatry, 3*, 216-237

INDEX

205